P9-DTY-565

Ethical Choices
in Research

Ethical Choices in Research

MANAGING DATA, WRITING REPORTS, AND PUBLISHING RESULTS IN THE SOCIAL SCIENCES

HARRIS COOPER

American Psychological Association • Washington, DC

Copyright © 2016 by the American Psychological Association. All rights reserved. Except as permitted under the United States Copyright Act of 1976, no part of this publication may be reproduced or distributed in any form or by any means, including, but not limited to, the process of scanning and digitization, or stored in a database or retrieval system, without the prior written permission of the publisher.

Published by
American Psychological Association
750 First Street, NE
Washington, DC 20002
www.apa.org

To order
APA Order Department
P.O. Box 92984
Washington, DC 20090-2984
Tel: (800) 374-2721; Direct: (202) 336-5510
Fax: (202) 336-5502; TDD/TTY: (202) 336-6123
Online: www.apa.org/pubs/books
E-mail: order@apa.org

In the U.K., Europe, Africa, and the Middle East, copies may be ordered from
American Psychological Association
3 Henrietta Street
Covent Garden, London
WC2E 8LU England

Typeset in Meridien by Circle Graphics, Inc., Columbia, MD

Printer: Edwards Brothers, Inc., Ann Arbor, MI
Cover Designer: Naylor Design, Washington, DC

The opinions and statements published are the responsibility of the authors, and such opinions and statements do not necessarily represent the policies of the American Psychological Association.

Library of Congress Cataloging-in-Publication Data
Cooper, Harris M., author.
   Ethical choices in research : managing data, writing reports, and publishing results in the social sciences / Harris Cooper.
      pages cm
   Includes bibliographical references and index.
   ISBN 978-1-4338-2168-4 — ISBN 1-4338-2168-0 1. Social sciences—Research—Moral and ethical aspects. 2. Social sciences—Authorship. I. Title.
   H62.C58587 2016
   174'.90014—dc23
                                    2015033465

British Library Cataloguing-in-Publication Data
A CIP record is available from the British Library.

Printed in the United States of America
First Edition

http://dx.doi.org/10.1037/14859-000

To my mountain perch and to the broad-tailed hummingbirds, pine siskins, mountain chickadees, white-breasted nuthatches, black-billed magpies, common ravens, wild turkeys, and their friends, who encouraged me to stop and think while I wrote this book.

Contents

III

IV

Acknowledgments

I thank the editors and authors of the American Psychological Association journals for what they taught me while I served as chief editorial advisor to the journals program.

I wish to thank David Becker, my development editor at the American Psychological Association, and two anonymous reviewers for helpful comments on the manuscript. Alison Koenka, my graduate student; Hannah Moshontz de la Rocha, a Duke graduate student; and Emily Cooper, my daughter and research assistant professor at Dartmouth University, made suggestions on specific chapters.

Ethical Choices

in Research

Introduction

The door closes and you breathe a deep sigh of relief. The final subject has been run. Things went well with hardly a glitch. The difficult part is over.

Not so fast. Maybe the hard part has just begun. You still have to run the data analyses. Examine the results. Maybe run more analyses. You have to write up the study; you think: "Let's see, the introduction is almost done. How much of the method section have we written? Do we have descriptions from other studies that used some of the same methods? What journal should we send the manuscript to? Are the data ready to show other people?"

Well, at least the ethical considerations are behind you. You have followed the prescribed rules of conduct in the way you treated the subjects. You used the approved consent form. You obtained informed consent from everyone who took part. All the subjects were debriefed and went away satisfied—okay, perhaps bored but not annoyed.

http://dx.doi.org/10.1037/14859-001
Ethical Choices in Research: Managing Data, Writing Reports, and Publishing Results in the Social Sciences, by H. Cooper
Copyright © 2016 by the American Psychological Association. All rights reserved.

Not so fast. Maybe there are still some tough ethical choices ahead: "When we write the study up, do readers need to know about the procedures we tried and modified *before* the ones we ended up using? Should we report *every* analysis of the data we performed? (Where are those files?) Let's see, do we know possible journals (and editors) to send this research to? Who might be asked to review the manuscript? If someone asks to see the data, did we write down somewhere the links between the data set variable names we used and their full descriptions? (Where are those notes?)"

Who Will Benefit From This Book

This book takes up ethical (and some etiquette) issues. These issues usually are addressed in only a few pages in typical introductory research methods texts that are aimed at those learning how to conduct research with human subjects. This book deals primarily with ethical and compliance issues that arise after the data have been collected, though some topics earlier in the process are also covered. Although the book is principally aimed at graduate students and new researchers in psychology, much of what I discuss is relevant to anyone learning to do research with humans in social and behavioral science disciplines, be they studying anthropology, sociology, political science, or economics, or applied disciplines such as education, public policy, and social services. New researchers in the health sciences and those doing research with animals also may find the topics covered valuable (e.g., how to assign authorship and avoid plagiarism and duplicate publication), but some topics important to them need to be explored elsewhere.

The book is written assuming that the reader has taken or is taking an introductory course in research methods, one that covers topics such as research design and measurement, and introductory courses in statistics that cover descriptive and inferential statistics, such as analysis of variance and multiple regression.

The book can be used as a supplemental text in a graduate-level (or an advanced undergraduate) course in research methods or professional behavior. It can also be used as an organizing text in an introductory course on research ethics in the social and behavioral sciences, supplemented by materials that explore each topic in more depth. Finally, new researchers (and maybe even some seasoned ones) may find the book important to have on their shelves and to share with the students they mentor.

The Ethical Treatment of Human Subjects and the Institutional Review Board

Because introductory methods texts typically cover the topic, this book does not get into issues regarding how subjects are treated while they are participating in a study. Of course, the ethical treatment of subjects in research is the researcher's most important obligation. So, let me spend a few paragraphs on this issue.

Put simply, ensuring that subjects leave experiments with no adverse effects for having taken part in the study is the *sine qua non* of scientific research with human subjects. And, to safeguard that this happens, research must not proceed without a community-validated certification that (a) this is the intention of the researchers and (b) proper procedures are in place to make it happen. This process is overseen by Institutional Review Boards (IRBs). If you are doing research at a university, before you begin you will be required to write a *research protocol* and submit it to the IRB for approval. Independent IRBs also exist for researchers not working in university settings.

IRBs must have at least five members, at least one of whom is a scientist and one a nonscientist. In addition to other elements, the IRB will require several topics be addressed in the research protocol. When you submit an IRB form, you will be asked for the names of the responsible researchers and assurances that the work will not begin until the protocol is approved and will not be changed without approved amendment. You must provide a description of the study's purpose and methods and an assessment of the study's risks and benefits. The protocol must include the procedures that will be used to ensure subjects have provided informed consent. You will be asked whether deception is being used, and if so, why and what procedures you have in place for debriefing subjects once their data have been collected. You will need to describe how you will ensure the confidentiality of the data after the subjects have gone.

Suppose you and some colleagues decide to do research on parents' involvement in their children's lives. You decide to go to a youth soccer match and ask parents about their children's after-school activities and how much they are involved in them. If you work for a university and this study is approved by your institution's IRB, you are good to go. If you did not get institutional approval, this is an ethical violation because the protocol and questionnaires have not been scrutinized by an independent group of community representatives. This is true even if you intend to ask parents for consent to interview them and their children. In addition, if you attempt to present or publish what you find in your study without securing IRB approval, you may find it difficult to get the paper accepted. Most psychology journals require that you indicate that a research protocol has been approved by an IRB before a paper can be considered for publication. If you cannot attest to this, most reputable journals will not publish your paper.

A Scientist's Responsibilities

That said, ethical considerations do not stop when the last subject leaves. However, the *focus* of ethical consideration does change. Now you must consider your obligations—ethically, as a scientist—to the scientific community and beyond to the people who provided support for your research. You also must consider your obligations to an audience around the world who will have access to your research report and might act on its results. Finally, let us not forget that you have obligations to your collaborators, to yourself, and to your career.

What are your responsibilities as a scientist? The National Academy of Sciences (NAS), National Academy of Engineering, and the Institute of Medicine (2009) prepared the monograph *On Being a Scientist: A Guide to Responsible Conduct of Research*. It speaks directly to a scientist's responsibilities:

> The scientific enterprise is built on a foundation of trust. Society trusts that scientific research results are an honest and accurate reflection of a researcher's work. Researchers equally trust that their colleagues have gathered data carefully, have used appropriate analytic and statistical techniques, have reported their results accurately, and have treated the work of other researchers with respect. (p. ix)

The monograph also says scientists have obligations to themselves. Responsible conduct in the laboratory is a prerequisite if you want your efforts to make a lasting contribution and want to maintain your personal and professional sense of integrity and advance professionally.

Clearly, the NAS sees "trust" as the essential element in the conduct of science. No argument there. But trust is essential in any source we might go to for knowledge about the world, be it scientists, parents, friends, teachers, political and religious leaders, and even our own senses and thought processes. What makes science unique is *how* scientists claim they have acquired the knowledge they share—the nature of the evidence the knowledge is based on.

For evidence to be considered scientific, it must have been collected in a particular way. It cannot be based on one person's observations or thoughts or something one person heard or read, no matter how author-itative the source may seem. For scientific knowledge to be trusted, the evidence for it must reside outside any given scientist; it must be observable by all and uncolored by the filters of belief of the person who collected it. When we learn research methods in psychology, we learn how to collect evidence scientifically.

Science is also self-critical. More than other sources that claim to provide knowledge about the world, scientists "trust, but verify." Even researchers who claim to have evidence establishing scientific knowledge remain critical of their own evidence ("What might I have done incorrectly"?). They encourage independent efforts—replications—that test whether findings stand up to rigorous scrutiny and repeated testing ("If others repeat my investigation, will they obtain the same result?").

For this reason, according to the NAS, the ethical considerations in the *process* of collecting scientific evidence emphasize honesty, accuracy, the careful execution of appropriate data collection and analysis, and respect for the contribution of others. I would add to this list transparency and completeness in how a study is described when it is shared with others. Without transparency and completeness in reporting, replication can be difficult (this topic is discussed in greater detail in Chapter 6).

These broad ethical principles may seem daunting. They should not. Here are a few reasons why. First, research methods rest on a theory of knowledge and evidence. The theory grows, is modified, and replaced, just like a theory in any substantive area of social science research. Today, things new researchers take as "givens" in the research process were once not only not *de rigueur* but they were controversial. For example, in your research you will calculate effect sizes (and confidence intervals) and report them alongside your results of null hypothesis significance tests. Today, you do this as a matter of course. Twenty years ago, not so much. In addition, if some researchers prevail, significance testing may disappear as a "given" (this topic is covered in Chapter 5). As another example, 50 years ago, experimenter expectancy effects were hardly a blip on methodologists' radar. Today, researchers are expected to report safeguards that were taken in the research protocol to ensure experimenter expectancies could not have influenced the data.

Second, new researchers are expected to adhere to the highest of standards of science. These often set benchmarks for evidence that were distant hurdles to their mentors. But it is also the case that new researchers are given more latitude than are their elders by many scientific journal editors and others who evaluate research. Of course, the rules cannot be relaxed; an attempt to collect unbiased evidence applies regardless of the scientific discipline, although how this is accomplished may differ somewhat from discipline to discipline. But evaluators of research and journal editors do have leeway in judging a mistake in a research report and submitted manuscript. They can label it as anything between "Here's a teaching moment, let's get this fixed and give this manuscript another chance" and "This person should have known better; reject." Peer review, discussed in Chapter 9, assists immensely in making this decision.

Third, whether you are new or experienced at conducting scientific investigations, you are human. All humans make errors, and honest mistakes are not viewed as ethical lapses; they are viewed as errors that need correcting. I have yet to see the perfect study and doubt anyone else has. What is essential is not that your work be perfect but that you look at it critically, identify its weaknesses, and report them. You must remain open and receptive to corrections suggested by others. Other scientists know this, and know even they make mistakes. This is the best way for science to progress. It is also how we become better scientists.

Fourth, different areas of research within psychology have different expectations about what makes for a sound contribution. Psychologists use methodologies ranging from ethnography to brain imaging. Each method has different sources of potential bias, some of which are better understood than others. The rigor of evidence for a contribution can be different depending on the level of sophistication in current explanations of the problem under study. Scientists know this.

American Psychological Association Ethical Principles

Many disciplines have written ethical standards. For this book, I rely heavily on the American Psychological Association's (APA, 2010a) *Ethical Principles of Psychologists and Code of Conduct* (hereafter referred to as the APA Ethics Code). The Ethics Code is quite exhaustive and covers most of what is covered in other social science ethical guidelines. I supplement APA's Ethics Code when appropriate with other disciplines' standards, such as those of the American Statistical Association, as well as guidelines prepared by some overarching organizations, such as the Department of Health and Human Services' Office of Research Integrity and the Committee on Publication Ethics.

The APA Ethics Code is divided into 10 sections. Although the main focus is on providing psychological services, ethics in research also is covered extensively. Appendix A reproduces sections of the APA Ethics Code that relate most directly to research ethics other than the treatment of subjects. Other APA principles are general and relate to psychologists regardless of whether they are engaged in clinical services or research. For example, some principles relate to competence. Chapter 1 discusses the topic of competence as it relates to the choice of a problem for research.

A Road Map for the Book

Every stage of the research process raises ethical issues. So, as an organizing device, I proceed through the stages of research, from the choice of a problem and methods, to data management and analysis, report writing, and (it is hoped) publication. I discuss ethical issues that can arise *after* an article is published. Of course, the *in vivo* process is never as linear as the textbook description suggests. As you proceed, you may find that decision points I covered at a later stage may influence your planning earlier in the research process. That is why it is good to be familiar with the contents of this book from start to finish, before you apply it to your research plans and activities. It is also why I visit some topics more than once. For example, issues associated with copyrighted material are discussed in Chapter 1, in relation to planning your research because you may want to use a copyrighted measurement device (e.g., a psychological scale) or stimulus (e.g., a video) in your study. Copyright issues also arise when you write a paper for publication if you use a table, figure, or long text excerpt from someone else's published article.

In Part I of the book, I deal with ethical and some legal issues that precede conducting your study but do not relate to the treatment of subjects. In Chapter 1, I ask you to consider whether you have the interest and competence to conduct the study you propose and whether you can do so without a conflict of interest. I also ask you to consider where the methods you plan to use came from and to ensure that you have obtained proper permission for their use. Before you begin, you also must consider your obligations to society and the people with whom you are working.

Chapter 2 deals with issues of authorship, both in terms of what constitutes authorship and how authorship credit should be assigned. Authorship issues appear in Chapter 2, which is about issues related to the early part of the research process, because they should be discussed among researchers as part of planning and then reconsidered throughout the process.

Part II of the book focuses on data collection issues that is not related to how subjects are treated while they take part in your study. Chapter 3 examines how you manage the data you have collected: how to keep records and how to keep records confidential. It also examines who owns the data you collect and how to store data sets. It discusses who should have access to data before your results are published. How long data should be retained and how it should be disposed also are covered. Chapter 4 looks at misconduct with data sets, in particular people making up data or altering it in unethical ways. Chapter 5 covers appropriate and inappropriate methods of data analysis.

Part III of the book deals with the preparation of a research report. Chapter 6 describes what details of the research need to be in a report so that your study can be properly evaluated and replicated by other scientists. Chapter 7 looks at plagiarism, using the words of others without attribution, how plagiarism can be avoided, and how it is uncovered.

Part IV of the book takes up ethical and etiquette issues in publication. Chapter 8 discusses what you need to do before you submit your manuscript to a scientific journal. It examines how to properly share your report before it has undergone scientific review, why you cannot submit a manuscript to more than one journal at a time, and why you need to avoid publishing the same results more than once (duplicate or redundant publication) or in multiple but small chunks based on the same subjects (piecemeal publication). Chapter 8 also provides guidance on choosing an appropriate journal and preparing submission materials in a professional manner. Chapter 9 describes the publication process, including its actors (editors and reviewers) and what their obligations are to you, as an author of a report under review. Chapter 10 tells you what to expect after your manuscript has been accepted, including how to share it properly and ethically handle errors that might be found after publication. In Chapter 10, I examine ethical considerations you may encounter once you are a published author of a scientific paper. These include how to appropriately interact with media interested in communicating your findings to a broad audience of nonscientists. Chapter 10 returns to when and how to share data with others who request it after publication of your study. It also looks at your ethical considerations and professional behavior if your contributions to science lead to an invitation that you serve as a peer reviewer for research papers prepared by others.

In the epilogue, I offer a broad but brief recap of the ethical obligations of a scientist. Finally, I describe some additional resources related to ethical issues in research.

All scientific research starts with an idea and someone asserting, "That's an empirical question."

PLANNING RESEARCH TO AVOID LATER ETHICAL PROBLEMS

Choosing a Topic and Methodology

1

You would think that choosing a problem to study happens long before the first subject in a study has been run. If you did, you would be correct. However, there are a host of issues unrelated to the treatment of subjects that need your consideration once you have in mind a problem to study. For example, it is essential to look ahead to all the stages of the research process and ask yourself whether you have the interest and skills (or are prepared to obtain the skills) necessary to see the research through to completion. In addition, you need to consider whether you have sufficient support, in terms of material and intellectual resources, to complete the work successfully. It is not ethical to start research if you are not committed or unable to complete it.

Once an idea for research has passed these thresholds but before you begin collecting data, it is important to assess whether you have a conflict of interest in pursuing the topic; that is, whether you have a personal stake in the results coming out in one way or another. In addition, as you consider what methods to use you need to obtain permission to use any

http://dx.doi.org/10.1037/14859-002
Ethical Choices in Research: Managing Data, Writing Reports, and Publishing Results in the Social Sciences, by H. Cooper
Copyright © 2016 by the American Psychological Association. All rights reserved.

copyrighted materials that will be part of your research protocol, such as any proprietary individual difference measures or stimulus materials developed by other researchers.

In this chapter, I discuss each of these issues. In addition, I briefly discuss two considerations with ethical implications that surround the choice of a problem. One concerns an assessment on your part of whether or what kind of contribution the research might make to the betterment of society. The other is the obligation of more senior researchers, especially the project director, to oversee the research and properly mentor people involved in the project who are still in training.

Completion as an Ethical Issue

You might wonder why bringing a project to completion is an ethical question. The answer: you will need the time and resources of others, beyond your research team, for your study to happen. If the people who supported and took part in your research were told the ultimate goal of the study was "to contribute to a body of scientific knowledge," that is the goal you are ethically bound to work toward.

The subjects in your study were likely told their participation would make a contribution to science. If undergraduates are subjects, their principal motivation for taking part in a study may be to fulfill a course requirement. Of course, being in a psychology experiment is a great way to learn about the research process but is rarely the sole rationale given to student-subjects. It is not uncommon for the rationale for enlisting undergraduate's participation to include: "It is because of the contribution of students before you that you have a textbook to learn from. This is your opportunity to contribute to the education of the next generation of students."

Other people take part in studies that involve new clinical treatments meant to improve their health and well-being. Yet others want to help in the development of broad social interventions. They get involved in these experiments not only for personal reasons but also with the expectation that their participation will improve the well-being of others. For example, teachers take part in studies of classroom innovations expecting to learn the results for themselves, but they also expect the results, positive or negative, to be disseminated to other teachers.

Other people participate in studies for monetary reward. These folks may have the least interest in what their data will contribute to knowledge. But "contribute to science" is implicit in signing up and may be contained in the informed consent agreement.

Participating in a study is not the only way people beyond the research team have contributed to the project. If the project received monetary

assistance, funders want to see not just research proposals but also progress reports and final reports as well. Many funders expect publication for
wide distribution.[1]

In fact, your track record will be a consideration in whether you get
funding again in the future. If your research is not directly funded by
others, someone—likely, the university or organization you work for—
is paying for the space, maintenance, and utilities used by your laboratory. Your funders may expect publication (certainly, universities do).
Receiving in-kind contributions (e.g., research materials or services other
than dollars) is a frequent part of research. Maybe you borrowed a piece
of equipment needed to collect your data. When the equipment lender
agreed to share, did he or she expect you to do more than collect data
simply to satisfy your curiosity?

Interest in the Topic

The first ethical consideration in your problem choice involves your
level of motivation or interest in the topic. Are your interest and commitment to seeing the project through sufficient to get the work done?
Conducting scientific research involves tapping several different motivations at different stages of the work.

You can start a project based on your simple desire to better understand the problem. For example, suppose you think that being in a state
of physiological arousal influences what people remember about a crime
they have watched being committed. Your curiosity about what these
effects might be is enough to get you started in the research process.
Curiosity is not the only reason research is undertaken, but it is a nearly
universal prerequisite. This motivation can inspire you to conceptualize
and operationalize the problem, design the method, run the subjects, and
analyze the data.

Curiosity can also comingle with other motivations. For example, you
might find an agency that funds research in a particular area and modify
your interest to meet the agency's program initiatives. Your study about
arousal and memory might be of interest to the Department of Justice, but
it might also be of interest to the Transportation Security Administration
(TSA). However, the TSA might want your topic studied in the context
of disruptions on airplanes. This might be a compromise you can make
to secure funds that does not lessen your interest or the study's potential
relevance to social issues.

---

[1]However, some may want no one to see your report except those they choose to
share it with. Other funders may want you to publish but to keep their support confidential.
These issues will be discussed in greater detail later in this book.

Similarly, you might be working with a team of researchers, and the context of the research on arousal and memory might be a collective decision. In such a case, the interest of those you work with can help sustain your own motivation.

But what happens next, once you know what the data say? To make a scientific contribution, your work will need to be shared with other scientists, preferably via publication in a peer-reviewed journal. Thus, your motivation to make a scientific contribution must sustain you to write up your work, cite and secure permissions for what you quote extensively and reproduce in your report, submit the paper to a journal, and revise it after it has been reviewed. You hope for the best, but you may need to revise and resubmit the paper multiple times.

To get from the beginning of a scientific research project to its end taps at least two principal motivations: (a) to better understand the problem and (b) to contribute to a body of scientific knowledge. Let me complicate things. First, there are lots of other motivations entwined in doing scientific research. Not the least of these are obtaining a new skill, gaining fame and fortune, and contributing to the betterment of society (which I will examine later).

A second factor related to motivation and noted previously is that often a study is undertaken by a team of scientists. Teams can be made up of professors or other principal investigators, postdoctoral fellows, graduate students, research staff, and/or undergraduates. They collaborate and share responsibilities for the different stages of research. Each contributes and takes the lead on different tasks. If you are part of such a team, an initial curiosity or desire to learn a skill might be all you need to complete your responsibilities successfully. In addition, your interest in the project might even be enhanced by your interpersonal dynamics with your coworkers. Being part of a team can expose you to the insights of others that stimulate your thinking. It can buoy your spirits through disappointments.

BARRIERS TO COMPLETING A STUDY

Figure 1.1 comes from a study that asked researchers about the fate of studies for which they had obtained Institutional Review Board (IRB) approval years earlier (Cooper, DeNeve, & Charlton, 1997). The question was not what motivated researchers to continue from one stage of the research to the next but what got in the way of bringing their studies all the way to publication. Note that the researchers who responded to our survey chose "lost interest" as a prevalent reason for stopping at all stages of research except the data analysis.

Another frequently cited reason for stopping was that problems with the study's design or operations suggested the study could not be conducted as planned or it might be difficult to interpret the outcomes. If

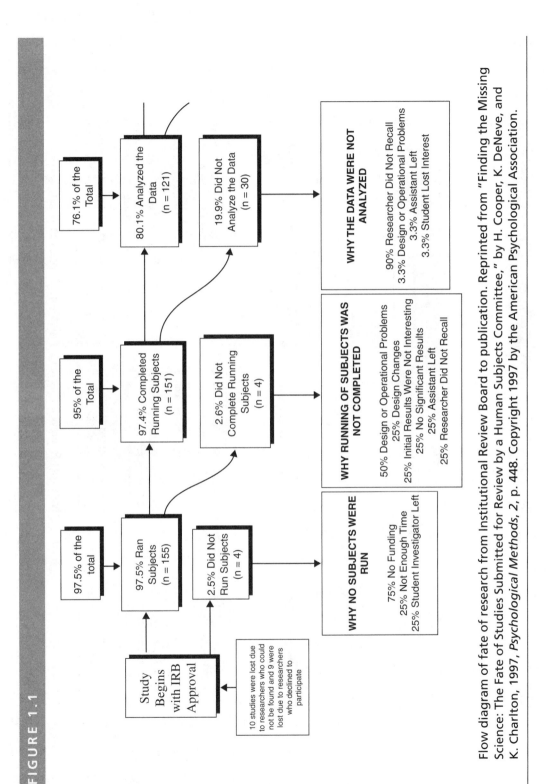

FIGURE 1.1

Flow diagram of fate of research from Institutional Review Board to publication. Reprinted from "Finding the Missing Science: The Fate of Studies Submitted for Review by a Human Subjects Committee," by H. Cooper, K. DeNeve, and K. Charlton, 1997, *Psychological Methods, 2,* p. 448. Copyright 1997 by the American Psychological Association.

FIGURE 1.1 (Continued)

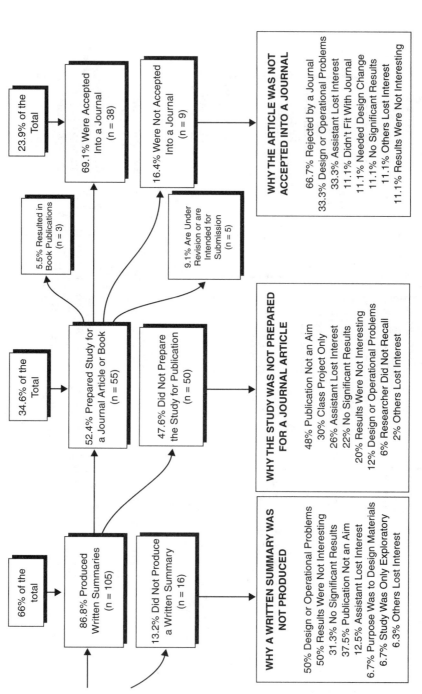

Flow diagram of fate of research from Institutional Review Board to publication. Reprinted from "Finding the Missing Science: The Fate of Studies Submitted for Review by a Human Subjects Committee," by H. Cooper, K. DeNeve, and K. Charlton, 1997, *Psychological Methods, 2*, p. 449. Copyright 1997 by the American Psychological Association.

motivation is high, this might lead to revision and resubmission of the IRB protocol, or if motivation is low, it might lead to abandoning the project entirely. A lack of interesting and/or statistically nonsignificant results was also a frequently cited reason for abandoning a project. In Chapter 5, I discuss the implications for science of abandoning projects after the data have been analyzed and no interesting or statistically significant results have been found. This speaks to the transition researchers must make from satisfying their curiosity for knowing an answer to communicating that answer to others. Finally, the survey revealed that many research projects are undertaken for purposes other than publication. The most frequently cited was that many projects are conducted as class assignments.

Competence in the Methods

Completing a research project involves not only whether your interest will sustain you but also whether you have the skills needed to successfully carry it out. The American Psychological Association (APA)'s standard of ethical practice related to competence states that psychologists who conduct research do so "within the boundaries of their education, training, supervised experience, consultation, study or professional experience . . ." (p. 4, Subsection 2.01; American Psychological Association, 2010a).

Competence can be viewed as having three components: knowledge, practice and what Epstein and Hundert (2002) call reflection or "habits of mind." Nagy (2012) broke this down further: "The metrics for competence stated in this standard are formal education, training, supervision, consultation and independent study, and professional experience" (p. 160).

Knowledge can be gained from a textbook but we know that is not enough. You can read a driver's manual and know *theoretically* how to maneuver a car from Point A to Point B. Actually doing so is another matter; that takes practice. And, when you do get behind the wheel, reflecting on your experience helps you hone your skills and learn to do things that are not in the driver's manual.

The same is true in research. Typically, you learn research methods first in classrooms. But it is the experience you gain actually doing research that fills in what the textbook left out. And, even practice will be of minimal value unless you process your experience correctly. As Epstein and Hundert (2002) wrote: "Competence depends on habits of mind that allow the practitioner to be attentive, curious, self-aware, and willing to recognize and correct errors" (p. 228).

Suppose you are interested in the effectiveness of an intervention to increase healthy eating. You are working with a dietician who agrees to provide her patients with information on your intervention. She agrees to use random assignment to choose half of her clients to give a brochure and encourage them to enroll in your workshops. When you look at the data (with the appropriate permissions, of course), you discover that most of the clients in the condition that received the intervention had higher initial body mass indexes than those in the control condition. Bad luck? When you speak with the dietician, she tells you her assistant gave out the brochures. The assistant decided to give the brochures to the clients she thought would benefit most. This is not an ethical lapse on the assistant's part because the assistant did not understand the meaning of "random assignment" in research and chose clients based on their perceived need for the intervention. But you have learned a lesson: You will make it second nature now to find out specifically who will assign subjects to conditions and be certain this person understands and is committed to carrying out your assignment procedures.

As with motivation, you are not ethically bound to feel competent *by yourself* to perform all the tasks in research, from conceptualization to publication. In fact, research teams are often constructed so that members have skills that complement one another. Some people's help can be enlisted for very specifics tasks, as when a statistical consultant is on the team. Other people, novices, are on the team not to carry out tasks themselves but to gain the experience and habits of mind that will build their competence and confidence. In fact, when a research method or instrument is new and innovative, all members of the team may be novices in its use. In this case, your team will seek the assistance of someone who knows the technique well and will take extra steps to ensure you can carry out the procedure or use the instrument successfully and without harm to subjects.

Also, at my institution I am required to take online training related to the treatment of human subjects and the protection of subjects' privacy. I must take this before I submit my first research protocol to my IRB and then renew my certification by periodically taking refresher courses. You should check to see whether this training is required at your institution.

Your level of the two motivations—interest in the topic and desire to contribute to knowledge—can suggest you be more active in some phases of the research than others. So, a question to ask yourself is not just about you but about your team as a whole. You need to realistically assess whether you and your colleagues are interested and capable of seeing the project through to completion and to meeting your commitments to others.

Personal Issues Beyond Interest and Competence

Finally, the APA (2010a) *Ethical Principles of Psychologists and Code of Conduct* (APA Ethics Code) asks that you consider whether personal problems, perhaps health or family issues, might interfere with your ability to carry out your responsibilities: "Psychologists refrain from initiating an activity when they know or should know that there is a substantial likelihood that their personal problems will prevent them from performing their work-related activities in a competent manner" (p. 5; Subsection 2.06).

When it comes to research, there is more than one way to deal with personal issues, in addition to refraining from beginning a study. These include (a) reducing your responsibilities and getting others to take them; (b) getting more support for the work you are committed to doing, such as having a coworker assist you in running subjects; and/or (c) seeking professional help (e.g., counseling, medical) to swiftly overcome barriers so the potential disruption to the research is minimized.

It is important that you inform your appropriate supervisors and collaborators if you have personal issues that might interfere with completing the tasks they expect from you. They can help you implement any of the strategies mentioned. For an undergraduate or graduate research assistant, informing supervisors may begin with a private conversation with the person who is one level of responsibility up from you and with whom you feel comfortable talking. For a principal investigator who may need to alter budgets, protocols, or ending dates on a grant, informing collaborators would involve a conversation with the program officer in the funding organization.

CONFLICT OF INTEREST

Sometimes, your motivation for doing a project extends beyond a desire to learn the answer to a question. You might be desirous of finding a *specific* answer to the question, such as finding support for a particular theory or showing that an intervention is successful. We almost always have a "bet" on an outcome, but sometimes the bet can be quite large. Therefore, another consideration in your choice of a problem to study should be the potential for others to question your ability to be unbiased in your choice of methods and analysis and your interpretation of the results. Saying "I can be fair in my treatment of the results" is not enough; you also need to consider whether others will *perceive* the possibility of bias and how you can allay their concerns.

Strictly speaking "conflict of interest" is a legal term, but it is fuzzy enough that it can be defined differently in different professional guidelines and employment conditions, as well as different laws and regulations. Most often, conflict of interest standards are applied to economic issues. Will you benefit financially if the results of the study come out one way but not the other? That said, in your thinking about topic choices, it is important to consider broader issues as well, especially those related to your professional reputation.

According to the APA Ethics Code (2010a), psychologists come up against concerns about conflict of interest when

> personal, scientific, professional, legal, financial, or other interests or relationships could reasonably be expected to (1) impair their objectivity, competence, or effectiveness in performing their functions as psychologists or (2) expose the person or organization with whom the professional relationship exists to harm or exploitation. (p. 6; Subsection 3.06)

For example, if you are the person who developed the intervention meant to improve eating habits and you travel the country giving workshops that promote its use, you have a personal and financial stake in the results of a study that tests its effectiveness. When you choose a topic to study, you need to consider whether you stand to gain more from one result than another. If the answer is yes, could this in some way bias—or be seen by others as biasing—your data collection, analysis, and interpretation?

Full Disclosure

People with a stake in a particular result are not necessarily discouraged from conducting research on that topic. We all recognize that protecting against conflict of interest often is a double-edged sword: the people who are most knowledgeable about a topic are also those who are most likely to have a stake in the outcome of research. For example, experts are most likely to have their own theory (or be closely associated with a theory) that makes a prediction the research is meant to test. Or, like our healthy eating example, experts are most likely to have a stake, even a financial one, in the effectiveness of an intervention.

Researchers are not discouraged from doing studies in their area of expertise. Rather, the profession expects researchers to be transparent about whether a conflict of interest *might* exist or be *perceived* to exist by others. Conflict of interest is as much a matter of perception as of reality. To this end, when you submit a manuscript for publication, you may be required to complete a form that asks you to disclose any possible conflicts of interest. APA calls this form "Full Disclosure of Interests." It is required to be completed by all authors of all papers published in APA journals. A copy is provided in Exhibit 1.1.

EXHIBIT 1.1

American Psychological Association Full Disclosure of Interests Form

Full Disclosure of Interests

This section to be completed by author(s):

Journal: _____ Issue: _____

Article title:

_____

Authors: _____

_____
_____

In psychology, as in other scientific disciplines, professional communications are presumed to be based on objective interpretations of evidence and unbiased interpretations of fact. An author's economic and commercial interests in products or services used or discussed in their papers may color such objectivity. Although such relationships do not necessarily constitute a conflict of interest, the integrity of the field requires disclosure of the possibilities of such potentially distorting influences where they may exist. The reader may then judge and, if necessary, make allowance for the impact of the bias on the information being reported.

In general, the safest and most open course of action is to disclose activities and relationships that, if known to others, might be viewed as a conflict of interest, even if you do not believe that any conflict or bias exists.

Whether an interest is "significant" will depend on individual circumstances and cannot be defined by a dollar amount. Holdings in a company through a mutual fund are not ordinarily sufficient to warrant disclosure, whereas salaries, research grants, consulting fees, and personal stock holdings would be. Being the copyright holder of and/or recipient of royalties from a psychological test might be another example. Participation on a board of directors or any other relationship with an entity or person that is in some way part of the paper should also be carefully considered for possible disclosure.

In addition to disclosure of possible sources of positive bias, authors should also carefully consider disclosure where circumstances could suggest bias **against** a product, service, facility, or person. For example, having a copyright or royalty interest in a competing psychological test or assessment protocol might be seen as a possible source of negative bias against another test instrument.

Please check one line only:
I have read the above APA policy on full disclosure, and I declare that

_____ Neither I nor any member of my immediate family have a significant financial arrangement or affiliation with any product or services used or discussed in my paper, nor any potential bias against another product or service.

_____ I (or an immediate family member) have a significant financial interest or affiliation with the following products or services used or discussed in my paper:

Name of product or service and nature of relationship with each (e.g., stock or bond holdings, research grants, employment, ownership or partnership, consultant fees or other remuneration).

Name of Product or Service   Relationship/Interest
_____

If an author note should be added to your manuscript in reference to any disclosure(s) noted above, please check the line below and attach to this form the text of the author note.

_____ Author Note Attached

_____ _____

Author signature *(All contributing authors must sign this form or a duplicate thereof)*   Date

There are a few key points to keep in mind when examining the Full Disclosure of Interests form. First, note that it defines conflict of interest in strictly economic and commercial terms. In my experience as the chief editorial advisor for the APA journals, conflicts of economic interests arose most frequently when

- researchers evaluated treatment techniques they developed, provided, or received compensation for training others to provide;
- researchers used proprietary software or measurement instruments without paying a licensing fee;
- researchers previously had served as an expert witness on the topic of the research; and
- researchers tested the effectiveness of an intervention using funds provided by the developer of the interventions, such as testing a new therapeutic approach using funds provided by the therapy's developer.

Economic interests can also include receiving compensation for consulting or sitting on advisory boards, gifts and gratuities, incentives for using particular instruments or brands of equipment, and so forth. In addition, remember that conflict of financial interests extends to members of your immediate family, so if your parents, spouse, or children work for a company that might benefit from the results of your study, such information needs to be disclosed.

The harm or enhancement to a professional reputation that might result from a study's findings is not covered on the APA Full Disclosure of Interests form. That does not mean these interests need not be disclosed. Rather, because potential financial conflicts are unlikely to be revealed in the manuscript when you discuss the theory that drove the study or the methods that were used, the form pays explicit attention to financial issues. Researchers are encouraged to disclose potentially problematic financial involvements in their manuscripts as part of the Author Note, as well as on the disclosure form. Potential reputational conflicts of interest, on the other hand, typically are disclosed in the manuscript proper. For example, if you are the developer of a theory or intervention, your introduction and methods should make reference to your related work that precedes the study. In the healthy eating study example, this might include reference to the procedural manual you developed.

Second, note how the second paragraph on the Full Disclosure of Interests form emphasizes full transparency. It is important that you err on the side of disclosing more rather than less. What you consider no ethical concern may not be so perceived by others. It is far better to disclose things that others will find irrelevant (and praise you for your openness) than to omit things that, should they come to light later, might be viewed by others as an attempt to keep hidden potential conflicts of interest, both financial and professional. If you are preparing a report or manuscript to submit to a journal, reveal anything that others might construe as a conflict of interest. The journal editor can help you decide what should be omitted and included in the Author Note and what should be noted in the body of the report.

Third, the form points out that conflicts of interest can be viewed as biasing research results in both positive and negative directions. Thus, you should not only disclose interests in the theory or intervention under study but whether you might have interests in a *competing* theory or intervention. This might be viewed as biasing you toward finding negative results.

Finally, note that all authors of the manuscript, not just the corresponding author, will be asked to disclose financial interests.[2]

Using Copyrighted Material in Methods

Once you have settled on a topic, you choose the methods to be used to carry out the study. Previous research on the topic will suggest methods you would like to use. Some materials you are considering using may be owned by others through copyright. The U.S. government defines *copyright* as a form of protection for "original works of authorship fixed in a tangible medium of expression" (Copyright.gov, 2014). *Copyright infringement* occurs "when a copyrighted work is reproduced, distributed, performed, publicly displayed, or made into a derivative work without the permission of the copyright owner" (Copyright.gov, 2014). If a work is copyrighted, this should be visible on the document you obtained, typically accompanied by the copyright symbol (©).

Some intellectual products are in the *public domain*, which means they have not been copyrighted (perhaps because the creators of the work wished to make it freely available), the copyright has expired, or the work failed to meet the requirements for copyright protection. There are also exceptions to copyrights that involve the doctrine of *fair use* (Teaching Copyright, n.d.). Fair use allows the use of copyrighted material for criticism and commentary, parody, news reporting, and art, among other uses. Some use of others' copyrighted work is legally permissible in research and scholarship. However, the courts have ruled about this in only limited

---

[2]Conflicts of interest also arise when you are asked to review manuscripts (or others are asked to review your manuscript) for potential publication. I will return to these issues when I discuss the publication process in Chapter 9.

circumstances (e.g., in scholarly presentations), so do not assume your use is fair use without consulting your organization's legal office or knowing that clear legal precedent exists.

If you intend to use a copyrighted scale, video, or other stimuli or measure in your study, you are ethically and legally obligated to obtain the permission of the copyright holders. Use of copyrighted material sometimes requires that you pay a fee. It is easy to ask permission to use a scale and pay a fee, but sometimes obtaining these permissions can be time consuming. It is important that you seek these permissions before you start collecting data. APA has a Permissions Alert Form for APA Journal Authors that is reproduced in the chapter on plagiarism (where I return to copyright issues). The form explains what material APA requires you to obtain permission for, be it a scale, a table or figure, or even a long quotation. As a paper's author, you will be asked to submit this form at the same time you submit your manuscript for review. It is especially important that you obtain permission for any copyrighted materials used as part of your methods before your study begins. If you wait, you may discover you have collected data that cannot be shared with others and must be destroyed.

As soon as you know that you will be using material for which you need permission, contact the work's publisher, author, and/or copyright holder. Many publishers have websites that can be used to submit such requests. Other permissions are harder to obtain, if only because the copyright holder is hard to locate or slow to respond. Typically, if a work, such as a psychological scale, is published, the publisher, not the author, holds the copyright. You contact the publisher, who will inform you if the author's permission also is needed. The copyright holder will also tell you if a fee for use is involved.

The content and availability of work by others will influence your choice of a topic. One ethical and legal issue occurs when your study's purpose requires you to translate or alter a work copyrighted by someone else. For example, you may want to use a scale that measures depression by giving it to a sample of subjects who speak a language different from the one originally used to validate the instrument. Or the depression scale may have been developed for adults, and you want to use it with children, requiring you to alter its wording. Here, the creators of the scale are likely to take a close look at what you plan to do. They will consider the fidelity of your translation ("Does this culture even have a concept akin to depression? Do the words used in the translation mean the same thing in both languages?") or adaptation ("Is depression, or put more simply, sadness, a concept that children of this age can understand?"). The copyright holders also will consider the implications of your proposed changes for their own work and the impact on what to them may be a source of income.

If the methods of your study suggest you alter and then use a scale copyrighted by someone else, it is critical that you contact the copyright holders before you begin. As an alternative, you might look for similar instruments that exist in the public domain. Using the more freely available version might be simplest, if the psychometric characteristics of instruments in the public domain are similar to those of copyrighted instruments.

Scales are not the only materials "fixed in a tangible medium of expression." Suppose you are an organizational psychologist working in a large company's personnel department. You have developed an algorithm that helps you predict the job satisfaction of new hires. You discover that the algorithm is highly successful, and thinking back to your course on social psychology, you realize your algorithm has implications for theories that predict future behavior based on attitudes. You decide to write and submit a manuscript to a scientific journal testing the algorithm using job interview data. However, your company views the algorithm and your data as proprietary. They may even copyright your work. Because it was developed as part of your job duties, the organization owns it. Therefore, you will need the organization's permission to submit your manuscript.

In this situation, you find yourself stuck between two competing interests. Your company might not want the algorithm revealed because it will lose a competitive advantage. The scientific journal might require that the algorithm be revealed because your paper is of little value to theory development unless readers know fully what was tested. When you consider doing research for which proprietary rights may restrict the information you can share, it is important that you understand and resolve these issues with the parties involved before you begin the research or submit it for publication. You should feel comfortable with how the issues surrounding proprietary rights and scientific transparency might (or might not) restrict your actions in the future. Terms of employment often spell out what you can and cannot do and whose permission is needed before you can proceed with collecting data and publishing the research.

Service to Society

The APA Ethics Code (APA, 2010a) states that psychologists "strive to benefit those with whom they work and take care to do no harm" (p. 3; General Principles, beneficence and nonmaleficence). They "are aware of their professional and scientific responsibilities to society" (p. 3, fidelity and responsibility) and take precautions that their potential biases "do not lead to or condone unjust practices" (p. 4; General Principle, justice). These principles echo the recommendations of the U.S. Department of Health and Human Services' Belmont Report (1979) on the protection of human subjects in biomedical and behavioral research and the subsequent Common Rule (U.S. Department of Health and Human Services, n.d.-a).

SOCIAL INEQUITIES

It is easy to see how these ethical principles relate to one-on-one relationships in clinical practice and how subjects are treated in experiments. It is important to remember that they relate to the choice of a research topic as well. When you do research, you are concerned not only about the implications of your work for any particular individual but also about the implications of your work for groups and subgroups within society. APA makes special mention of the importance of attention to several specific factors that distinguish individuals and subgroups in society. These include people's age, gender, gender identity, race, ethnicity, culture, national origin, religion, sexual orientation, disability, language, and socioeconomic status (APA, 2010a, Principle E). Before you make a decision about your topic, APA asks that you be familiar with how differences among people might interact with your treatment. You are asked to consider the implications of the research you propose as it relates to creating or alleviating social inequities based on these distinctions. You should ask yourself whether your study, should you conduct it, may place certain social groups at a disadvantage; will it contribute to social inequities or serve to ameliorate them?

CONFLICTS OF CONSCIENCE

In addition, a topic can give rise to what Macrina (2005) called a *conflict of conscience* "when the convictions of an individual are allowed to override scientific merit in reaching a decision" (p. 164). This is different from conflict of interest; you may have nothing personal to gain from finding a specific outcome other than the affirmation of a strongly held belief. If you hold this belief so strongly that you doubt you would be able to accept a negative outcome, you need to ask whether you can truly be impartial in carrying out the research you are considering.

This does not necessarily mean you should shy away from studying topics you think are of societal concern or you feel are meant to combat social injustice. A desire to "do good" is an excellent motivation for undertaking research and is encouraged by the professions. For example, APA gives an award every year for distinguished contributions to research in public policy. In 2013, the award was given to Michelle Fine, whose research "addresses theoretical questions of social injustice that sit at the intersection of public policy and social research" (APA, 2013, p. 686). Her award citation stated that her "school-based participatory action research, conducted in collaboration with her students and members of the local community, has led to changes in school policies, increased engagement in schools by both teachers and parents, and enhanced community pride and optimism" (p. 686). One of her most influential reports examined the impact on women inmates of going to college while in prison. The dependent variables she examined included changes in both the prison environment and the subjects' postrelease outcomes, including effects on the prisoners' children. Wishing to do good for society is not antithetical to wishing to do good science. However, having so strong a desire to do good that the scientific process is compromised does no one any good.

The APA Ethics Code (2010a) related to justice speaks of both the person doing the research and those who become aware of the research once it becomes public. Either group might use a study for personal gain or to hurt others. Therefore, "Psychologists exercise reasonable judgment and take precautions to ensure that [their work does] . . . not lead to or condone unjust practices" (pp. 3–4).

How can you be held responsible for what others do with your work? Generally, you are not. But you are obligated to try to anticipate the good and bad that might arise from your study and to guard against any harm your study might cause. You need to do this for any result you might find. The key to ethical behavior is to do all you can to ensure your results are interpreted correctly by others (this topic will be discussed in greater detail in Chapter 10).

DOING GOOD

Another broad social issue in your choice of a problem concerns the ethical principle of beneficence. The IRB applies the principle of beneficence to the subjects who participate in studies. When you submit your study proposal, the IRB will ask you to describe the benefits of your study and to weigh them against the risks. In your application to the IRB, you undoubtedly will describe the potential impact of your work on theories of human behavior or the well-being of the general population or some subgroup of it (including other scientists). Beneficence relates first to the subjects in your study, but it also relates to science and society.

In sum, considering the impacts on society your research might have, it is important to ask whether your research could lead to the amelioration or exacerbation of a social problem and to consider what might be the societal ramifications of one result or another.

A Note on Leadership and Mentoring

Although ethical issues that arise when you are a team leader are not directly related to your choice of a problem, the planning phase of research is a good point to take a brief digression into the areas of mentoring and leadership. Leadership issues are not the sole province of people who hold doctorate degree. Graduate students can be the leaders and mentors on their master's theses, dissertations, and self-initiated projects. For example, they often mentor undergraduates who help collect data and prepare it for analysis.

If you are the project's leader, you are also the one who made promises to others. It is your responsibility to fulfill these agreements. The research must be completed and shared with others as you promised.

It is also likely that there are people working for you who you have empowered to carry out some tasks related to the project. Some of these people may be quite knowledgeable about the task you assigned them and were hired specifically to do it. This group might include someone to run a complex piece of machinery, such as an magnetic resonance imaging machine, or to collect data (a DNA analyst), or to conduct the data analysis. The APA Ethics Code (2010a) says the following about the delegation of work to others:

> Psychologists who delegate work to employees, supervisees or research or teaching assistants or who use the services of others, such as interpreters, take reasonable steps to (1) avoid delegating such work to persons who have a multiple relationship with those being served that would likely lead to exploitation or loss of objectivity; (2) authorize only those responsibilities that such persons can be expected to perform competently on the basis of their education, training or experience, either independently or with the level of supervision being provided; and (3) see that such persons perform these services competently. (p. 5; Subsection 2.05)

What constitutes "reasonable steps" is open to interpretation. What may be "reasonable" to one person could be "inadequate" to another. For example, suppose you publish an article and then discover that a research assistant made undetected errors when coding the data. Were there steps that could have been taken (e.g., have the data coded twice) before the data were analyzed that might have uncovered the mistakes earlier? If you are responsible for assembling the research team, you should consider whether you have assembled a team with the motivation and competence to bring the project to fruition.

The APA principles also cover ethical issues in teaching and mentoring. It is likely there will be people working on your project who have little previous experience with the task you ask them to do. Most obviously, many laboratories employ undergraduates and others to help run subjects and code and enter data in research contexts that are unfamiliar to them. If these students have undertaken these tasks as part of their education and you are the laboratory leader, it is your obligation to make this an educational experience. Section 7 of the APA Ethics Code (2010a) covers education and training, and Section 3 covers human relations. These relate to relationships with students and research assistants, as well as to clinical practice and with subjects in studies.

Conclusion

In this chapter, I cover ethical and legal issues that relate to your planning of a study. These begin with whether the interest in the topic and skill in the conduct of research possessed by you and your research team are sufficient to successfully complete the study. Completing and sharing the results of studies involve ethical issues because you will have asked for help from others and made commitments to them that include the expectation of a contribution to knowledge. You also need to consider whether the topic you choose raises concerns, real or perceived, of conflicts of interest and whether you will benefit more from some potential results of the study than from others.

You also need to consider whether your chosen methods involve materials or stimuli that are the copyrighted property of others. Although many methods are in the public domain, others require permission from and perhaps fees paid to their originators before they can be used. You must also consider the impact on society of your planned study. Finally, if you are leading a team of researchers, you must meet your responsibilities and appropriately mentor those on your research team who are less knowledgeable and experienced than you.

Related to the issues of choosing a topic and methods and mentoring is how authorship will be assigned once the research is completed and the paper is written. You may think authorship is an issue to be decided when the research is completed, but leaving this decision until late in the research process leads only to disputes and charges of ethical impropriety. For this reason, the issue of authorship is discussed in the next chapter.

Authorship

Responsibility and Credit for Research

2

One of the more sensitive issues you will encounter in the course of publishing research involves the assignment of authorship credit. Who deserves authorship, and in what order should the authors be listed? Answering these questions is a task that should not be left for late in the research process because doing so will make disagreements harder to resolve.

When authorship is assigned, it expresses a judgment of peoples' contributions to the research. But it does more than that. First, the judgments influence the relationships among people who work or have worked together closely. Disagreements about authorship credit can arise among coworkers who otherwise get along swimmingly.

Second, the decisions about authorship have consequences for people's careers. For researchers in university settings, scientific publication is a coin of the realm, often its largest denomination. In other research settings, being an author of published articles can have implications for job advancement and longevity.

http://dx.doi.org/10.1037/14859-003

Ethical Choices in Research: Managing Data, Writing Reports, and Publishing Results in the Social Sciences, by H. Cooper
Copyright © 2016 by the American Psychological Association. All rights reserved.

Third, along with authorship credit comes authorship responsibility. Authors of an article are accountable for its contents, both its contributions and mistakes. Of course, because research projects have become so collaborative, it is not expected that every author be able to justify each decision made in the course of the research. But authors should be well versed in their contribution(s) and have a comfortable understanding of the contributions of others. American Psychological Association (APA) journals require that all authors sign a statement to this effect before an article is published. Other journals in psychology and other disciplines require the same.

Types of Authorship Disputes

How often does a sense of unease about authorship happen? Several researchers have provided answers to this question. Martinson, Anderson, and de Vries (2005) sent surveys to 7,760 researchers whose work had been funded by the National Institutes of Health. About 3,250 usable questionnaires were returned. The authors found that about 1 in 10 researchers admitted they had engaged in some form of "inappropriate" authorship credit. Geelhoed, Phillips, Fischer, Shpungin, and Gong (2007) surveyed 300 authors of empirical research in psychology journals and received 109 responses. About one of five thought authorship was given when it was not warranted, and one of 10 thought someone was left off the author list that should have been credited (this result was consistent with findings in psychology many years earlier; Spiegel & Keith-Speigel, 1970). Sandler and Russell (2005) surveyed 604 authors of psychology articles that had both a faculty member and a student as authors. They found little difference between faculty and students or men and women with regard to the reported frequency of unethical authorship incidents. Sandler and Russell asked those who thought an unethical incident had occurred whether they reported it to an authority figure. Only 7 of 185 authors said they did so. The most frequent reason for not reporting the incident was fear of negative consequences (25.4%). Marušic, Bošnjak, and Jerončić (2011) provided an impressive systematic review of 123 studies looking at authorship concerns and related publication issues across multiple disciplines (primarily in health-related fields). They found authorship disputes are not confined to any one discipline. However, it is important to reiterate that the studies reveal no disagreement about authorship for most social and health sciences articles; Geelhoed et al. (2007) reported that nine of 10 authors of published articles said there was never a disagreement about authorship, and four of five said they were completely or very satisfied with the authorship order.

WHO DESERVES AUTHORSHIP?

Authorship disputes arise because there is room for subjectivity in assigning credit. Disagreements about authorship credit can be divided into two types. First, people can differ regarding what kinds of contributions they define as deserving authorship. This can lead to people not being listed as authors who others think merited authorship. This is frequently referred to as a *ghost authorship*. Alternatively, people can be listed who other authors think should not have made the cut. This is referred to as *gift, honorary*, or *guest authorship*. Barnett and Campbell (2012) suggested gift authorships arise (a) to enhance the credibility of a study, (b) from pressure by individuals in authority (to include their name), (c) to compensate someone for efforts not related to the particular project, or (d) to enhance the scholarly record of more junior researchers. There is an accepted practice in medical research that the principal investigator (PI) on a grant be listed as an author on any research supported by the grant funds, regardless of the PI's level of contribution to the particular study. This practice was followed less frequently in the social sciences but is becoming more common. It is not an example of gift authorship because the grant proposal that made the work possible was authored by the PI.

What if someone you invite to be an author feels he or she has not contributed sufficiently to merit authorship? For example, suppose in the course of your research you consulted an expert in the field for suggestions about your hypotheses, design, and/or data analysis. She was kind enough to share her thoughts. When the project is completed, you offer her authorship. What if she feels her contribution does not rise to authorship or has qualms about the research methods, interpretation, or manuscript? Perhaps your results run counter to the results she is finding in her laboratory. This can lead the reluctant "author" to ask that she not be listed. If the potential source of disagreement is known to you early in the manuscript preparation process, this person should be given the opportunity to have input into the manuscript or remove his or her name from it. Needless to say, an individual's request to be removed from a list of authors should be honored. However, to avoid the potential for future disagreement, you should get such a request in writing.

In addition to disagreements over content, a situation that sometimes leads to authors being listed without their consent involves reports that are being written sometime after the research was conducted. For example, a graduate student deserving authorship on your study may have moved on to a professorship, or a professor has changed institutions. An undergraduate or paid research assistant may have taken up a different profession entirely, perhaps going to law school or medical school. In such a case, it is the obligation of the research team to make every effort to track down the relocated author. Locating people has become surprisingly easy with the aid of the Internet and the resources of the institution where the research was conducted. In fact, in my experience, when a corresponding author has said that a listed author has not approved the manuscript because he or she has moved, we were always able to find that individual.

Many journal publishers, including APA, require that the cover letter submitted by the corresponding author state that all authors agree with the content of the manuscript and the order of authorship. Should the manuscript be accepted for publication, publishers also may require that all authors sign an agreement that transfers the copyright to the publisher. If your efforts to locate an author have been exhaustive but fruitless or if you have found a relocated author who does not respond to your communications, share this information with the editor and publisher. Together you can come to an agreement about the proper course of action. You should keep records of all your communication attempts.

IN WHAT ORDER SHOULD AUTHORS BE LISTED?

A second type of authorship dispute involves the order in which authors are listed. In the social sciences, authors typically are listed in descending order of their contribution. (I mentioned that PIs on grants often are listed as authors of works for which they provide minimal input. Convention suggests the PIs be listed last.) This type of dispute occurs because authors disagree about the relative magnitude of each author's contribution.

Definition of a Scientific Contribution

The APA's *Ethical Principles of Psychologists and Code of Conduct* (2010a) guideline on publication credit begins as follows: "Principal authorship and other publication credits accurately reflect the relative scientific or professional contributions of the individuals involved, regardless of their relative status" (p. 11, Subsection 8.12). The American Educational Research Association's (AERA; 2011) ethical standards state

> Education researchers ensure that all who have made a substantive contribution to an intellectual product are listed as authors . . . [they] ensure that principal authorship, authorship order, and other publication credits are based on relative scientific and professional contributions of the individuals involved, regardless of their status. (pp. 153–154, Section 15)

Osborne and Holland (2009) collected definitions of "authorship" from 12 science organizations and societies. These are summarized in Table 2.1, which is reproduced from their article. Osgood and Holland

TABLE 2.1		
Definitions of Authorship and Authorship Credit From Various Scientific Organizations		
Organization	**Authorship**	**Authorship credit**
American Chemical Society	The coauthors of a paper should be all those persons who have made significant scientific contributions to the work reported and who share responsibility and accountability for the results.	An administrative relationship to the investigation does not of itself qualify a person for coauthorship (but occasionally it may be appropriate to acknowledge major administrative assistance).
American Counseling Association	When conducing and reporting research, counselors give full credit to those to whom credit is due.	
American Educational Research Association	All those, regardless of status, who have made substantive creative contribution to the generation of an intellectual product are entitles to be listed as authors of that product.	Clerical or mechanical contributions to an intellectual product are not grounds for ascribing authorship. Authorship and first authorship are not warranted by legal or contractual responsibility for or authority over the project or process that generates an intellectual product.
American Physical Society	Authorship should be limited to those who have made a significant contribution to the concept, design, execution, or interpretation of the research study. All those who have made significant contributions should be offered the opportunity to be listed as authors.	All collaborators share some degree of responsibility for any paper they coauthor. Some coauthors have responsibility for the entre paper as an accurate, verifiable report of the research. Coauthors who make specific, limited contributions to a paper are responsible for their contributions but may have only limited responsibility for other results.
American Psychological Association	Psychologists take responsibility and credit, including authorship, only for work they have actually performed or to which they have substantially contributed.	Principal authorship and other publication credits accurately reflect the relative scientific or professional contributions of the individuals involved, regardless of their relative status. Mere possession of an institutional position, such as department char, does not justify authorship credit.

(*continued*)

TABLE 2.1 (*Continued*)

Definitions of Authorship and Authorship Credit From Various Scientific Organizations

Organization	Authorship	Authorship credit
American Sociological Association	Sociologists take responsibility and credit, including authorship credit, only for work they have actually performed or to which they have contributed.	Sociologists ensure that principal authorship and other publication credits are based on the relative scientific or professional contributions of the individuals involved, regardless of their status.
American Statistical Association	Maintain personal responsibility for all work bearing your name, avoid undertaking work or coauthoring publications for which you would not want to acknowledge responsibility.	Conversely, accept (or insist upon) appropriate authorship or acknowledgment for professional statistical contributions to research and the resulting publications or testimony.
British Sociological Association	Everyone who is listed as an author should have made a substantial direct academic contribution to at least two of the four main components of a typical scientific project or paper; (a) conception or design, (b) data collection and processing, (c) analysis and interpretation of the data, and (d) writing substantial sections of the paper. Authorship should be reserved for those, and only those, who have made significant intellectual contribution to the research.	Participation solely in the acquisition of funding or general supervision of the research group is not sufficient for authorship. Honorary authorship is not acceptable.
International Committee of Medical Journal Editors	Authorship credit should be based on substantial contributions to conception and design, acquisition of data, or analysis and interpretation of data. As persons designated as authors should qualify for authorship, and a those who qualify should be listed.	Acquisition of funding, collection of data, or general supervision of the research group and does not constitute authorship.

TABLE 2.1 (*Continued*)

Definitions of Authorship and Authorship Credit From Various Scientific Organizations

Organization	Authorship	Authorship credit
National Academy of Sciences	Authorship should be limited to those who have contributed substantially to the work.	All collaborators share some degree of responsibility for any paper they coauthor. Some coauthors have responsibility for the entire paper as an accurate, verifiable report or the research. Coauthors who make specific, limited contributions to a paper are responsible for their contributions but may have only limited responsibility for other results.
National Institutes of Health	For each individual, the privilege of authorship should be based on a significant contribution to the conceptualization, design execution, and/or interpretation of the research study.	
Society for Neuroscience	It is properly assumed that all authors have had a significant role of the creation of a manuscript that bears their names. The Society for Neuroscience believes that authorship must be reserved for individuals who have made a significant contribution to the conception and design of the analysis and interpretation of data.	Although researchers are strongly encouraged to share materials such as reagents, animals, and tissues, the provision of such materials in and of itself does not constitute sufficient grounds for inclusion as an author.

Note. From "What Is Authorship, and What Should It Be? A Survey of Prominent Guidelines for Determining Authorship in Scientific Publications," by J. W. Osborne and A. Holland, 2009, *Practical Assessment, Research & Evaluation, 14*, pp. 1–19. Copyright 2009 by PARE. Reprinted with permission.

concluded from their policy analysis that authorship requires a contribution to "some combination of one or more of the following: (a) conception or design, (b) data collection and processing, (c) analysis and interpretation of the data, and (d) writing substantial sections of the paper" (p. 4). Note as well that many of the guidelines state directly that status—be it high or low—is not an appropriate criterion for determining authorship credit. Check your university or workplace documents for guidelines about assigning authorship and your laboratory's website because some lab directors (e.g., university faculty) post guidelines online for how authorship will be determined in the research they direct.

The unaddressed question in all these guidelines is a big one: exactly what is a scientific, professional, substantive, or creative contribution? These definitions are left unaddressed because the answer is both complex and contextual. Bebeau and Monson (2011) examined documents (e.g., journal instructions to authors, ethical codes) from the AERA, APA, and the American Sociological Association (ASA). Osborne and Holland (2009) performed a similar investigation. These authors suggested that all three professional societies do not define authorship but rely on "research mentors to communicate normative practices" (Bebeau & Monson, 2011, p. 372).

Let us see if we can get closer to a more consensual definition or at least raise and clarify some of the issues that need to be considered in such a definition. A contribution meriting authorship can come from anyone involved in the project. The questions to ask are

- Did this person make a contribution that clearly influenced how the study was conceptualized, conducted, analyzed, and/or interpreted?
- Did this person's contributions somehow change the course of the research?
- Did this person write the report or significant sections of it?

Thus, simply moving the research forward is not enough. Washburn (2008) provided an excellent list of contributions that *do not*, of themselves, rise to the level of meriting authorship. These are reproduced in Exhibit 2.1. For example, research assistants hired to run subjects or distribute questionnaires have helped move the research along, but they have not contributed to its development or changed its course. This does not merit authorship. Note that the British Sociological Association recommends that to merit authorship a person "should have made a substantial, direct academic contribution to at least two of the four main components of a scientific project or paper" (see Table 2.1). This is the only guideline that suggests a person must contribute to more than one stage of research to merit authorship.

Authorship decisions can be less than clear-cut when they involve people with special expertise not shared by others on the research team. Professionals are people with special training and skill in the area of their contribution to the project. At one end of the professional contribution dimension would be an expert in statistical analysis (who was not involved in developing the study's design and data collection) but who contributed the data analysis strategy used in the research. In psychology and most social sciences, this person would be considered to have made

---

EXHIBIT 2.1

Examples of Contributions That Do Not Independently Meet Criteria for Authorship

---

. . .

C) Examples (not exhaustive) of contributions that do not independently meet criteria for authorship include:
1) Holding a position within [an organization] or any other institution
2) Implementation of an intervention
3) Acquisition of funding
4) General supervision of the research project
5) Entering data
6) Carrying out data analyses specified by the supervisor
7) Editing, typing, or other administrative assistance
8) Primarily technical contributions

> Individuals that have contributed to the production of a specific manuscript or presentation, but do not meet criteria for authorship, will be acknowledged in a format appropriate to the publication or presentation (e.g., Acknowledgments section of a manuscript).

D) The amount of time and effort contributed to a project does not, in and of itself, determine authorship. Instead, authorship is based on the scholarly importance of the contribution . . .
E) Authorship decisions are not affected by payment for contributions or employment status. It is the nature of the contribution to the paper or presentation that determines whether authorship credit is warranted and not whether participants received compensation for their efforts.
F) Honorary authorship (gift or guest authorship), in which authorship is provided without contribution sufficient for authorship, as previously defined, is prohibited. Ghost authorship, in which authorship is withheld when a contribution sufficient for authorship is provided, is also prohibited.

Note. From "Encouraging Research Collaboration Through Ethical and Fair Authorship: A Model Policy," by J. J. Washburn, 2008, *Ethics & Behavior,* 18, pp. 44–58. Copyright 2008 by Taylor and Francis. Reprinted with permission.

a scientific or creative contribution that typically deserves authorship. At the other end is a statistical expert who simply runs an analysis strategy principally developed by others, perhaps making a few suggestions along the way or writing the computer code. In this case, the creative or scientific contribution is minimal and typically not sufficient to merit authorship. That said, the line between the two cases often is not this well-defined and can vary from discipline to discipline. Thus, it should be clear to all from the beginning how this person will be recognized.

THE AUTHOR NOTE

Remember that you have the opportunity to thank, in the Author Note, those whose contribution does not rise to the benchmark for authorship. This should include granting or contract agencies that provided funds to pay staff. It should also include people who provided in-kind resources, such as laboratory equipment, measures, and access to subjects. However, before you do this, be certain these individuals and institutions wish to be acknowledged. Sometimes, your benefactors may wish to be anonymous. If a benefactor wishes to be anonymous, be sure that this will not conceal what others might view as a potential undisclosed conflict of interest. Funders who wish to remain anonymous should share their desire with you as part of the funding agreement. You can consider its implication for creating a potential conflict of interest before you accept the conditions for funding.

Intellectual Theft

In addition to your interest in the topic, competence in methods and possible conflict of interest, another issue that may arise as you consider a topic to study concerns where the idea for the research comes from and how closely it is associated with the work of other people. For example, if you attend a paper session at a conference and one of the speakers concludes the talk with a few suggestions for future research (what paper does not?), the speaker has no copyright on the ideas shared. Suppose you are interested in attention disorders. Based on what you heard at a conference, you might come home and begin a project to test the generalizability of an attention treatment in rural populations. These ideas are fair game for others to take and begin to study.

In such a case, it would be good etiquette for you to contact the person who suggested the need for a test in a rural area, tell them of your intention, and perhaps invite collaboration. In fact, people who make these suggestions at meetings may be hoping this happens. Alternatively, the paper presenter may already be at work doing this research. Therefore, it is in your best interest to make your intentions known to her or him. You may think you are doing groundbreaking work, but by the time you are done, your work is a replication.

More trouble ensues when readers of reports think their ideas have been taken without their knowledge or proper acknowledgment; they think *intellectual theft* has occurred. This happens when scholars read reports they think present versions of ideas they are closely associated with and the ideas have been changed in only inconsequential ways and are presented without attribution to the scholars' earlier work. Intellectual theft can be distinguished from plagiarism, in which someone's actual words have been copied. I discuss plagiarism in detail in Chapter 7 because it arises as an issue when reports are written, whereas intellectual theft can be an issue in problem formulation.

Claims of intellectual theft most often involve the reader's concern about who gets priority for the discovery or development of novel theories or methods. These disputes often surface during the manuscript review process. For example, it would not be surprising to find that someone aware of the earlier work is used as a reviewer for your report on rural populations when it is subjected to almost any form of peer review.

Disputes involving intellectual priority that arise when reports are undergoing peer review can still be resolved amicably and privately. If the parties agree, many such disputes can be resolved with the addition of new references to the report. If references are added after publication, an erratum is appended to the original work (see Chapter 10). This is an action that makes more public a possible dispute between the parties. For journals available online, the erratum is placed at the end of the electronic copy. In printed journals, errata are published in later issues.

Of course, it is also possible that you believe your work derives from an entirely different intellectual lineage than that claimed by the reader. You think your work is properly referenced. If the reader remains unconvinced, she or he may go to the publisher, your home institution, or your funder for action. Typically, publishers will not alter journal articles without the permission of the author or someone acting on the author's behalf (e.g., a university or the Department of Health and Human Services Office of Research Integrity). Publishers await the outcome of the investigation by the authors' institution or funder before altering the scientific record.

Needless to say, it is important that you avoid claims that you have missed key references, whether knowingly or not. This is why it is critical to do a thorough literature search on your topic before you begin collecting data.

It is also critical that you not ignore work by others you know is relevant. You might be tempted to do this because you want your findings published and you think the manuscript has a better chance of being published if it seems more original. Alternatively, you might have a bone to pick with the person whose work you decide not to cite. This decision might be based on intellectual arguments (okay) or personal animosity (not so okay). In these cases, my advice is to be inclusive and not jeopardize your scientific integrity. You should understand the intellectual heritage of your ideas and be ready to clearly acknowledge this in the report's introduction.

Finally, remember that we are thinking about intellectual theft here from the point of view of the history of the problem. Later, we will return to this important subject when we discuss plagiarism (Chapter 7).

CRYPTOMNESIA

An instructive line of research has emerged from the notion of theft of ideas. It concerns the phenomena referred to as *cryptomnesia*, or *unconscious plagiarism*. According to Brown and Murphy (1989), cryptomnesia refers to

> generating a word, an idea, a song, or a solution to a problem, with the belief that it is either totally original, or at least original within the present context. In actuality, the item is not original, but one which has been produced by someone else (or even oneself) at some earlier time. (p. 432)[1]

Brown and Murphy experimentally demonstrated how people remember ideas generated by others as their own. Perfect and Stark (2008) showed that cryptomnesia can be influenced by the evaluation of the idea; ideas labeled excellent are more likely to be misremembered as one's own. Another manipulation in their study asked subjects to "improve upon" some idea, and once improved, the ideas became more susceptible to unconscious plagiarism.

Perfect and Stark's (2008) procedure requires us to consider the difference between legitimate collaboration, an activity that happens all the time in laboratories as people throw around ideas, and intellectual theft. You should consider whether such a circumstance really constitutes "theft" or, given the opportunity to acknowledge all authors appropriately, the idea is described best as a collaborative product. In such group settings you should not hold back from offering an idea or improving on another's suggestions because you fear your contribution might be "stolen." If the rules for appropriately assigning authorship are followed, they should encourage sharing and brainstorming, not discourage it.

Schemes for Assigning Authorship

As I mentioned, in most social sciences, a person's position in the order of authorship reflects the amount or importance of their contribution relative to those of other authors, although different disciplines have different norms in this regard. Some disciplines list the PI last; some list authors in alphabetical order. We can get a better idea of what might

---

[1]The term *cryptomnesia* dates back many years before it was first applied to plagiarism. See Taylor (1965) for a brief history. The term was initially used to label the ability of mediums to uncover hidden memories.

constitute a sufficient contribution to merit authorship by looking at some of the methods developed to make the assignment process more standard, consensual, and transparent. These methods operationalize how the order of authorship might be determined.

What is involved in determining effort worthy of authorship? Clearly, the professional organization policies (see Table 2.1) indicate it is not simply time spent on the study. It is also not seniority or contractual responsibility. Marušic et al. (2011) drew the following lessons from their overview of articles and reviews:

> The review of 118 studies reported in 123 articles revealed . . . universal themes: there was a common perception that the conception of research/research design and writing the manuscript were the most important qualifying contributions for authorship—across disciplines, geographical regions and time. Also, respondents from most disciplines would grant authorship not only to the researchers but also to all members of the research team who had made an important contribution. Authorship order emerged as an important but formally undefined issue across disciplines. (pp. 13–14)

Winston (1985) presented a scheme delineating 12 activities that might merit authorship (see also Foster & Ray, 2012). These are reproduced in Table 2.2. He provided a weight for each activity to help distinguish "how critical each category typically is to successful research studies" (p. 516). Winston noted, of course, that his scheme is no substitute for good judgment and professional integrity. The scheme is based on his experience, and he encouraged research teams to use it as a starting point for their discussion of authorship.

DESCRIBING CONTRIBUTIONS IN THE AUTHOR NOTE

In the medical sciences, some journals have established the practice of requiring authors to describe the specific contributions made by each in the Author Note or the Acknowledgments (Rennie, Flanagin, & Yank, 2000). Thus, not only would the Author Note contain thanks to those who made a contribution not rising to authorship but it also would include a brief description of each author's major areas of contribution. For example, I found an article in the *Journal of the American Medical Association* that had 13 authors (Bennell et al., 2014). The article information contained the subsection "Author Contribution." This section had seven subheadings, not unlike the contributions suggested by Winston (1985), and after each was listed the last name of each author who had contributed to that activity. This practice remains rare in the social sciences.

TABLE 2.2

Activities Associated With Data-Based Research Manuscripts: Points and Method of Assignment of Authorship

Activity category	Points	Method of assigning points[a]
Conceptualizing and refining research ideas	50	Q
Literature search	20	T
Creating research design	30	Q
Instrument selection	10	Q
Instrument construction/questionnaire design	40	Q/T
Selection of statistical tests/analyses	10	Q
Performing statistical analyses and computations (including computer work)	10	T
Interpretation of statistical analyses	10	Q
Drafting manuscripts		
First draft	50	T
Second draft	30	T
Redraft of a page (on later drafts)	2	T
Editing manuscripts	10	T

Note. From "A Suggested Procedure for Determining Order of Authorship in Research Publications," by R. B. Winston, Jr., 1985, *Journal of Counseling and Development, 63,* pp. 515–518. Copyright 1985 by Wiley and Sons, Inc. Reprinted with permission.
[a]Q = points assigned on a qualitative criteria; T = points assigned based on proportion of total time expended on the tasks or on proportion of total pages drafter or revised; Q/T = points assigned partly on the basis of time spend on the task and party on qualitative criteria.

Talking About Authorship Throughout the Research Process

The worst approach you can take with regard to assigning authorship credit is to not talk about it at all. In most instances, it is the responsibility of the senior person or PI to initiate this conversation. But it is not inappropriate for anyone involved in the project to ask for clarification if it is unclear who should first broach the topic (because researchers are relatively equal in status) or if the conversation seems overdue. You should avoid having everyone (or anyone) involved in the research learn who or what the order of authorship only when the project is complete. The second worst approach is to begin a discussion of authorship when the project is complete. The third worst approach, regardless of when it happens, is to talk about authorship only once.

The best time to begin talking about authorship is as soon as the project is real enough that sitting down with Winston's categories could lead to a friendly and fruitful discussion. The first conversation might even be about whether these categories are adequate for your project and whether you think the weights are appropriate. The categories can be used not only to focus a conversation on authorship but also to help ensure that who is responsible for which task is clear and all responsibilities are discussed in advance.

It is important to revisit your agreement occasionally. This should certainly happen (a) at critical junctures of the research (e.g., before data collection or analysis begins), if only to confirm that everyone is still in agreement; and (b) if and when there is a change in responsibilities. Suppose a project takes longer than expected and a team member moves. Who will take over that person's remaining responsibilities? Are there implications for the order of authorship?

Some scholars have suggested that a written contract is a good way to make sure agreements are explicit and to avoid misunderstandings (e.g., Foster & Ray, 2012). My experience suggests that except for large and complex projects, such a contract might be overkill. Written contracts suggest a degree of formality that might be inconsistent with the relationships in the collaboration. Still, it is always a good idea after roles, responsibilities, and authorship are assigned for the PI (or a person designated by the group) to summarize these in a written communication that goes to all team members. The document should include an invitation for questions and clarification, if needed.

Mentoring and Authorship

It goes without saying that there is a power differential between students and their professors and between junior and senior investigators. In the context of assigning authorship, this imbalance has the potential to create grievances when those with less status feel their contribution has not been acknowledged properly. This is probably the topic that has received the most attention in the literature on authorship (e.g., see Fine & Kurdek, 1993; Sandler & Russell, 2005; Welfare & Sackett, 2011).

Oberlander and Spencer (2006), two students at the time they wrote, reiterated the importance of many of the points discussed above (e.g., attention to ethical principles, frequent and open discussion of authorship issues) as means for assisting in ensuring students feel they have been treated fairly in the assignment of authorship. In addition, they suggested that mentors remain aware of the power differential and commit themselves to obtaining the professional development needed to understand the best way to make authorship decisions. They also pointed out that mentors need to give students the chance to act creatively because that is part of the mentoring process. This means mentors should allow students to initiate research and take on the additional responsibilities that merit authorship as the students' training progresses.

If a dispute does arise and cannot be resolved by the people involved, the mentor should feel comfortable discussing with the student or junior collaborator the appeals process that is available. Appeals typically begin by talking with other authors (if only to get additional perspectives before moving to the next level), then with other professors, the department chair, and the dean. I emphasize here the importance of (a) faculty remaining aware of their role as mentor, keeping the best interest of the student in mind, and being empathetic; and (b) students raising any concerns as soon as they develop. It is better for the faculty–student relationship and less disruptive of the research if these concerns are aired and resolved early in the research process.

THE DISSERTATION

A special case in authorship credit involves a student's dissertation. By definition, a dissertation is meant to be an independent project conducted by the student. Thus, students who successfully complete dissertation research should be first, if not sole, author of any resulting publication. Authorship for others should be determined based on an assessment of the extent of their scientific contribution. Complicating circumstances occur when (a) the data analyses change significantly between the dissertation and the submitted manuscript and the person responsible for these changes (e.g., the dissertation advisor) is different from the dissertation's author; (b) the writing of the paper for publication is undertaken by someone other than the dissertation's author; and/or (c) the dissertation project becomes part of a larger publication involving other projects. Again, it is best to discuss the impact of these circumstances when they first arise.

Conclusion

Because published articles have such value for those involved and the context is so complex, deciding authorship of scientific papers can result in difficult interpersonal circumstances and personal grievances. Perhaps it is most remarkable how often the process occurs without incident. What is clear is that the best way to avoid difficulties is to start with agreed-upon criteria, roles, and responsibilities; remain flexible; and talk about author agreement early and often.

DATA MANAGEMENT II

Data Collection and Handling of Data Sets

3

Because introductory methods texts typically cover well the ethical treatment of human subjects when they are participating in studies, I touch only briefly on this topic here. Instead, I focus on other ethics-related issues in collecting data that receive less attention. I describe methods of data collection and record keeping, in particular the unique issues raised by collecting health-related data and data collected using the Internet. Next, I discuss protecting the confidentiality of data once they have been collected and why doing so is important to fulfilling your promises to subjects after they have left your study. In addition, I briefly discuss why it is important to secure a promise from your subjects to not speak about your study with others.

Then I turn to the management of your completed data set. In the *APA Handbook of Ethics in Psychology*, Fisher and Vacanti-Shova (2012, p. 362), wrote the following:

> Psychologists conducting research must create and maintain records in a manner that allows for replication of the research design. . . . Raw data should

http://dx.doi.org/10.1037/14859-004
Ethical Choices in Research: Managing Data, Writing Reports, and Publishing Results in the Social Sciences, by H. Cooper
Copyright © 2016 by the American Psychological Association. All rights reserved.

be stored in a form accessible to analysis or reanalysis by the psychologist or other competent professionals who seek to verify substantive claims. (p. 362)

Managing data sets concerns not only how records and data are kept (e.g., to keep them confidential and protect them from loss or tampering) but also who owns and has access to data, where the records and data are stored and protected, how long data should be retained, and when data can be destroyed.

Definition of Data

Merriam-Webster defines the term *data* as "facts or information used usually to calculate, analyze, or plan something" (Data, n.d.). Clearly, the definition is extremely broad. For example, your research meeting notes might contain the statement "Jane [a research assistant] had the idea to examine the taped interviews by looking at the transcripts and counting the number of times subjects used the pronoun 'I' and determining whether persons of higher status use it more often." Jane's suggestion contains reference to at least six types of data: the originator of the idea (Jane), the taped interviews, the transcriptions, the frequency count of each subject's use of "I," the determination of which subjects were of low and high status, and the results of the statistical test. Note that the data take different forms, but all are an important part of the scientific record.

It may seem odd at first, but record keeping and data management begin on the day the research project begins. It is not unusual for researchers, even some seasoned ones, to think of data only as the numbers they collect and/or their field notes, questionnaire responses, transcripts, and videos of interviews. However, to avoid ethics-related problems you should think of all the records regarding a research project as data, even the notes and descriptions that relate to the development of an idea, the research design, and the assignment of responsibilities to team members.

The Office of Research Integrity (ORI) published a guide, authored by Coulehan and Wells (n.d.), for responsible data management in scientific research. It is an excellent introduction to the issues surrounding the handling of data and keeping data confidential. It also covers data sharing and how to apportion and monitor data responsibilities among members of a research team. The ORI scheme for organizing concepts in data management is reproduced in Table 3.1. Although the ORI guidelines are aimed primarily at researchers who may wish to use

TABLE 3.1

Key Concepts in Data Management From the Department of Health and Human Services Office of Research Integrity

Key concept	How it relates to responsible conduct of research
Data ownership	This pertains to who has the legal rights to the data and who retains the data after the project is completed, including the principal investigator's right to transfer data between institutions.
Data collection	This pertains to collecting project data in a consistent, systematic manner (i.e., reliability) and establishing an ongoing system for evaluating and recording changes to the project protocol.
Data storage	This concerns the amount of data that should be stored—enough so that projects results can be reconstructed.
Data protection	This relates to protecting written and electronic data from physical damage and protecting data integrity, including damage from tampering or theft.
Data retention	This refers to the length of time one needs to keep the project data according to the sponsor's or funder's guidelines. It also includes secure destruction of data.
Data analysis	This pertains to how raw data are chosen, evaluated, and interpreted into meaningful and significant conclusions that other researchers and the public can understand and use.
Data sharing	This concerns how project data and research results are disseminated to other researchers and the general public, and when data should not be share.
Data reporting	This pertains to the publication of conclusive findings, both positive and negative, after the project is completed.

Note. From "Guidelines for Responsible Data Management in Scientific Research," by M. E. Coulehan and J. F. Wells, n.d., developed by Clinical Tools Inc. for the Office of Research Integrity. Reprinted with permission. Table contents are attributed as follows: "ORI introduction to the responsible conduct of research," by N. H. Steneck, 2007. Available at http://ori.dhhs.gov/documents/rcrintro.pdf.

health records, the rules are thorough and should be followed in all human subjects' research regardless of whether or not health-related issues are under study. In this chapter, I discuss the first five rows in the ORI table. The remaining topics are covered in other chapters.

Data Collection

Data collection refers to the mechanics of how data will be obtained, recorded, and documented. The ORI data management guidelines (Coulehan & Wells, n.d.) suggest that before data collection begins a written plan should be in place that answers several questions. All members of the research team should know and feel comfortable with the plan. The questions are

■ What is the purpose of the research?
■ What methodologies were chosen for the research and why?
■ What are the methods' strengths and weaknesses in relation to inferences you want to draw?
■ How will these methods be implemented?
■ What forms will the data take? What instruments will be used to collect data?
■ How will data be analyzed?
■ Were unexpected events encountered while the data were being collected?

Answering these questions in writing before you begin collecting data may seem like lots of work and the last thing you want to do when you are excited about getting the study started. However, it is also likely the case that you have written most of the answers to these questions; all but a few questions need to be answered as part of your Institutional Review Board (IRB) application. The first two questions are standard on any IRB form. The third question should be answered as part of your assessment of the risks and benefits of your study. If your study's method is not well matched to the inferences you wish to make with your data, the study's benefits are smaller, and it is harder to make a good case for why subjects should be exposed to any potential risks. You also likely will include in the IRB proposal a description of your initial strategy for analyzing the data.

Your records of how and when you collected data should be more detailed than will be requested on the IRB form. If you are running subjects in a laboratory, your subject log-in sheets should do much of this for you. However, if you are collecting data in the field, such as a community setting or a clinic or classroom, the data collectors should keep records of when and where they went to collect data. For example, if you are going to youth soccer matches to interview parents about their involvement in their children's after-school activities, records should be kept of the date, time, and place each interview was conducted, along with who conducted the interview.

In the soccer match example, the interview record itself (the raw data) should be kept. The second form these data will take might be a spreadsheet that contains a transfer of many parents' responses (or a coding of them) to one document. This should be kept as well, along with a code book that explains all codes in the spreadsheet and links each column heading on the spreadsheet back to the original interview question whose responses that column contains. If videotapes were used (e.g., you taped the soccer match and later coded for parent behaviors on the sideline), the tapes are also data, just like open-ended questions, and should be kept.

CHANGES IN DATA COLLECTION AFTER IRB APPROVAL

Not included on the IRB form you submit before you start collecting data but important to record are the changes that occur in your data collection and analysis plan once you have begun collecting data. Some of these changes will require you to amend your IRB form and resubmit it for approval before the change is implemented. For example, if you change data collection instruments (e.g., you find a measure of parental expectations for their children that you like better than the one mentioned in the IRB proposal) or you change subject populations (e.g., you find the 12-and-younger soccer league had too few players, so you add the 12-and-older league) these changes must lead to IRB protocol amendments, a new approval by the IRB, and documentation in your research logs.

Once your data are collected, you may change your analysis strategy, perhaps adding age to the example above or deciding that behaviors are nested within games, something you had not thought of earlier. These kinds of changes typically do not need new IRB approval, but check with the IRB staff before proceeding. However, your research logs should contain this progression of thinking, especially if you actually conducted one type of analysis and then changed to another (see Chapter 5 on statistical analysis and Chapter 6 on reporting standards).

Again, you may find this level of detail bothersome when you think about doing it before or during collecting your data. However, you will be rewarded for doing it when you begin writing your study. You will discover that the introduction and method sections are largely drafted and primarily need to be updated, organized, and fine-tuned. Decisions you forgot you made will be in the written record. When someone requests a detail of your study, even perhaps after it is published, the answer will be right there.

The ORI data management guidelines (Coulehan & Wells, n.d.) include a nice summary of record-keeping tips. This is reproduced in Exhibit 3.1.

CONSENT TO USE OTHER DATABASES

There are circumstances that will require you to obtain permission to use data collected by others. Suppose you would like to collect data from the application forms parents filled out to enroll their children in

EXHIBIT 3.1

Best Practices in Record Keeping Suggested by the Office of Research Integrity

Pop up Page: Best Practice Tips—Record Keeping

Diligent record keeping is essential to ensuring the integrity of research data. To help maintain data validity and reliability, consider these tips when planning or completing data collection:

- **Include notes:** Your records should allow you not only to account for what occurred during the course of research but also to reconstruct and justify your findings. It is important that records include notes about what methods did or did not work, observations, and commentary on the project's progress. Keep notes according to the research team's predetermined communications plan.
- **Personal notebooks:** For smaller projects using handwritten data, each team member should have his or her own personal notebook for recording project data, observations, etc. Entries should be made in a chronological and consistent manner—for instance, each new workday should begin on a new page. Try not to leave blank lines between entries.
- **Noting errors:** Use a consistent system for noting errors or adjustments. In written records, make entries in indelible pen so that records cannot be altered or damaged. If information needs to be changed or amended, mark through the entry with one solid line and initial and date the change. The records can thus reflect what has occurred during the course of a project.
- **Recording information:** Record anything that seems relevant to the project, its data, and the standards of the project. At a minimum, records should include the following information:
  - date and time
  - names and roles of any team members who worked with the data
  - materials, instruments, and software used
  - identification number(s) to indicate the subject and/or session
  - data from the experiment and any pertinent observations from the data's collection
  It may also be helpful to include a summary of the day's data collection activities and a task list for the next day.
- **Transferring information:** When transferring records from written to electronic format, use a double entry system to reduce rates of incorrectly entered electronic data. To implement such a system, have two different Research Assistants enter all of raw data into the software program, then cross-check the data to identify and remedy inconsistencies at the time of data entry. Use our printable worksheet to help track your data collection and entry activities. This handout is included at the end of the document.

Note. From "Guidelines for Responsible Data Management in Scientific Research," by M. E. Coulehan and J. F. Wells, n.d., developed by Clinical Tools Inc. for the Office of Research Integrity. Reprinted with permission.

a soccer program. Such data belong to the soccer program and were not collected with the parents' understanding that the data might be used for research purposes. Your use of the data requires the permission of the soccer program officials and parents. In some cases, securing parent permission may be unnecessary if, for example, a program official agrees to aggregate the data for you in a fashion that cannot be used to identify the program and the children who take part in it. Whether your protections in such a case meet standards for confidentiality and informed consent is an issue you should take up in consultation with your IRB and include in the protocol you submit for approval.

Protecting the Confidentiality of Subjects' Data

There are several steps you should take to ensure that your subjects' identities and the link between their identity and data remain confidential:

- Assign each subject a unique identification number that is unrelated to her or his data. Keep the key that relates the numbers to identifying information in a separate and secure location.
- Keep informed consent documents separate from the data sheets.
- If your subjects' responses are on paper, keep the original data together in a secure place. If the paper sheets are needed for coding (for example, categorizing open-ended responses) make copies on which any identifying information has been removed. Be sure to collect all copies.
- If your data are collected on the computer, make a copy of the unique identifier with the identifying information and put this is a secure place. Remove the identifying information from the data set you will use for analysis.
- If your data are collected over the Internet or on a shared computer server, be sure to employ up-to-date encryption, password, and firewall techniques.
- Destroy the identifying information as soon as it is no longer needed.
- Train anyone who will see the identifying information in why confidentiality is necessary.
- Allow access to data only to those who need it (a topic I return to in the next chapter).

If a subject withdraws from your study before he or she completes participation or if errors make a subject's complete responses unusable (e.g., you discover the subject has a characteristic not permitted by your sampling frame or failed to correctly complete a questionnaire), the subject's data should be immediately destroyed and not entered into your data set. Of course, records should be kept of this occurrence, and your paper should detail how often this happened and why. If the subject withdraws after the study has been completed, this should be noted in the original data set, but the data set used for analysis should not include the subject's data.

HEALTH-RELATED INFORMATION AND CONFIDENTIALITY

The U.S. Department of Health and Human Services has developed guidelines for the collection and use in research of health-related information about subjects (U.S. Department of Health and Human Services, n.d.-a). The Common Rule (U.S. Department of Health and Human Services, n.d.-a, -b), discussed in Chapter 2, also pertains to this topic. These rules fall under the Health Insurance Portability and Accountability Act (HIPAA) of 1996 (U.S. Department of Health and Human Services, n.d.-c).

The HIPAA rules protect personal health information (PHI), which includes subjects' physical or mental health in the past, present, or future, and any health-related treatments received by subjects. The HIPAA rules require that before health records can be used in research:

> (a) a patient signs an authorization to release information that is project specific (*not* a general authorization for PHI for future unspecified research); (b) an institutional review board (IRB) or privacy board approves in writing a waiver of the requirement for such authorization, and the investigator provides the covered entity with written assurance that HIPAA-compliant procedures are in place to protect confidentiality; or (c) the records are de-identified, as specifically defined in HIPAA regulations. (Fisher, 2009, pp. 135–136)

Although most research in psychology does not have the goal of treatment for a particular individual, psychology researchers using PHI must comply with HIPAA rules. With regard to item (b), if you have applied for a waiver from your IRB and it has been approved, you still need to provide the covered entity with assurance that your procedures to protect confidentiality are robust. A *covered entity* includes health care providers (including individual caregivers, clinics and hospitals, clearinghouses) and health insurers. The state in which your study is being conducted may also have privacy rules for use of PHI, and these may be stricter than HIPAA rules. You must comply with state rules.

In addition to the U.S. Department of Health and Human Services website (n.d.-a), a clear description of how HIPAA rules relate to psychological research can be found in Fisher and Vacanti-Shova (2012). They include circumstances that may require you to reveal some information you learn from subjects. These situations can vary from state to state, so be sure to check the regulations in the state governing your institution. The American Psychological Association (APA) published a book that goes into detail about "duty-to-protect" situations (Werth, Welfel, & Benjamin, 2009). The circumstances that universally require disclosure include instances in which the subject reports child or elder abuse or the intent to harm himself or herself or commit violence against a specific other person. Even in an interview seemingly as innocuous as parent involvement in a child's activity, you should remain vigilant for disclosures that require reporting.

You can obtain a certification of confidentiality from the National Institutes of Health or a U.S. Department of Health and Human Services agency if you think that your substantive topic requires extra protection from disclosure for you to collect data. This certificate protects you from having to reveal certain types of information, even under subpoena. However, it relates to only some types of information that might prove harmful to the subject, such as financial dealings or damage to personal reputation; it does not include the instances I mentioned in the preceding above. It also does not require you to keep this information confidential if you feel revealing it would prevent imminent danger to specific others.

Because there are limits to your ability to keep information confidential, it is important that your informed consent procedures explain this to subjects. In addition to the exclusions mentioned, limitations to confidentiality caused by the means of data collection (e.g., data will reside on common computer servers) should be noted. Although this disclosure may lead some subjects to decide not to participate, your truthfulness and transparency will begin to build trust with your subjects even before the study begins. It is likely that a representative of your IRB can provide you with language that meets this obligation without causing undue reluctance on the part of potential subjects.

INTERNET DATA

Collecting data from subjects over the Internet presents complex ethical issues that are only now being identified, debated, and resolved. Issues surrounding Internet research that collects data from subjects who have agreed to take part in your study are relatively straightforward as long as the informed consent was clear about its intended use; the safeguards for confidentiality and informed consent are the same as those in place to protect subjects who provide data in your presence or through the mail (for an example, see Reips, 2012). Treat Internet subjects no differently than subjects who come to your laboratory. Also, when data are collected over the Internet, it is not as easy to establish that informed consent is authentic, that is it has come from the person who actually takes part in the study.

Ethical issues that arise from using the contents of the Internet, such as the Facebook pages of the soccer program and the children who take part in it, are less clear. What you can and cannot use will depend on whether the Internet is viewed as a public space or private mailbox. This designation remains under debate. The answer to this question will depend on the nature of the information you are retrieving. For example, information on the schools which soccer players attend, the schools' sizes, and the economics of the populations they serve (e.g., the percentage of students eligible for free lunch programs) are public records and can be retrieved from the Internet without concern. But personal information on soccer players is less clearly public. This is especially true for qualitative data. For example, suppose you find a quote you want to use on a soccer player's Facebook page that helps you make the point that some children do not like it when their parents attend their soccer games; the parents' attendance makes the children anxious. A direct quote might be traceable to the specific child and harm her or his relationship with parents. Because the quote was in a comment the child made on a Facebook page, is it "fair game"? Probably not; you may have compromised the child's confidentiality even if you do not use names in the paper. The concern is that sophisticated search engines might be able to retrieve with good accuracy the name of the child who posted the quoted material, whereupon the following questions arise: "Was the statement public because it was on the Internet? Are you being unethical by simply drawing attention to it?"

My own advice in this case is simple: if you can, find some other way to emphasize the point or find a quote that is clearly in the public domain. Still, if you want to use the Internet (or any data collected by others for other purposes) as a source of information, your best safeguard against a charge of an ethical breach is to carefully consider whether you need informed consent from the person who provides the data and how you will protect that person's confidentiality. These should be spelled out in your IRB protocol. Speak with a member of the IRB staff before you prepare your protocol. Your IRB's approval is not just an acknowledgement that your procedures meet ethical standards. It is also a protection against claims of unethical behavior that might arise after the fact.

A MORE GENERAL NOTE ON THE INTERNET AND CONFIDENTIALITY

The growing presence of the Internet in our lives and the way it has linked us together is rapidly changing our notions of privacy and how privacy is protected. What information about us is confidential and how that information can be used is an ongoing debate. Today, you can be a subject in an experiment without knowing it or at least without realizing you gave blanket consent when you signed an agreement to receive an online service. For example, when you visit a website or make an online inquiry or purchase, the information you view may be one condition in an experiment. That is, someone making the same or a similar query a few miles away from you may get a different, experimentally controlled response. Your subsequent web behavior may be used to make your next click more useful or efficient for you (or increase your likelihood of making another purchase). All of your behavior may be contributing to an enormous database that will be used for research in the future.

Your use of the Internet as a research tool also raises a set of unique issues. Several of these issues are discussed by Hoerger and Currell (2012). For example, suppose you recruited families for your soccer study by sending a mass e-mail to parents, and you received their agreement to take part via a response e-mail. These communications are likely not available only to you. They can be collected and read by others. Printing them out and deleting your electronic version probably will not be sufficient protection of confidentiality because your organization may back up computer files on a daily basis. In addition, many such electronic communications are open to subpoena, and your employer will tell you they should not be destroyed. Similarly, you may use a survey application on the Internet to collect parent or child questionnaires. The survey application may be administered by your institution. If so, there are likely administrators who can view your account and data.

Burbules (2009) has suggested that the new technologies require us to think about privacy in entirely different ways. He proposed that we adopt a context of *networked ethics*, "a rethinking of how one makes ethical judgments in an environment that is structured by a complex, interdependent, and rapidly changing set of relations" (p. 537). Burbules contended that

> many of the elements of typical human subjects review (privacy, anonymity, the right to "own" information about one's self) need to be rethought; as do the procedures by which the well-being of research subjects is, we hope, to be served. (p. 538)

That said, the "old" human subject privacy protections are still in place and, if anything, have grown more comprehensive in recent years. As Fisher and Vacanti-Shova (2012) noted, in many studies the possibility that data will become public or be shared with inappropriate people is the greatest risk to subjects. That is why an important rule of data collection is to not collect more information from subjects than is needed for your study, especially information of a sensitive nature. In Appendix A, I have reproduced the section of the APA's *Ethical Principles of Psychologists and Code of Conduct* (APA Ethics Code, 2010a) that relates to privacy and confidentiality (Standard 4: Privacy and Confidentiality).

Fulfilling Obligations and Promises to Subjects

Any promises you make to subjects should be fulfilled in a timely fashion. Not to do so is unethical. One example of this is monetary payments. Your institution should have rules about how subjects are paid, especially with regard to how payments can be made and the documentation you need to show the payments were made.

Obligations can also include sharing copies of your report once it is complete. This is less likely to be part of your obligations if you are using subjects from a university subject pool. It is more likely to be the case if you are conducting a study in school classrooms, for example. Both school administrators and individual teachers may want to see your report. Sometimes teachers (or heads of departments at businesses) may want to see the full report or the piece that relates to their responsibilities. If you made these commitments, follow through on them. However, be sure when you make these types of promises that you are complying with the ethical standards for confidentiality and any unique agreements you made before you began collecting your data. For example, it is okay to show a company manager the results of analyses you did that reveal a relationship between age and productivity, assuming that you disclosed on the subjects' consent forms the possibility of sharing aggregated data with managers that cannot be used to identify individuals. It is not okay to show managers the raw data, even if the names of employees have been removed. The manager might have access to records that pair ages to names.

Asking Subjects to Keep Your Study Confidential

Confidentiality is a two-way street. You need to keep confidential your subjects' participation in your study and the information you learn about them. But in many instances it is also critical that your subjects keep confidential the information they learn about you and your study. This is especially important if your study involved some form of deception or misdirection that allows your manipulation to work. For example, a foundational study in social psychology involved influences on conformity (Asch, 1951). In that study, groups of subjects were presented a perceptual task with a clear correct answer. However, all the subjects but one in a group setting where confederates of the experimenter and began giving wrong answers in the presence of the real subject. The dependent variable was whether the real subjects would give similar wrong answers. Clearly, your study's validity will be ruined if subjects relate their study experiences to others who might later take part in your study.

Experiments involving deception are not the only ones that need subjects to maintain confidentiality. In some experiments, you might want subjects' reactions to be spontaneous and uninfluenced by prior thought or practice. Subjects might practice or think about their response if they know your objective before they take part your study.

Asking a subject to keep the methods and purpose of a study confidential should occur during the debriefing process. Your success at this will be an accumulation of how well you treated the subject. If deception was used, you should make it clear to subjects that the manipulation was constructed, often through extensive pilot testing, to be credible to nearly everyone (note that I did not use the word "fooled," see APA Ethics Code, 2010a, Subsection 8.07 regarding deception in research). You should also make certain it is clear what the purpose of the study was, why the purpose is important, and how much you value the subject's contribution. It should be clear that subjects are viewed as collaborators and their contribution to psychological knowledge, as well as your contribution, depends on them keeping the procedures and purpose of the study confidential. Of course, subjects cannot be forced to keep the details of your study confidential. This makes it all the more important that they understand your respect for them and the value of their efforts and when you request their cooperation.

Ownership of Data Sets

It is important to be clear about who owns the data you have collected. According to ORI (n.d.-a) data ownership

> refers to both the possession of and responsibility for information. Ownership implies power as well as control. The control of information includes not just the ability to access, create, modify, package, derive benefit from, sell or remove data, but also the right to assign these access privileges to others. (p. 1)

Principal investigators (PIs) sometimes assume that they own the data they collect. In most cases this is not true. If you are doing research while holding a position at a university, another type of research institution (such as a contract research firm, a hospital or clinic that conducts research, or a school system), or a private foundation or business (whether profit or nonprofit), the data you collect as part of your job typically are owned by your employer. ORI refers to these as *sponsoring institutions*. If you have a grant to conduct the research, the funder may own the data. This information should be found in the terms of the funding agreement.

DATA COLLECTED UNDER CONTRACT

Suppose you work not for a university but for a child welfare agency. The agency owns the data you collect under its auspices. Suppose as well that the agency receives funding for your study from a philanthropic foundation. The foundation wants the agency (and you) to collect data on parent involvement in their children's after-school activities and explore its correlates. Who owns these data and who can make the results public undoubtedly are spelled out in the agreement between the funder and the agency. Your job description also should refer to these rules.

This type of arrangement is called *contract research*. In this case, you and your agency have agreed to collect the data as specified in the research protocol and to answer the questions it is meant to answer. Institutions can object to the restrictions put on the use of the data in a contract. Agreements can go through several iterations before a final version is reached. All signers must approve any changes to the agreement. Typically, the report you produce in contract research is the property of the funder and for its use only. Unless otherwise agreed to, the funder decides who else will see it. Often, disputes about agreements deal with the investigator's right to make the results public. If you are doing contract research, be sure you understand what you can and cannot do with the data you collect. You should secure explicit approval if you want to publish the report.

At all types of institutions that conduct scientific research, if you are the PI, you are the *steward* of the data on its behalf. Further, PI is not just a title used to designate the steward of a funded project; it refers to the person with overall responsibility for a project regardless of its funding source. This means you are responsible for the data and have "physical custody" of it (on behalf of your employer), even if it resides on a common institutional computer with limited rights to access. Macrina (2005) summarizes the role of the PI as follows:

> The principal investigator assumes the primary responsibilities for data collection, recording, storage, retention, and disposal. Grantee institutions (e.g., universities) usually operate so as to give maximum latitude and discretion to principal investigators. However, the discharge of these duties does not impinge upon, nor should it cloud, the issue of data ownership. (p. 273)

DATA COLLECTED ON A RESEARCH GRANT

Research grants also provide funds or other resources for research but are different from contracts. Depending on the funding source, PIs on grants typically have more liberty to revise grant research protocols after the award is made. PIs can make such alterations if it will improve the studies or answer questions more clearly. They can substitute new questions related to the topic of the grant. These questions might arise as the research progresses. Grant PIs are also free to publish as they like, the more the better. These conditions generally are true, but it is always important to read the funding agreement to ensure the funding agency agrees to these terms.

PROPRIETARY DATA

At most universities, you are free to publicly present and publish the research you conduct as part of your work without specific prior institutional permission, assuming (a) doing so is consistent with agreements if the research is funded by outside sources and (b) the study has been properly vetted by the university's IRB. This freedom might not be true at other institutions that conduct research, such as contract research firms, nonprofit organizations, or businesses. In those situations, PIs likely need permission before they present or publish data, regardless of funding from outside sources.

For example, studies conducted for businesses often use proprietary information that can give the company (or the company that contracted with your research firm) an improved position in the marketplace. Suppose you work for a company that helps people find compatible partners, and it uses a proprietary algorithm as part of the dating service. You conduct a study to see whether changes in the algorithm your company uses might lead to better dates, with the important dependent variable being the users' interest in the matches the algorithm produces for them. The revised algorithm you test is derived from basic notions of "liking" or "attraction" that were gleaned from published books and articles. Your results are relevant to the validity of theoretical formulations found in the scientific literature, and you wish to prepare a paper for publication. It does not matter that this purpose is different from the purpose for which the data were collected (to improve an older algorithm). The data are still proprietary and owned by your company.

You would need to obtain your company's approval before submitting this study for publication. (I would not even start writing until I had approval.) It is important to know what your employer's rules are before making public statements about what your research found.

The employer may not want others to know the company is changing its algorithm. Certainly, they would not want the details of how the new algorithm works or its components and weights to be public. This could be a big sticking point in your attempt to get the paper published. You may also discover that your paper is hard to publish unless you can make the algorithms you used public because the algorithms are needed if others are going to be able to evaluate your claims and replicate what you found.

CHANGING INSTITUTIONS

When you work at a university and get a grant to do your research, the grant is made to the sponsoring institution, not to you, and the institution legally owns the data. What happens if you change jobs? Often if a grant is in progress when you leave, you may request of your sponsoring institution that the remainder of the grant and any data already collected go with you. You will also need the consent of the funding agency (if the research has a funder other than just your old institution) and your new institution. Most often the old institution will agree to let you take the project with you. But it is possible, especially if the grant is large and ongoing and there are competent people involved in it who are staying behind, that the sponsoring institution will want to hold it and assign a new PI. They then may *subcontract* with your new institution for that particular part of the data collection and analysis that you will take with you.

Regardless of the fact that you have moved, your old institution should receive credit on the title page as your affiliation for any studies you conducted while there. The ownership of the data remains at the place it was collected unless a negotiated agreement suggests otherwise. You can alert readers that you are no longer at the old institution in your Author Note. In addition, if you plan to collect new data at your new institution, be sure to reapply for approval to do so with your new IRB, even if you have obtained permission from your old IRB.

Data Storage and Protection

You have worked hard to collect and create your data set. The last thing you want to see happen is your data getting lost, stolen, or tampered with in some way that compromises its validity. I learned this lesson early in my career when I entered a colleague's office while he was meeting with collaborators regarding a study they were conducting in several countries. A research assistant responsible for collecting data from one country had informed them via e-mail of her decision to leave school. The collaborators did not know why she made this decision, and she was unresponsive to their queries. She had the only copy of the data for her country. The data set was never recovered, and the collaborators had to explain the loss of data (and the waste of resources for its collection) to their funding agency.

Clearly, data should be stored in duplicate, in separate locations, and with documentation complete enough that the data can be interpretable and replicable by others. The record should also permit you to establish who "owns" the data, when it was collected, and by whom. Steneck (2007), writing for ORI, suggested the following rules:

- Laboratory notebooks should be stored in a safe place. When written notebooks are used, you should keep two copies in different places.
- Computer files should be backed up. You can do this using a dedicated hard drive separate from group servers. Needless to say, any data that resides on a computer should be protected by up-to-date antivirus software. Data on the Internet should use software that allows you to monitor access to your files.
- Original data, such as questionnaire responses and videos, should be saved in a medium that will not degrade over time. For example, in chemistry and biology laboratories, this rule might dictate that written records use a specific type of ink and paper. Social scientists should consider their options as well.
- Care should be taken to reduce the risk of fire, flood, and other catastrophic events destroying your data.

DATA ENCRYPTION

You should consider encrypting your data regardless of whether it resides on your own computer, a removable drive, a shared server, or the Internet. Data encryption involves applying an algorithm to your data that prevents others from reading it unless they know a password that allows them to decode the data file. The entire disc on which the data resides can be encrypted, which is called *full disc* or *whole disc encryption*, or only the data file. Essentially, encryption adds gibberish to your file. Your computer's operating system may have a program that allows you to do this (e.g., Apple computers have a program Filevault II). If not, there are free programs available on the Internet that perform encryption (search using the keywords "data encryption" to find the latest of these). Encryption is becoming the norm for data that reside on computers. Your IRB may ask about your data encryption plan when you submit your protocol for approval.

Access to Data Sets

Who has rights to see your data? This is a question that should be answered before a project begins. You should first make this clear with the responsible officers of your institution and funder, should you have one. Know the names of those given access rights by your ownership agreements. If the people overseeing your project change (for example, your program officer leaves and a new one is named) be sure that the change is reflected in the agreements, if needed. Most often, however, these people will be specified in agreements by their position, not the names of individuals.

In addition to access through ownership, there may be several members of your team who have permission to access data. These will include data collectors and data analysts. All members of the team should understand

- what their roles and responsibilities are,
- how they are permitted to use the data and for what purpose,
- how to document their use, and
- that they are not to make unauthorized copies of the data.

ORI (Coulehan & Wells, n.d.) again provides some good advice for keeping access to your data limited to the right people:

- use unique user IDs and passwords that cannot be easily guessed,
- change passwords often to ensure that only current project members can access data [and change passwords whenever someone leaves the project],
- provide access to data files through a centralized process,
- evaluate and limit administrator access rights [e.g., your institution's IT specialist], and
- ensure that outside wireless devices cannot access your system's network. (p. 15)

Retention of Data

How long should you retain data? The rules vary and may be different for the different entities with some claim to the data. For example, if you have a grant from the U.S. Department of Health and Human Services, the agency's current rule is that data should be retained for at least 3 years after you submit your final financial report or any special report that follows that (U.S. Department of Health and Human Services, n.d.-d). Your institution may have a policy that dictates an even longer retention period. A publisher may also have rules for articles in its journals. For example, if you publish a paper in a journal of the APA, the raw data described in the article should be kept "for a minimum of five years after publication of the research" (APA, 2010b; p. 12).

Data retention rules are ever changing, and no one set of rules prevails for all data sets. It is important for you to understand the rules in your particular circumstance. Most notably, the movement toward data sharing promotes the idea that, once published, data should be publicly available. This might require that you post it on a website and/or place it in a data repository (see the section in Chapter 10 on data sharing). There, it will be available to future generations of researchers.

Disposal of Data

Disposing of your data when your project is complete also must be handled with care. All records on paper files should be destroyed after you have made notification and permission has been granted by the data owner, your employer, and/or funder. Computer records might need to be handled by experts who can ensure that "erased" data truly cannot be reconstructed. For example, as mentioned some institutions routinely back up their servers, so even if you have removed your copies, other copies may exist.

Depending on its size, your institution may have an office of information technology. Before your project begins, it is a good idea to contact the office and ask whether assistance is available for setting up a data management system that will include collection, record keeping, storage, retention, access, and confidentiality. Asking these questions before you begin your project should save you much time later. If your project is large enough, you may also have at no cost to you another member of your team, an information technology specialist, whose primary purpose is to assist you with these issues and make them work for you.

Conclusion

In this chapter I have addressed numerous issues surrounding the collection and handling of data sets that raise ethical issues beyond those related to how research subjects need to be treated while they participate in your study. These issues relate primarily to (a) actions you should take to ensure you understand the lines of authority over the data you collect, (b) how to protect the confidentiality of individual subjects' data after the study is complete, and (c) how to handle the complete data sets.

Now that you have your data set, let us turn to the issue of data misconduct.

Misconduct With Data 4

The Federal Research Misconduct Policy of the Office of Science and Technology Policy (Federal Register, 2000) defines research misconduct as "fabrication, falsification, or plagiarism in proposing, performing, or reviewing research, or in reporting research results" (p. 76262). I cover the falsification and fabrication of data in this chapter and plagiarism in Chapter 7. *Data falsification* involves the manipulation or alteration of a data set, such as changing or omitting the responses of subjects. Because we define data so broadly, data falsification can include altering the records of how a study was conducted or even "rigging" a study's methods so that a particular result is more likely. *Data fabrication* occurs when an entire data set is made up. An example would be if the reported study never was run; the entire data set is faked. I examine the causes of data misconduct, how frequently it occurs, and what the scientific community does to prevent and uncover it. Then, I provide examples of actual cases of data fabrication and falsification. These are meant to illustrate the causes of data misconduct and how it is uncovered,

http://dx.doi.org/10.1037/14859-005
Ethical Choices in Research: Managing Data, Writing Reports, and Publishing Results in the Social Sciences, by H. Cooper
Copyright © 2016 by the American Psychological Association. All rights reserved.

as well as provide cautionary tales illustrating why you do not want to engage in such behavior. Finally, I describe specific circumstances in which you can create new data sets that contain modifications of your original data.

It is important to emphasize again here that the scientific community and federal policy make a distinction between *deliberate* data falsification and fabrication and *honest* errors with data. Honest errors are not research misconduct. If you make an honest error in your data set or data analysis, you should correct it as soon as possible. Obviously, honest errors that are detected before publication can be corrected before they become a part of the scientific record. Chapter 10 covers honest errors and how to correct them after publication.

Along with mistreating subjects, misconduct with data is the most serious ethical breach. The American Psychological Association's (APA, 2010a) *Ethical Principles of Psychologists and Code of Conduct* (APA Ethics Code) state simply that "Psychologists do not fabricate data" (p. 11, Substandard 8.10) and "Psychologists do not knowingly make public statements that are false, deceptive or fraudulent concerning their research, practice or other work activities or those of persons or organizations with which they are affiliated" (p. 8, Substandard 5.01). The National Academy of Sciences (NAS), National Academy of Engineering, and Institute of Medicine (2009) point out why data misconduct is so bad. They take the position that data falsification and fabrication are

> so at odds with the core principles of science that they are treated very harshly by the scientific community and by the institutions that oversee research. Anyone who engages in these behaviors is putting his or her scientific career at risk and is threatening the overall reputation of science and the health and welfare of the intended beneficiaries of the research. (p. 15)

Causes of Data Misconduct

The causes, prevention, and uncovering of data misconduct have been topics of discussion almost since the birth of science (Babbage, 1830). Today, the reason most often cited as the cause of scientific misconduct is the pressure scientists feel to establish and maintain a research career. This pressure comes in several forms depending on the stage of the scientist's career. First, there is the need to complete research to receive a degree. Next comes the pressure to publish for career advancement, whether in the form of receiving tenure and promotion at universities or job security and career advancement in other research settings. In addition, the competition to obtain funds to continue ones' work can be an impetus for data misconduct. Prominent researchers are not immune to these pressures. As they become more recognized professionally, researchers may feel even greater pressure to maintain a position of prestige (and funding) and produce proof that their theories and ideas are correct. The inducements for misbehavior continue to grow as the criteria for advancement become more stringent and the competition for funds becomes more intense.

Another factor increasing the incentive to commit data misconduct can be simply to reduce the workload. Whether it is in the form of making up an entire data set or changing some numbers to make results look better or reduce the need to run more subjects, data misconduct is the easy way out, at least until the misconduct is discovered.

Frequency of Data Misconduct

In the book *On Fact and Fraud: Cautionary Tales From the Front Lines of Science*, David Goodstein (2010) noted that, "For years it was thought that scientific fraud was almost always restricted to biomedicine and closely related sciences, and although there are exceptions, most instances do surface in these fields" (p. 3). Although this may or may not be true, it is certainly the case that fraud and misconduct are not confined to any one field of science or, indeed, to any one area of human endeavor.

Martinson, Anderson, and de Vries (2005) conducted a survey that was responded to by 3,247 scientists (about 47% of delivered surveys) who had received funding from the National Institutes of Health. About 0.3%, or 3 in 1,000, said they had engaged in falsifying or "cooking" research data. About 6% said they had failed to present data that contradicted their own previous research, and 10% had withheld details of their methods and results. About 15% said they had dropped data points because of a "gut feeling" that they were inaccurate. The authors noted that these estimates might be conservative because researchers who had engaged in these questionable activities might be less likely to have returned the survey. Martinson et al. (2005) found no differences on these self-reports between early career and middle career scientists. Fang, Bennett, and Casadevall (2013) found similar results in the occurrence of misconduct reported by the Office of Research Integrity (ORI). In addition, they found that male researchers were disproportionately represented in the cases. It is only a matter of speculation what portion of the instances of misconduct reported on these surveys were eventually uncovered and corrected.

It also appears that misbehavior with data is increasing. Fanelli (2009) found that the frequency of self-reports of data misconduct was increasing, based on seven surveys conducted over the years. Recent cases indicate that psychology is not immune to misconduct with research data and results. In a survey of more than 2,000 academic psychologists (36% of e-mailed surveys) at major U.S. universities, John, Loewenstein, and Prelec (2012) found that the rate of self-admission of data falsification ranged from 0.6% to 1.7%, depending on the level of incentive they provided respondents for telling the truth. In fact, several highly visible cases of misconduct, two of which are detailed in this chapter, have led to some serious self-reflection in psychology (e.g., Bartlett, 2012; Stroebe, Postmes, & Spears, 2012).

Detecting Data Misconduct and Minimizing Unintentional Errors

Data misconduct in science is detected largely through self-policing. Researchers themselves are the first line of defense against the commission of intended misconduct. This defense is accomplished first through the training and supervision provided by principal investigators, laboratory managers, and employers, all of whom can set a tone for a lab that explicitly conveys that bad practices will not be tolerated.

Minimizing unintentional errors also can be accomplished through training and by creating a laboratory culture that emphasizes care and collaboration. How research records are kept and how data collection and analysis are documented are the first safeguards against both intentional and unintentional errors. A laboratory atmosphere that encourages double-checking numbers and analyses by multiple lab members is less likely to make mistakes. Creating a laboratory culture that emphasizes collaboration also can be a safeguard against misconduct. The more eyes that see data sets, the less likely it is that a cheater will go undetected.

The second mechanism for detecting intentional errors and unintentional ones missed by the researchers involves the broader scientific community. Research reports, especially those submitted for publication, are carefully scrutinized during the peer review process. Peer reviewers do not necessarily review raw data (although they can request to) but often find inconsistencies within reports that suggest an error may have been made. For example, the reviewer might discover that the sample sizes and degrees of freedom used in reported inferential tests are inconsistent. In my experience, peer reviewers also cast a spotlight on research results they find "too good to be true."

After publication, results are open to scrutiny by any reader. The more important or controversial the area of study, the more closely results will be scrutinized (and the more likely that researchers seeking recognition will be tempted to misbehave?). In addition, regardless of the area of study, it is becoming more common for researchers to be required by the journal publishing their study or their funders to make their data public and/or available to other researchers who want to verify the results. I will discuss data sharing more fully in Chapter 10.

Finally, others may attempt to replicate what was found. A successful replication does not necessarily mean that no misconduct has occurred; simply because the data have been fabricated or falsified does not necessarily mean the hypothesis is incorrect. Likewise, a failure to replicate results is not evidence of misconduct. Such failures can result from subtle changes in methods, differences in subject characteristics, time and circumstance, and by simple chance alone. That said, multiple failures to replicate results lead to added scrutiny of the work.

Peer review, expanded access to data, and replication are far from foolproof methods for detecting data misconduct. In fact, as you will see in the examples that follow, misconduct often is uncovered and reported by colleagues of the cheater. These colleagues are peers, and surprisingly often they are research assistants and graduate students. This raises the concern that reporting misconduct may be distressing for the reporter. It can be difficult to do because it will involve reporting misconduct by a supervisor, mentor, or personal friend. It might have negative consequences for one's own career. For this reason, large institutions typically have policies that cover procedures for reporting and conducting investigations into charges of research misconduct. They may also have related protections in place that allow these reports to be initiated anonymously and protected against reprisals. (For example, see the University of Wisconsin–Madison's [2010] policy for reporting misconduct that protects graduate students and postdoctoral research associates.) Whether these protections exist depends a lot on organizational culture. You should check to see if your organization has such protections. Still, if you know something is amiss, especially if you are or will be listed as an author, remember that the consequences are most dire if the misconduct is uncovered by someone not affiliated with the study after it is published.

If you work for a university, your institution may also have a research integrity officer (RIO), as does the Office of Research Integrity (2014a). In Exhibit 4.1, I have reproduced some excerpts from the ORI sample policy on research misconduct that should parallel your institution's policy. Note that if you suspect misconduct with data, you should be able to talk with your RIO confidentially and even present your concerns as hypothetical scenarios. Be aware that respondents, the people accused of

EXHIBIT 4.1

Excerpts From the Office of Research Integrity Sample Policies and Procedures for Responding to Allegations of Research Misconduct: Section IV: General Policies and Principles

A. Responsibility to Report Misconduct

All institutional members will report observed, suspected, or apparent research misconduct to the RIO [Research Integrity Officer]. If an individual is unsure whether a suspected incident falls within the definition of research misconduct, he or she may meet with or contact the RIO at [telephone number] to discuss the suspected research misconduct informally, which may include discussing it anonymously and/or hypothetically. If the circumstances described by the individual do not meet the definition of research misconduct, the RIO will refer the individual or allegation to other offices or officials with responsibility for resolving the problem.

At any time, an institutional member may have confidential discussions and consultations about concerns of possible misconduct with the RIO and will be counseled about appropriate procedures for reporting allegations.

B. Cooperation With Research Misconduct Proceedings

Institutional members will cooperate with the RIO and other institutional officials in the review of allegations and the conduct of inquiries and investigations. Institutional members, including respondents, have an obligation to provide evidence relevant to research misconduct allegations to the RIO or other institutional officials.

C. Confidentiality

The RIO shall, as required by 42 CFR § 93.108: (1) limit disclosure of the identity of respondents and complainants to those who need to know in order to carry out a thorough, competent, objective and fair research misconduct proceeding; and (2) except as otherwise prescribed by law, limit the disclosure of any records or evidence from which research subjects might be identified to those who need to know in order to carry out a research misconduct proceeding. The RIO should use written confidentiality agreements or other mechanisms to ensure that the recipient does not make any further disclosure of identifying information. [Option: The institution may want to provide confidentiality for witnesses when the circumstances indicate that the witnesses may be harassed or otherwise need protection.]

D. Protecting Complainants, Witnesses, and Committee Members

Institutional members may not retaliate in any way against complainants, witnesses, or committee members. Institutional members should immediately report any alleged or apparent retaliation against complainants, witnesses or committee members to the RIO, who shall review the matter and, as necessary, make all reasonable and practical efforts to counter any potential or actual retaliation and protect and restore the position and reputation of the person against whom the retaliation is directed.

E. Protecting the Respondent

As requested and as appropriate, the RIO and other institutional officials shall make all reasonable and practical efforts to protect or restore the reputation of persons alleged to have engaged in research misconduct, but against whom no finding of research misconduct is made.

Note. From Office of Research Integrity Sample Policies and Procedures for Responding to Allegations of Research Misconduct: Section IV: General Policies and Principles. Retrieved from http://ori.hhs.gov/sites/default/files/SamplePolicyandProcedures-5-07.pdf. Reprinted with permission.

misbehavior, have the right to confidentiality and the right to respond to charges. ORI also has a rapid response technical assistance program that can help your institution conduct a thorough and fair investigation (Office of Research Integrity, 2014b).

If the research report in question has been published and intentional misconduct is involved, the publisher, upon learning of the misconduct, likely will forward such information to the institution that owns the data or the funding agency. Unintentional errors can be corrected through retraction of the article or, when less severe, the placement of errata at the end of the published article. (I discuss retractions and errata in Chapter 10, which covers matters that arise after a manuscript has been published.)

An Example of Data Falsification

Data falsification occurs when the data for a study have been collected legitimately but are altered in some way to make the results look better. This can occur by changing or omitting data, sometimes called *data censoring*, that goes against the hypothesis the researcher wants to confirm.

Writing in *The Nation* magazine, Charles Gross, an emeritus professor in the Department of Psychology at Princeton University, provided an excellent summary of one of the most highly visible recent cases of data falsification and censoring (Gross, 2012; see also Bartlett, 2010). This case involves Marc Hauser, professor of psychology, organismic and evolutionary biology, and biological anthropology at Harvard University. He had published more than 200 papers and several books on animal cognition and the similarities and differences between animal and human cognitive capabilities. It was his position that rhesus monkey and human infant cognition had much in common. Thus, this is a case of data fabrication perpetrated by a prestigious researcher.

The experiment that appears to have led to accusations that Hauser had falsified data involved auditory pattern recognition in monkeys. In the study, monkeys were exposed to a pattern of sounds that was repeated over and over again. Then, the pattern was modified. Videotapes were coded looking for whether the animals reoriented themselves in a way that indicated they noticed the change. Such behavior, if it exists as Hauser believed, would be a precursor to language acquisition.

A research assistant unaware of the sound pattern being played coded the videotapes for instances of reorientation toward the speakers. The fact that the assistant was unaware of the monkey's condition protects against experimenter expectancy effects unconsciously biasing the data in favor of the hypothesis. A second research assistant analyzed the data and found no support for the hypothesis, which was that monkeys were more likely to look at the speaker when the original repeated sound pattern was played. Hauser also coded the tapes, and these data produced a statistically significant finding supporting the hypothesis. Thus, a discrepancy in findings was found because more than one person coded the data. The second assistant suggested that the tapes be coded again by a third coder who was unaware of the sound pattern. Had the discrepancy been unintentional error, this would have been a reasonable way to check for accuracy. However, Hauser resisted forcefully and told his assistant to proceed with the data Hauser had provided. Uncomfortable with reporting the data as Hauser had presented it, the assistants decided to conduct the third coding, unbeknownst to Hauser. This coding again showed no effect of the manipulation. When word of the discrepancies spread through Hauser's laboratory, other lab members reported similar instances, which suggested data falsification on other experiments. Thus, a culture that valued checking results and sharing concerns prevailed among Hauser's laboratory assistants, if not with Hauser himself. He had something to hide.

The research assistants went to the university ombudsman and their dean. This led to a formal investigation and a committee report (Committee on Professional Conduct of Harvard's Faculty of Arts & Sciences, 2010). The investigative committee followed exhaustive procedures. It met 18 times over 2 years, interviewed 10 people, met with Hauser and his attorney, and impounded the Hauser laboratory's notes and computers. They considered the allegations, responses to them, and explanations other than misconduct. They found evidence that Hauser had committed in multiple experiments "falsification and reckless handling of data that in our opinion constitutes research misconduct as defined by federal regulatory standards" (p. 1). They found that Hauser's shortcomings consisted of

> repeated instances of cutting corners, of pushing analyses of data further in the direction of significance than the actual findings warranted, and of reporting results as he may have wished them to have been rather than as they actually were. (p. 84)

The committee drew this lesson from the case: "Skepticism above all toward the veracity of one's own hypotheses is of course an essential virtue of scientists, one that must be modeled for the benefit of trainees" (p. 84).

Ultimately, Hauser resigned his position (Bartlett, 2011). Subsequent attempts to partially replicate the findings in question provided support for Hauser's hypotheses.

An Example of
Data Fabrication

In common usage, *data fabrication* refers to instances in which the data reported have been entirely, or mostly, made up. The conception and design of the study may or may not be carefully worked out, but then the actual collection of data never occurs.

A high profile example of data fabrication involved Diederik Stapel, a professor of social psychology at Tilburg University in the Netherlands who had also worked at the University of Groningen. At Tilburg, Stapel was the founder of the Institute for Behavior Economics Research and the dean of faculty for social and behavioral sciences. In 2009, he won the Society for Experimental Social Psychology's Career Trajectory Award. Thus, this is another instance of misconduct by a prestigious researcher.

Stapel's work focused primarily on cognitive priming. For example, in one of his experiments, subjects were exposed to a brief visual image of an attractive or unattractive person. Subjects then completed a rating of their own attractiveness. The hypothesis was that the priming (contrast) effect would lead to subjects rating themselves as less attractive when exposed to the more attractive image, even if they did not consciously process the picture. In another study, elementary school students were asked to color a picture of a person exhibiting either no emotional expression or shedding a tear. The children were then given candy and an opportunity to share it. The hypothesis was that coloring the picture with the child crying would lead children to feel more empathy for others and therefore be more likely to share their candy.

Both of these experiments were allegedly conducted and the results subsequently published. Both were based on data sets that Stapel had fabricated. In fact, an investigative committee, the Levelt Committee (Levelt Committee, Noort Committee, & Drenth Committee, 2012), composed of faculty at three universities (his two employers and the university at which he received his degree), found evidence of data fabrication or falsification for a total of 55 publications and 10 dissertations with which Stapel was affiliated. No one else was found complicit with his actions. To conduct their investigation, in addition to poring over Stapel's publications and enlisting the aid of statisticians to examine his articles, the committee interviewed more than 90 individuals.

How did it happen, and how was it uncovered? Yudhijit Bhattacharjee (2013) wrote a piece for the *New York Times Magazine* that not only explored these questions but also delved into the psychology of the perpetrator, based on interviews with him, his family, and colleagues.

What is unique about Stapel's deception was he would tell collaborators that he would collect the data himself (which is unusual for a prestigious professor) or that he already had in his possession data relevant to the hypotheses. He would take the study materials home and, rather than distribute them as agreed to, construct the data sets by himself.

Several researchers working with Stapel sensed that something was not right. Stapel often told them data were not available for additional analyses even, for example, for checking the reliability of measures or running moderator analyses (e.g., looking for differences between the sexes). Thus, there was no opportunity in his laboratory to check data. When data were shared, other researchers found anomalies, including rows of numbers in different conditions that were nearly identical and too little variability in numbers from one study to the next.

The investigative committee wrote that the misconduct was discovered by three young researchers who, after months of observation, reported their suspicions to the head of the department. The committee wrote, "The researchers all deserve praise for reporting these suspicions. It is noted that they were in a dependent position and had much to lose" (Levelt Committee et al., p. 9).

Without excusing Stapel's behavior, the investigative committee also held the lack of oversight by the science community responsible for allowing this misconduct to happen. They made recommendations about how oversight could be improved. These recommendations included that newly appointed faculty sign a code of conduct, dissertation data must be collected by the degree candidate, the research culture look more askance on "minor massage" of data (p. 57), more emphasis be placed on replication, details be published about which author was responsible for what part of the research, and journal editors use statistical procedures to identify possible irregularities in data. Stapel himself likened the lack of oversight to sitting next to a cookie jar without a lid (Bhattacharjee, 2013).

Stapel eventually admitted to the misconduct, but not until after he examined potential ways to cover his tracks. What led Stapel to commit the misbehaviors? Borsboom and Wagenmakers (2013) quote Stapel as explaining the factors contributing to his behavior as "The need to score, ambition, laziness, nihilism, want of power, status anxiety, desire for solutions, unity, pressure to publish, arrogance, emotional detachment, lowliness, disappointment, ADD, addiction to answers" (p. 1). Bhattacharjee (2013) elicited this explanation from Stapel for his behavior:

> Stapel did not deny that his deceit was driven by ambition. But it was more complicated than that, he told me. He insisted that he loved social psychology but had been frustrated by the messiness of experimental data, which rarely led to clear conclusions. His lifelong obsession with elegance and order, he said, led him to concoct sexy results that journals found attractive. "It was a quest for aesthetics, for beauty—instead of the truth," he said. He described his behavior as an addiction that drove him to carry out acts of increasingly daring fraud, like a junkie seeking a bigger and better high. (p. 1)

New Data Sets With Modified Data

There are three circumstances for which you can construct new data sets based on the original data: to delete problematic cases, impute missing data, or modify data identified as statistical outliers. In all three instances, the modifications must be thoroughly justified, infrequently applied, and explicitly documented in your research log and research report. In addition, the original data set should *never* be modified or deleted; it should be kept so that the changes you make can be verified.

If you are going to use any of the techniques described below, create a new data set and give it a new name. If you use more than one modification technique on the same original data set, keep a copy of each new data set as it emerges in the order the techniques were applied. You do this so that the progression of changes, from the original data set to the one you use in your analyses, can be open to inspection and verification. Be sure to carefully and completely document how each new data set was altered from the one before it. Give each data set a distinct name that explicitly communicates how it differs from the original data set. For example, you can label data sets with the modifiers "as collected," "subjects deleted," "missing data imputed," and "outliers modified." You might also consider using an Internet-based application, such as REDCap (2015) to manage your data set. REDCap provides an "audit trail" for tracking data modifications and user activity.

Finally, you need to document the order in which data sets with modifications (labeled with compound modifiers) were made because the modifications you make may depend on which is done first, second, and so on. For example, the results of an analysis to identify statistical outliers may be different if it comes before or after subjects with some incomplete data are removed. Generally speaking, it probably is best to conduct the examination of your data in the order they are presented later in this chapter.

When analyses are conducted it is critical that the analytic record specifically contain the name of the data set analyzed. In larger studies in which more than one person may be analyzing data, it is important to restrict access to data sets to ensure that different analysts are using the same data. It is not good to allow analysts to independently decide what modifications to use.

DELETING CASES

If a respondent has many missing data points, you can consider dropping all of that person's responses. Here, the threshold for deletion of subjects should be made before the data are analyzed. If you decide this before the data are collected or analyzed, the decision to delete the respondent is not based on how the deletion will affect the results but rather on whether you think the completed responses become untrustworthy.

It also is important to consider whether deleted respondents are unique in some way such that multiple deleted subjects might result in a study that is relevant to only a particular type of subpopulation: for example, to parents who are highly involved in their child's afterschool activities. It might be possible to get some indication about whether generalizability is restricted because of the deletion if the deleted subjects can be compared with other respondents on variables to which the deleted subjects did respond. For example, you might discover parents who omitted answers to questions about specific soccer skills were more likely to be mothers than fathers.

Sometimes participants can have complete data, but you may decide they should be omitted from the analyses for other reasons. Two frequent reasons for dropping subjects are that you think they (a) did not understand the study's instructions or (b) they did not take the study seriously. In experimental studies, researchers include a *manipulation check* that is meant to gauge whether the manipulated conditions were attended to and believed by the subject (Cozby, 2009). If you use a manipulation check, before you begin the study and certainly before you conduct any analyses related to your primary hypotheses, you should establish criteria for dropping subjects based on responses provided. What constitutes inattention is hard to gauge before data collection, but again, you should not develop and apply any such rule after you have conducted data analysis.

If you deleted cases, your report of the research should include (a) the number of cases deleted and (b) the reason for deleting each case. You should also say whether the deletion criterion was established before the experiment began or adopted post hoc, after the data were collected, but not analyzed, and a problem discovered.

MISSING DATA

A problem that arises in many studies, especially those conducted in field settings, involves subjects who have missing data but not so much that their entire set of responses is called into question. In a study conducted in a health clinic or with children at a soccer game, you may not be able to monitor responses closely, and subjects may accidentally skip a question, turn two pages together, or not answer a question because they do not understand it or because they wish to keep their thoughts and feelings to themselves. Students may be sick on the day one questionnaire or test is given but not on other data collection days. If you are conducting a follow-up to an earlier study, you may not be able to locate all the people who completed the early measures. Study equipment may fail on a particular day of data collection. If this happens, you have some of the data on these subjects but not all of it. Is it possible to retain these data, perhaps estimating how the respondent *might* have answered?

If you have missing data, it is important to consider what caused it. Little and Rubin (2002) grouped missing data problems into different types depending on the cause. My description of their scheme is simple and brief. When data are missing completely at random, it means that the reason the data are missing has nothing to do with the data's value or to the value of any other variable in the data set. Thus, if you lost data in your soccer study because one match was rained out or the video camera battery died, this could be considered data that was missing completely at random. If data are missing not at random, it means that the reason the data are missing is related to the variable's values. For example, you might ask a soccer parent if his or her child is taking a medication. Some parents may find this question intrusive and decide not to answer. Is it possible that parents are less likely to respond if their answer would be "yes"? Finally, the trickiest reason is called missing at random. In this instance, the data point is not missing because of the value of the variable itself but because of another variable in the data set. Suppose you asked soccer parents to state their child's "pass success percentage." Some parents may be able to answer, and some may not. The missing/not missing attribute of responses to this question could be related to parents' responses to another question in your data set. For example, it might be related to the question, "How involved are you with your children's soccer team?" but not to the child's actual passing success.

How to handle missing data presents you with several options. First, you can recontact subjects and ask them again to provide the missing values. This request should make responding as easy as possible, perhaps by approaching parents at the next soccer match, phoning, or sending an e-mail. For data that cannot be retrieved in this way, you can consider conducting the analyses with the value blank. You can also decide to delete the subject entirely.

Finally, you can use a method to impute missing data or estimate its missing value given other values for that respondent in your data set. If you choose to do this, you must be particularly careful. For example, filling children's soccer scoring for a rained-out match (missing completely at random) with the child's average score in completed ones might be acceptable. This would depend on how reliable the average score might be, so you would consider the number of matches for which scoring data are available. You should also consider how many matches were cancelled.

Missing values might also be filled in with the mean of all known values on the characteristic of interest. For example, if a parent did not answer the question, "How many of your child's soccer matches do you attend?" you might fill this with the average of all the parents in the sample. This strategy does not affect the variable's mean in any cumulative analysis, but it does affect the variance and raises the power of inferential tests using it. The legitimacy of such an approach will depend in part on how often it is used.

Alternatively, a missing value might be predicted using regression analysis based on all respondents with known values. In that situation, the resulting equation is used to predict the most likely value for the missing data point. The value of this approach rests on the number of missing values and the credibility of the regression model.

There are more complex approaches to estimating missing values, and numerous books and articles have been written that can help you with such estimations (e.g., Enders, 2010). There are even specific computer programs for estimating missing values.

Again, the legitimacy of using these approaches will rest on assumptions you make about why the data are missing. The appropriateness of the approach for your situation also is a function of the quantity of data missing and how important the variables exhibiting blank values are to the questions you wish to ask. Perhaps, for example, asking parents about a child's medical prescriptions is interesting but not central to your hypothesis.

The most critical point is that if you confront a missing data problem in your study you describe it in your report. The peer review process will give you feedback about how credible your approach was. Your description of any missing data problems you encountered should include:

- the frequency or percentages of missing data;
- any empirical evidence and/or theoretical arguments for the causes of data that are missing; and
- the methods you used for addressing missing data and why it was chosen.

With that information, the scientific community has what it needs to consider whether your procedures were legitimate. Remember that a difference of opinion is not misconduct. However, you cannot undertake to impute values for missing data and not report doing so.

STATISTICAL OUTLIERS

A final reason for modifying a data set involves the identification of *statistical outliers*. Statistical outliers are values on a variable that are so extreme they suggest they were inappropriately drawn from a population different from the one you intended to sample (Barnett & Lewis, 1994). This can happen for reasons you can identify (e.g., measurement errors, values outside the permissible range) or for unknown reasons. In the latter case there are ways to test whether the value is so extreme it is unlikely to be part of the population (e.g., Grubbs, 1950). In this case your sample estimates will be more accurate if the outlying data are omitted or modified (e.g., moved to their next nearest neighbor) so that your sample parameter estimates are more accurate.

Again, this can be done if your reasons are well justified, your procedures are appropriate and used infrequently (numerous statistical outliers in the same data set suggest they are not outliers), and your report includes the details of what you did.

Checking for Errors

According to the NAS, National Academy of Engineering, and Institute of Medicine (National Academy of Sciences et al., 2009), "A crucial distinction between falsification, fabrication and plagiarism (sometimes called FFP) and error or negligence is the intent to deceive" (p. 17). Although unintentional errors may be forgivable, when you collect data it is critical to adopt procedures meant to minimize errors. There are several actions you can take to reduce and remove errors.

In the case of responses that need to be categorized, such as answers to a free response question by parents regarding why they think their child's soccer team won or lost a match, your methodology should contain a mechanism for training coders and having each response coded independently by more than one person. The Hauser case provides an example of an instance in which coding discrepancies led to the uncovering of data misconduct. In most cases, the honest errors made in coding can be identified by having more than one person code the same data, through a double-coding process. If double coding is not possible (because of limited resources), your methodology needs to include some procedure for estimating and demonstrating coder reliability (e.g., Freelon, 2010).

You also need some checks to ensure that any transfer of data from one document to another has been done without error. If your study is being conducted entirely on computers, you can look for programs that transfer data directly from your subjects' responses to spreadsheets and then to statistical analysis. There are both web-based applications and stand-alone software that allow you to do this (e.g., Microsoft Access). If your data must be transferred by humans, such as from printed questionnaires completed on the sidelines of soccer fields to computerized spreadsheets, you should have a second person check the transfers or, if possible, have two people do the transfers independently and run an automated check for discrepancies.

Finally, even the subjects in your study can make mechanical errors, such as accidentally missing a question on an answer sheet. Check for this. You also should check for any *wild values*, that is, instances in which a subject has used a value not within the permissible range. These can be caused by subject mistakes or inaccurate data transfer. You can check for wild values by making your first statistical run a frequency count of responses.

Conclusion

The joint NAS, National Academy of Engineering, and Institute of Medicine monograph (National Academy of Sciences et al., 2009) sums up nicely the potential impact of scientific misconduct:

> Within the scientific community the effects of misconduct—in terms of lost time, damaged reputations, and feelings of personal betrayal—can be devastating. Individuals, institutions and even entire research fields can suffer grievous setbacks from instances of fabrication, falsification and plagiarism. Acts of misconduct also can draw the attention of the media, policymakers, and the general public, with negative consequences for all of science and, ultimately, for the public at large. (p. 18)

When you accept an assignment on a science project, be it as a principal investigator, research assistant, or even as a peer reviewer, you accept the obligation to remain truthful in all aspects of your undertaking and to do all you can to make the scientific record of your activities as free of error as possible. Scientists understand that unintentional human errors will happen. Intentional lack of truthfulness is inexcusable.

In this chapter I defined misconduct with data, why it is unethical, and when the creation of a new data set with modifications might be acceptable. Now, I turn to ethical concerns and misbehaviors that occur when the data are analyzed.

Data Analysis

5

I n the previous chapter, I outlined different ways that data can be manipulated to make results look more to the liking of the researchers. These behaviors, in particular fabricating and falsifying data, are verboten. In this chapter, I turn to techniques for analysis of data that may raise ethical questions. Some of these procedures are clearly unethical, whereas others are permissible under specific circumstances.

American Statistical Association "Ethical Guidelines for Statistical Practice"

The American Statistical Association (ASA; 1999) adopted guidelines for ethical statistical practice. The guidelines are a good complement to the American Psychological Association's

http://dx.doi.org/10.1037/14859-006
Ethical Choices in Research: Managing Data, Writing Reports, and Publishing Results in the Social Sciences, by H. Cooper
Copyright © 2016 by the American Psychological Association. All rights reserved.

(APA, 2010a) *Ethical Principles of Psychologists and Code of Conduct* (Ethics Code) because although both documents embrace the same broad principles (e.g., professionalism, responsibility), the ASA guidelines directly address the behavior of those doing statistical analyses, a topic the APA Ethics Code does not specifically address. The ASA guidelines are broad in their application, encompassing statistical issues not only in psychological research but also in economics, agriculture, health care and pharmaceuticals, public policy and business, and any area in which statistics may be applied. Regardless of the area of application, the rules for ethical behavior are the same.

Appendix B contains the ASA guidelines in their entirety. Many of the guidelines address issues covered in this book. Seeing that different disciplines must speak to the same ethical quandaries serves to demonstrate their universality and reinforce their importance. Some of the ASA prescriptions guide behavior specific to how data analysis should be done. In this chapter, I delve a bit more deeply into some of these circumstances as they apply to research in psychology and the social sciences.

Competence in Analysis Techniques and the Subject Matter

Often, people are recruited to a research team for the specific task of conducting the data analysis. It is the obligation of both the team and the statistician to ensure that the person doing the analyses knows how to get software to conduct analyses and understands the statistical concepts and assumptions upon which different analyses are based (see Chapter 1 for discussion of competence). Gardenier (2011), in his chapter in *Handbook of Ethics in Quantitative Methodology,*[1] states the issue well:

> Necessary concepts for statistical work include probability, randomness, error, distributions, variables, variance, and populations. For applied statistics, we need to add data sampling as a necessary concept. Often useful but not always necessary concepts include independence, outliers, exactness, robustness, extrapolation, bivariate and multivariate correlation, causality, contingency, and risk. Although it is tempting simply to apply statistical software

---

[1]The Panter and Sterba (2011) book is full of excellent chapters on ethical issues in quantitative analyses that might arise at different stages of the research process or in the conduct of numerous specific types of analyses, including factor analysis, multilevel modeling, causal modeling, and meta-analysis. Many of these issues are not discussed here, only the ones that are generally and frequently encountered.

to real world problems without any training in these underlying concepts, that is misleading, error prone, and certainly far from professional. It is also necessary to bear in mind that, in statistical usage, the words describing these concepts have more precise and technical definitions than the same words in everyday usage. (p. 24)

In addition to having confidence in your data analyst's statistical expertise (or your own if you are conducting the analyses), you should not think of statistical analysis as simply number crunching. The data analyst should have a working understanding of the theoretical and/or practical context of the research. This can be critical to the choice and interpretation of analyses.

For example, suppose you were studying the relationship between loneliness and depression. If you used a measure of loneliness that revealed an internal consistency estimate of $rr = .60$, this might raise some concerns about the measure's reliability, its validity (because reliability sets an upper limit for validity), and its ability to reveal relationships with other variables. However, if you also knew that the measure was taken on 9-year-old children, the estimate might be close to the best you could expect at such an age for most individual difference measures tapping broad constructs. If your loneliness measure was given to a sample of adults, the reaction might be quite different. This estimate of internal consistency is toward the low end of what might be expected of measures taken on people of such maturity and might suggest a different measure be used. If your data analyst knows about the age characteristic of your sample, the analyst perhaps would alert you to this possible problem.

In addition, without understanding the broader context of the research, it is questionable whether you or your statistician can make an optimal decision regarding the best analytical approach to the data. For example, suppose you were deciding whether adjusting a correlation for attenuation because of the low reliability of the loneliness measure is appropriate in your study. Here, the answer depends on the study's purpose. An adjustment for attenuation might or might not be called for depending on whether the purpose of the research was (a) to test a theoretical prediction about the relationship or (b) to predict future depression-related behaviors (e.g., attempts at suicide). For theoretical purposes, adjusting for attenuation might be informative. In this case, you do not want measure error to reduce the size of the loneliness–depression correlation to the point that when you analyze the data a Type II error occurs; you fail to reject the null hypothesis when it is, in fact, likely false. But adjusting for attenuation is of little help and may be misleading if you want to use the loneliness scale to predict who might be depressed. The disattenuated correlation will make the measure look more useful than it actually is for this applied purpose.

Descriptive, Exploratory, and Confirmatory Data Analysis

The lesson to take from the preceding discussion is that the choice of statistical methods for analyzing data might depend on (a) characteristics of the sample and (b) the purpose of the research. It also extends to the stage of development of knowledge about your topic. By stage of development, I mean both (a) how well the problem itself is already understood and how often it has been researched and (b) how precisely the hypotheses can be specified in your particular study. If you are the first to study the topic, your analytic strategy might be different than if the area is well studied. Although the ASA guidelines use the terms "exploratory," "intermediate," and "final" to distinguish different analyses at different stages of discovery, in the social and behavioral sciences, the corresponding terms would be "descriptive," "exploratory," and "confirmatory" analyses (Cooper, 2012).

Descriptive analyses are just that: descriptions of the data that typically are used to characterize the sample of people and measures used in a study. For example, you would use descriptive statistics to describe your sample and assess whether the participants in your study of loneliness and depression constitute a representative sample from the population of interest. You might also use them to discover how frequently loneliness and depression occur. Typically, descriptive statistics do not involve any inference tests or tests of correspondence.

Exploratory analyses can be undertaken for several reasons, principally to (a) help you consider whether assumptions about the distribution of the data are appropriate, (b) identify outliers, (c) suggest specific relationships to test again in future research, and (d) help you decide what hypotheses can to be pursued with the your data using what tests. John Tukey's (1977) book *Exploratory Data Analysis* has been influential in setting the rules for exploratory analyses and appropriate use of techniques. Tukey wrote that exploratory data analysis

> is a critical first step in analyzing the data from an experiment . . . [it is used to carry out] detection of mistakes, checking of assumptions, preliminary selection of appropriate models, determining relationships among the explanatory variables, and assessing the direction and rough size of relationships between explanatory and outcome variables. Loosely speaking, any method of looking at data *that does not include formal statistical modeling and inference* [emphasis added] falls under the term exploratory data analysis. (p. 61)

Tukey's use of the phrase "formal statistical modeling and inference" corresponds to the ASA's use of the term "final" and my use of the term *confirmatory analysis*. You cannot pass judgment on the explanatory value of a hypothesis if you are examining your data from an exploratory point of view. In a confirmatory analysis, the hypothesis is precisely stated before the analysis begins. It must not be influenced in any way by the findings of the data you are about to use to test it. It is tested with assumptions that result in statements of the probability that your hypothesis might be correct or, more formally, the probability that the hypothesis of no relationship between the variables, the *null hypothesis significance test*, is true. If the data contributed to the choice of hypotheses, the probabilities cannot be accurately estimated. As Gardenier (2011) stated,

> One of the most important assumptions underlying statistical methods is randomness in the sense of lack of bias . . . we cannot subsequently decide that we do not like the result we have calculated and then reperform the estimate on the same sample using a different method in hope of getting a more pleasing result. (p. 24)

Hypotheses presented as if they were tested in a confirmatory framework can result in faulty results when the procedures used were actually exploratory in nature. For now, the important ethics-related point is that the delineation of which of your analyses are descriptive, exploratory, and confirmatory in nature must be made in advance of the analysis of data. The type, number, and interpretation of your results rest on this determination. Not to make this determination and then report, for example, exploratory analyses as if they were confirmatory would be an ethical breach.

Pitfalls in Data Analysis

Gardenier (2011) used the term *shopping around* to describe the practice of looking at multiple estimates of a statistical parameter and then choosing to report only the one that conforms most closely to the researcher's expectations. This questionable approach to analysis of data seems to be most prevalent when the researcher's objective is to reject the null hypotheses that no relation exists between two or more measured variables in a sample from a population. This phenomenon has also been called *fishing for significance, probability pyramiding, data dredging, data mining, data snooping, p-hacking,* and *opportunistic bias.*

Simplistically, you can think of a hypothesis as predicting the roll of a die. If you predict "6" before the die is thrown but then change the prediction to "5," the odds of you getting it correct are 1 in 6 regardless, although you may have learned something about the weighting of the die that led you to change your hypothesis. But suppose you wait until after the die is thrown, you get it wrong, and try again, this time predicting "5." Your chances of being correct at least once in the two tries are 1 in 3. In scientific studies, you cannot change hypotheses after you have seen the results without reporting both attempts. You also need to critically appraise what *dependence* there might be between your two tosses or how the former throw might have affected your later prediction.

The systematic categorization of how researchers carry out analyses that make suspect their reported estimates and probabilities of rejecting the null hypothesis can be traced back at least four decades to Theodore X. Barber's (1976) monograph *Pitfalls in Human Research: Ten Pivotal Points*. Among the 10 pitfalls (many of which parallel questionable behaviors covered elsewhere in this text) was "Investigator Data Analysis Effects." With some reorganization on my part, these pitfalls included:

- Researchers "eyeball" their data before deciding how it will be analyzed.
- Researchers find that the hypothesis the research was meant to confirm was not supported and then substitute a new hypothesis but do not report the failed hypothesis or that the substituted hypothesis (actually exploratory in nature) needs to be confirmed with independent data. (This practice is often referred to as HARKing—Hypothesizing After Results are Known.)
- Researchers collect data on many variables, some only tangential to the hypothesis of primary interest, and then perform a large number of statistical tests and report only the significant results. These new results are incompletely reported (some nonsignificant tests are not reported) and are not labeled as exploratory in nature.
- After finding that the a priori hypothesis was not supported, researchers analyze the same data by conducting moderator analyses or analyses on subsamples of data that were not planned and for which no a priori hypotheses were stated. Barber (1976) pointed out that "This kind of postmortem [exploratory] analysis can provide hypotheses to be tested in further research but it leads to misleading conclusions when the results are accepted without replication" (p. 21). For example, suppose you were to find no overall relation in your sample between loneliness and depression but then you divided the data into subsamples. You found the relationship did exist among older men who did not attend church (even though your statistical power to test this relationship was reduced). This seems quite reasonable, but it is clearly a post hoc result that needs independent replication.

If I said the relationship between loneliness and depression was found only among young, female churchgoers, could you construct an equally plausible explanation?

▪ Researchers capitalize on chance by performing a large number of null hypothesis tests without adjusting for *experimentwise error* rates, that is, without adjustment for the number of tests being conducted on the same data. In such cases, even if the numbers were generated at random and 20 null hypothesis tests were conducted using p < .05 as the rejection criterion in each case, thus treating each test as if it alone were conducted, at least one significant result would be expected.

▪ Researchers obtain results that fail to confirm the original hypothesis and then check for computational errors, but the same checking procedure is not conducted on results that do confirm the original hypothesis. Thus, if errors remain in the analyses, they are not random but rather favor the original hypothesis.

▪ Researchers find a statistically significant outcome but "fail to point out that the degree or strength of association between the two variables is actually very small or negligible" (Barber, 1976, p. 23). This pitfall is one of the primary reasons the reporting of *effect sizes*,[2] the strength of the relationship, is now encouraged along with null hypothesis tests in the reporting of research findings.

With regard to Barber's (1976) last point, it is important to note the ASA ethical guidelines also say that sampling methods should allow valid inferences, and many studies in the social sciences are *underpowered*; that is, they have sample sizes too small to give the researchers a reasonable chance to reject the null hypothesis (Maxwell & Kelley, 2011). In the quest for statistically significant results, having an inadequate sample size (given the expected strength of the relation under study) can be a major impetus for the questionable behaviors outlined above.

But that is not all. DeCoster, Sparks, Sparks, Sparks, and Sparks (2014) suggested other ways experimentwise error rates can go unacknowledged in the statistical analyses reported by researchers. These include

▪ Researchers run analyses that test multiple main effects and interactions without specifying which effects were predicted. The number of these tests increases rapidly from, for example, three sources of variance if two main effects and one two-way interaction

---

[2]Cohen (1988) defined an *effect size* as "the degree to which the phenomenon is present in the population, or the degree to which the null hypothesis is false" (pp. 9–10). For example, a correlation coefficient is an effect size. You can also find descriptions in Cooper (2011, 2016).

are tested, to seven sources of variance for three main effects and all possible interactions, to 15 sources for four main effects and their interactions.

▪ Researchers measure the same variables in multiple ways (e.g., use two measures of loneliness), and when the first measure does not reveal the hoped-for relationship, they test the other measures and report the measure that provides the most favorable results. This approach is open to capitalizing on random variations (errors) in measurement so that the chosen measure reveals significant relations by chance. The results may be difficult to replicate with a new sample.

▪ Researchers transform data in different ways *after* analysis of the original data did not confirm the hypothesis. Data transformations need to be planned or based on the distribution of the data (perhaps discovered in exploratory analyses) before any confirmatory analyses are performed. For example, this ethical breach would happen if you discovered a nonsignificant relationship between loneliness and depression that was not moderated by whether subjects regularly attended church. However, you then discover that your depression variable was skewed to the right (positive skew), you conduct a square root transform, a natural logarithm transform, and an inverse transform and find a significant result using one of these methods. Although it may have been legitimate to transform your data before you knew the result of the untransformed analysis, it is not legitimate to do because the first result was not significant. The need for transformation must be driven by an inspection of the data before any confirmatory analyses are conducted.

▪ Researchers collect data until desirable results are found. Ideally, before you begin collecting data, a power analysis is conducted using an anticipated effect size and a prespecified error probability at which the null hypothesis will be rejected. This effect size used in planning is based on the results of a pilot study, previous studies, or what size of effect would be considered practically or theoretically meaningful. The number of subjects for the study is based on this power analysis before the study begins. That said, in some limited instances other methods are used to determine when to stop running subjects.

STOPPING RULES

The term *stopping rule* typically refers to setting criteria for deciding what obtained statistical results would be satisfactory to stop running more subjects. This typically relates to the significance of a null hypothesis test because, all else being equal, *p* levels will decrease as the numbers of subjects increase. However, the rule cannot be that "subjects will be run until the null hypothesis is rejected." For example, you should not decide to run subjects in the loneliness and depression study until your *t*-test of the correlation between them rejects the null hypothesis at the $p < .05$ level of significance. You cannot run some subjects, conduct a *t*-test, repeat until the $p < .05$ level is reached, and then stop.

The use of stopping rules is rare in most areas of psychology because of the possibility that the significant results have capitalized on chance; you might have stopped after a particularly fortuitous run of subject responses. Had more subjects been run, the observed relationship between loneliness and depression could be weaker, but closer to the population value than when you stopped running subjects. That said, there are some methods of *sequential analysis* that are meant to minimize distortions in the final test of the null hypothesis (Lakens, 2014).

Why should stopping rules be permitted? They are used most often in medical research when researchers are evaluating a treatment for illness. Stopping rules most likely would lead to stopping a study *before* running the planned number of subjects, not adding additional subjects (although it is possible chance has had an effect on the statistically significant results). In this kind of medical research, ethical concerns are raised by *not* stopping the research if the preliminary results indicate the treatment could have an important positive effect on peoples' lives. Lives might be negatively affected by withholding the treatment while further evidence is collected.[3]

PILOT STUDIES

It is better to conduct a *pilot study* than to use stopping rules. A pilot study involves conducting your study as planned using a limited number of subjects and then not using those subjects in your final data analysis. You decide that you will run a limited number of subjects in each of your experimental conditions or will give the loneliness and depression questionnaires to a small sample. Then you use the resulting effect size to conduct the power analysis. You might even conduct a test of the null hypothesis in a pilot study. The result of this power analysis is used to decide how many subjects to run in the final study.

Pilot studies can assist in a power analysis when effect size estimates are not available from previous studies or there is no way to estimate what effect size would be meaningful (Cooper, 2008). There

---

[3]A brief treatment of ethical and statistical issues related to stopping rules and interim analyses in medicine is provided by Pocock (1993).

are other good reasons to do pilot studies. They can help you discover manipulations that do not have the intended effects by including in the pilot study appropriate manipulation checks. Pilot studies can help you identify measures that are problematic, such as a measure that is unreliable when used with your particular sample. Of course, estimates from a pilot study are likely to be rough. If you conduct a pilot study, you must say so when discussing the procedures in your research report.

SOLUTIONS TO FISHING FOR SIGNIFICANCE

There have been many proposed solutions to the undesirable effects of fishing for significance. Consistent with the advice I have given in this chapter, the APA's "Journal Article Reporting Standards" (covered in the next chapter and presented in Appendix C) recommend that researchers be required to distinguish confirmatory analyses from exploratory analyses and provide a log of all the analyses run. In addition, researchers are increasingly being asked to make their data available along with their manuscript when they submit it for publication (e.g., see the requirements for submission to *Archives of Scientific Psychology*, APA, 2015a), although this does not directly disclose the full number and type of analyses conducted. Another simple approach is for editors and reviewers to require that researchers report experimentwise error rates when data are analyzed and reported (DeCoster et al., 2014).

It has been suggested that the use by editors of statistical significance as an important criterion for accepting a paper coupled with the pressure to publish has distorted the value of fishing for significance. Thus, some have argued for a de-emphasis of null hypothesis significance testing in publication decisions (cf. Kline, 2013) or doing away with it completely (cf. Harlow, 1997). In fact, one journal, *Basic and Applied Social Psychology* (Trafimow & Marks, 2015), has banned its use in the articles it publishes.

Other solutions include (a) preregistration of studies and their intended analyses before studies are begun and (b) placing more value on replications. For example, the journal *Perspectives on Psychological Science* (Association for Psychological Science, n.d.) has begun a publication mechanism, called Registered Replication Reports, whereby replications of classic studies in psychology are registered and approved for publication by the editors before data collection begins. Acceptance for publication is based principally on the fidelity of the methods. Researchers are guaranteed publication regardless of the results. The preregistration of studies and their methods as a prerequisite for publication is an idea that is likely to spread.

When all else fails and there is suspicion that fishing for significance has occurred, procedures have been proposed to help detect it after the fact (e.g., Hedges, 1992; Simonsohn, Nelson, & Simmons, 2014). This happens after a manuscript has been submitted for publication or has been published. It will not protect you against suspicions of deliberate incomplete reporting and misleading presentation of results.

THE VALUE OF DATA SNOOPING

Now that I have cataloged the many ways in which reported *p* values can be distorted to make them look more supportive of confirmatory hypothesis tests than they actually are, it is important to provide the case for judicious use of exploratory analysis. Rosnow and Rosenthal (2011) made the case well:

> snooping around in the data (sometimes referred to as data mining) is technically advisable (in the sense of being transparent, informative, precise, accurate, and well grounded), and it can be a way of increasing the utility of data insofar as it is likely to turn up something new, interesting and important. (p. 52)

Rosnow and Rosenthal (2011) made the case for data snooping on ethical grounds:

> Data are costly in terms of time, effort, money and other resources. The antisnooping dogma makes for bad ethics because it is a wasteful consumption that betrays the public trust that scientists will be prudent in their use of funding, material, people's time, energy, and other resources. (p. 52)

Rosnow and Rosenthal (2011) made the point that if your research is primarily initiated to test a priori hypotheses, it should do so. But it is wasteful to stop there. When you have less well-formed queries to explore, you also should test those. You should even plan such explorations before data are collected so that you collect the variables of interest and make the most efficient use of your resources. It is okay to "follow your nose" if intriguing paths of inquiry present themselves. But this is different from using a "shotgun approach" to data analyses, in which a multitude of tests are conducted on a mass of data with no suspicions about what the data might contain.

For example, you might hypothesize that loneliness and depression are correlated but also be curious about how they might relate to peoples' patterns of social interaction with others. So you ask your subjects questions about social interactions with friends, school or work mates, family, and organized social groups. Your thinking and past research can take you no further than the suggestion that depression might be more closely associated with a lack of some of these kinds of social interactions but perhaps not others. You might also be curious about whether the relationship between loneliness and depression might be moderated by social interactions. To conduct these exploratory analyses is perfectly legitimate. What is critical is that your strategy, rationale for it, and results be fully presented in your manuscript.

What about the effect of data snooping on tests of the null hypothesis? Rosnow and Rosenthal (2011) wrote

> It is true, of course, that snooping around in the data can affect p values obtained, but we can use well grounded statistical adjustments to deal with this problem, in case getting a more accurate p value is important to the investigator. . . . If no adjustment is made for p values computed post hoc, we can all agree that replication will be required. (p. 52)

Thus, they recommend that researchers pay careful attention to experimentwise error rates when data are mined. By labeling tests a priori as confirmatory or exploratory, researchers can preserve the power of their central tests. In our example, no objection would be raised to your testing your depression—loneliness relation as if it were a singular hypothesis and then following the test with more exploratory analyses that appropriately adjust for the number of tests you performed. The key to acceptance of your results resides in your justification for the strategy and the care you use in interpreting the results, in particular, noting the need to replicate exploratory findings.

Frequency of Misbehaviors in Data Analysis and Reporting

The frequency of questionable behaviors in data analysis and reporting by psychologists was examined by John, Loewenstein, and Prelec (2012). Some of their results for nine different misbehaviors are presented in Table 5.1. These researchers found that failing to report all of the dependent measures collected in a study was the most frequently admitted misbehavior among psychology researchers, and they also felt it was the most defensible. The least defensible (after falsifying data, see Chapter 4) was reporting that there was no effect of demographic variables on the results when the researchers (a) did not know whether this was true or (b) knew it was not the case. John et al. (2012) also developed a technique for adjusting the frequencies of questionable data analysis behaviors that suggested they were higher than admitted to by the researchers. They concluded that the frequency of questionable data analysis and reporting was "surprisingly

TABLE 5.1

Mean Self-Admission Rates of Questionable Research Practices, Comparison of Self-Admission Rates Across Groups, and Mean Defensibility Ratings

	Self-admission rate (%)		Defensibility rating (across groups)
	Control group	BTS group	
1. In a paper, failing to report all of a study's dependent measures	63.4	66.5	1.84 (0.39)
2. Deciding whether to collect more data after looking to see whether the results were significant	55.9	58.0	1.79 (0.44)
3. In a paper, failing to report all of a study's conditions	27.7	27.4	1.77 (0.49)
4. Stopping collecting data earlier than planned because one found the result that one had been looking for	15.6	22.5	1.76 (0.48)
5. In a paper, "rounding off" a *p* value (e.g., reporting that a *p* value of .054 is less than .05)	22.0	23.3	1.68 (0.57)
6. In a paper, selectively reporting studies that "worked"	45.8	50.0	1.66 (0.53)
7. Deciding whether to exclude data after looking at the impact of doing so on the results	38.2	43.4	1.61 (0.59)
8. In a paper, reporting an unexpected finding as having been predicted from the start	27.0	35.0	1.50 (0.60)
9. In a paper, claiming that results are unaffected by demographic variables (e.g., gender) when one is actually unsure (or knows that they are)	3.0	4.5	1.32 (0.60)

Note. Items are listed in decreasing order of rated defensibility. Respondents who admitted to having engaged in a given behavior were asked to rate whether they thought it was defensible to have done so (0 = *no*, 1 = *possibly*, and 2 = *yes*). Standard deviations are given in parentheses. BTS = Bayesian truth serum (a condition in which incentives were provided for self-admission of the behavior). From "Measuring the Prevalence of Questionable Research Practices With Incentives for Truth Telling," by L. K. John, G. Loewenstein, and D. Prelec, 2012, *Psychological Science, 23,* pp. 524–532. Copyright 2012 by Blackwell Publishing. Adapted with permission.

high [and] may constitute the prevailing research norm" (p. 524). Further, they suggested

> the prevalence of QRPs [questionable research practices] raises questions about the credibility of research findings and threatens research integrity by producing unrealistically elegant results that may be difficult to match without engaging in such practices oneself. This can lead to a "race to the bottom," with questionable research begetting even more questionable

research. If reforms would effectively reduce the prevalence of QRPs, they not only would bolster scientific integrity but also could reduce the pressure on researchers to produce unrealistically elegant results. (p. 531)

Pitfalls in Data Interpretation

Hubert and Wainer's (2011) statistical guide for the ethically perplexed described numerous other mistakes that might be made in data analysis and interpretation. Many occur more as a function of poor training or forgetfulness than because of ethical lapses. Here I briefly describe two errors in interpretation mentioned by Hubert and Wainer that researchers often make.

ECOLOGICAL FALLACY AND SIMPSON'S PARADOX

First is the phenomenon referred to as the *ecological fallacy* (Robinson, 1950). The ecological fallacy occurs when data collected at one level of analysis are used to infer a relationship at another level. For example, suppose you collected from 40 countries around the world the national percentages of clinical depression and the frequency with which people report going to church. You found a correlation of r = .30 (n = 40). You interpreted this to mean depression and church attendance were positively correlated *among individuals.* This inference would be wrong because the data were not collected at the individual level; it is possible that both variables are caused by economic factors that vary *across countries*: that is, a weak economy causes both a higher countrywide mean depression and higher church attendance. However, *within* each country, the relation might be in the opposite direct: given the shared economic conditions, people who go to church more often are less depressed.

Related to the ecological fallacy is another phenomenon called *Simpson's paradox* (Simpson, 1951). This occurs when the result of an aggregate analysis is compared to results within meaningful subgroups and the results are found to differ. Perhaps the best-known example involves a lawsuit brought against the University of California at Berkeley alleging that its selection of graduate students was biased against women applicants (Bickel, Hammel, & O'Connell, 1975). The aggregate analysis done without regard to graduate departments revealed that 44% of male applicants and 35% of female applicants were admitted. However, when the data were analyzed separately for each of the 85 individual graduate admitting units, the data showed few units departed significantly from expected frequencies of admissions for the two sexes. About the same number of units admitted higher percentages of females as males. How could this happen? Women tended to apply to units with lower rates of admission.

The ecological fallacy and Simpson's paradox suggest that there is no a priori reason to expect that the results of group-level analyses and subgroup analyses will be similar in either magnitude or direction. This argues for the careful examination of the fit between your unit of analysis in the data collection and the inferences you wish to draw. Different causal processes may be operating on data collected on different levels of aggregation. The determination of which analysis is "correct" depends on the level at which you wish to make inferences. It also argues for the judicious (that is, theoretically justifiable) use of subgroup analyses.

Statistical Issues in Program Evaluation

Leviton (2011) highlighted the need for additional emphasis on several statistical issues when you are conducting an evaluation of an intervention, such as a treatment for depression that attempts to increase and improve clients' interactions with others. First, Leviton pointed out the need for adequate statistical power and the avoidance of Type II errors:

> A Type II error means declaring a program as unsuccessful when in fact it is successful. The consequence can be a chilling effect on innovation and the perception that "nothing works" . . . A frequent Type II error problem in evaluation is a lack of statistical power to detect outcomes at conventional significance levels. . . . The ethical evaluator should explain [to funders and policy makers] the need for the sample in detail and explore options for assessment, including not conducting an evaluation that is sure to set up the program for failure. (p. 252)

Leviton (2011) also noted that unreliable and insensitive measures of outcomes can diminish the estimated size of a program's effect, so evaluators are obligated to use the best measures available or create measures that allow estimation that meets acceptable standards. The American Psychological Association, American Education Research Association, and National Council on Measurement in Education (2014) jointly developed standards for psychological testing. You should be familiar with these when you choose measures (see also Cizek & Rosenberg, 2011).

Finally, Leviton pointed out that in treatment evaluations, it is especially important to (a) have detailed protocols before a study begins,

(b) thoroughly train staff, and (c) attentively manage data collection. This, of course, is true for all scientific research. However, unlike laboratory experiments, for example, researchers conducting program evaluations rarely have an opportunity to learn from their mistakes (that is, conduct pilot tests) and undertake the project again.

Conclusion

Two themes occur repeatedly throughout my discussion of ethical issues in data collection, misconduct, and analysis: (a) research reports need to be transparent and comprehensively detail the methods used in data collection and analyses, and (b) the validity of research findings rests on their ability to be replicated. These are related themes in that complete reporting is needed if replication studies are to be conducted with fidelity.

The importance of replication has gained increased attention in psychology, as evidenced by a special section of the journal *Perspectives on Psychological Science* (Pashler & Wagenmakers, 2012) and scholarly discussions about how best to promote and interpret the results of replications (Novotney, 2014; see also National Institutes of Health, 2015, for an example of a federal agency tackling the same problem). These efforts can only improve the science of psychology and related disciplines, but their success rests on a continuous examination of the nature of researchers' rewards. The training and oversight of researchers and the criteria for publication must coincide with the search for valid conclusions about human behavior. In the next chapter, I discuss reporting standards and how they are meant to facilitate this search.

REPORT PREPARATION |||

Contents of a Research Report | 6

n the introduction, I noted that the National Academy of Sciences (NAS), National Academy of Engineering, and Institute of Medicine, in a joint monograph, listed accurate reporting of results as one of four fundamental elements if the scientific enterprise was going to maintain the trust of members of society (along with careful gathering of data, accurate statistics, and respect for the work of others; NAS, National Academy of Engineering, and Institute of Medicine, 2009). More than other sources of knowledge, scientific evidence must be open to verification and replication. That is why the report you write about your research needs to be complete and accurate and the description of your methods transparent.

Barnett and Campbell (2012) suggested that American Psychological Association's (APA) *Ethical Principles of Psychologists and Code of Conduct* (APA, 2010a; APA Ethics Code) contained two ethical principles that address the issue of reporting accuracy and transparency. Substandard 8.10 is meant to protect the integrity of the scientific enterprise. It states that psychologists do not fabricate data, and if they discover errors

http://dx.doi.org/10.1037/14859-007
Ethical Choices in Research: Managing Data, Writing Reports, and Publishing Results in the Social Sciences, by H. Cooper
Copyright © 2016 by the American Psychological Association. All rights reserved.

after data have been published, they take steps to remedy the situation. Substandard 5.01 states that, "Psychologists do not knowingly make public statements that are false, deceptive, or fraudulent concerning their research, practice or other activities or those of persons or organizations with which they are affiliated" (p. 8).

The principles also point out that this admonition is not just about accuracy in data analysis but in all aspects of publications. It says you should accurately report your training and experience, academic degrees and other credentials, and professional affiliations. Thus, you should not give in to the temptation to exaggerate your credentials because you think it will bring added credibility to your work. Your work will have no credibility if it is discovered that your claims about yourself are not accurate. The title page and Author Note of your manuscript must be as accurate as the body of your report.

I would add a third section of the APA principles to the two mentioned by Barnett and Campbell (2012). Subsection 6.01 of the APA Ethics Code relates to "Documentation of Professional and Scientific Work and Maintenance of Records":

> Psychologists create, and to the extent the records are under their control, maintain, disseminate, store, retain, and dispose of records and data relating to their professional and scientific work in order to (1) facilitate provision of services later by them or other professionals, (2) allow for replication of research design and analysis, (3) meet institutional requirements, (4) ensure accuracy of billing and payments, and (5) ensure compliance with law. (p. 8)

Obviously, some of the listed circumstances relate to providers of psychological services, but others are directed toward those conducting research. Perhaps most importantly, and to reiterate what I discussed in Chapter 3 regarding data management, this section highlights that keeping accurate records extends beyond the material you present in the research report. Other aspects of research—for example, videos presented to subjects in a study of reaction times, raw data, and the code books needed to make your results meaningful to others and capable of verification—may not appear in the report per se but also should be kept accurately and made available if they are requested.

Journal Article Reporting Standards

There are numerous guidelines available to help ensure your research reports contain the information your readers will find valuable in evaluating the quality and interpretation of your research and needed to assist others who wish to replicate it. For example, the Consolidated Standards of Reporting Trials (CONSORT, n.d.) have been used since 1996 in medical research to guide reports of experimental studies and are still undergoing revisions and extensions related to other types of research. The Equator Network (n.d.) lists at least 10 guidelines for health-related research.

Psychology also has such guidelines. In anticipation of the sixth edition of its *Publication Manual* (APA, 2010b), the APA Publications and Communications Board formed the Journal Article Reporting Standards (JARS) Working Group. The group was charged to learn about reporting standards in other fields and develop standards for psychology and related social science disciplines. The resulting report and guidelines were first published in the *American Psychologist* (APA Publications and Communications Board Working Group on Journal Article Reporting Standards, 2008), and the guidelines were reproduced in the sixth edition of the *Publication Manual* (APA, 2010b). A brief monograph more fully explains many of the suggested guideline elements and why they are important to report (Cooper, 2011). The focus of the JARS is on reports written for scientific journals. Obviously, conference papers will be less comprehensive. Of course, when presenting a conference paper, you should have the JARS-required information available for anyone who requests it.

Appendix C presents the JARS. The entries in Table C.1 outline items to include in all research reports on new data collections. They are categorized into the sections of a research report used by APA journals. Table C.2 presents the information that needs to be reported if the study involved an experimental manipulation or intervention. It presents the guidelines for experimental and quasi-experimental studies using random and non-random assignment of subjects to conditions. For example, if you ran a randomized experiment on the effects of fear-inducing advertisements meant to encourage people not to smoke, you would use Tables C.1 and C.2. Table C.3 presents two separate sets of reporting standards for studies (a) that randomly assigned participants to conditions of the study (Module 1) or (b) in which participants were assigned to conditions using a non-random process (Module 2). Figure C.1 is used to report the flow of participants through a study that used an experimental manipulation.

JARS modules are becoming available for other research methods. For example, standards for reporting meta-analysis were part of the original JARS report (APA Publications and Communications Board Working Group on Journal Article Reporting Standards, 2008) and also can be found in the *Publication Manual* (see also, Cooper & Dent, 2011). Standards for studies that use structural equation models are now available (Hoyle & Isherwood, 2013). Additional information to report could be added to the existing JARS modules (see Davidson et al., 2003), as could additional research designs.

The rationale for most of the elements in the JARS and their ethical implications are readily discernible. In Chapter 5, I discussed why certain procedures should be performed and why their results need to be reported. In this chapter, I highlight a few of the ethical issues that underlie aspects of research design to be reported in other sections of a research manuscript. I refer you to Cooper (2011) for a more in-depth treatment of the elements of the JARS.

Title Page and Author Note

Previously, I mentioned the importance of providing accurate information on yourself and co-authors on the title page and in the Author Note. In Chapter 3, I mentioned that one question that often arises concerns what to do when you have changed affiliations since the research you are reporting was conducted. Generally, the affiliation "credit" on the list of authors should go to the institution at which the research took place. Thus, if you are reporting your dissertation, it is the institution at which you received your degree that should follow your name on the title page. In the Author Note, you can then alert readers to any change in your affiliation. You can say "[Author name] is now at . . ." and if the corresponding author has moved the new address can be given.[1]

It is also important to alert readers in the Author Note to any other previously published versions of the paper or data that occurred before this manuscript. This most often arises when you are reporting a longitudinal study in which data collected earlier are part of a new data collection. For example, suppose in an earlier publication you asked subjects their attitudes toward smoking immediately after they see different ad campaigns. Then you followed up with subjects a year later and want to publish both the earlier and new data in a new publication. You should refer to the earlier publication in your Author Note. If you have earlier published different data on different variables from the same data set, this also should be mentioned. In both instances, the previous publications should be noted in the body of the paper, typically in the introduction and/or the Method section.

It is not necessary (although sometimes authors choose) to include in the Author Note presentations at conferences unless the conference proceedings were published. Often, these proceedings include brief papers that are available online. In all these instances, you should

---

[1]If the report is your dissertation, you should also say this in the Author Note. Typically, your dissertation will include more details about your research, and readers should be able to access this as well.

tell the editor of the journal to which you are submitting your report about the earlier works. Do this in the cover letter. The editor will help you determine whether this constitutes prior publication. I delve more deeply into this issue in Chapter 8.

Introduction

In Chapter 1 and again in Chapter 7, on plagiarism, I discuss the need to cite in the introduction to your paper the previous works, both those of others and your own, that contributed to your thinking and research. You need to cite the work that underpins what you did and how your work builds on it.

DISTINCTIONS IN HYPOTHESES

Let me return again to a topic I covered in the previous chapter. You need to state in the introduction your hypotheses and your rationale for them. One of the questions I am most frequently asked concerns what to do if you change hypotheses after you have collected data. Typically, when I am asked this question, I follow up by asking: Did you change hypotheses before or after you tested the original hypotheses?

If your answer is "before," there is no problem. If the answer is after, in scientific reporting you must report both results. You also need to critically appraise what *dependence* there might be between your two analyses or how the former analyses affected your later prediction. Your first hypothesis, the confirmatory one, failed to be supported. Your second hypothesis is post hoc, exploratory. As such, it is a much more tenuous assertion and needs repeated verification that it truly describes the state of nature.

Your key consideration is what impact the first set of results might have had on your change of hypothesis. Here is one more example. Let us return to your study on fear-inducing advertisements and attitude change toward smoking. First, you simply hypothesized more negative attitudes after a fear message. You found no main effect. But you used a variety of message lengths in both the fear and no-fear conditions. You follow a "hunch" and add the length of the message to the analyses. You then discover a significant interaction, suggesting shorter messages were effective but longer messages were not. After the fact, you reason, "Well of course, the longer messages turned people off, leading them to attend less closely and to forget the message more quickly." Conversely, perhaps you found that longer messages were more effective. You reason, "Well of course, the longer messages would have more impact with more time to sink in." You did not predict either of these in the beginning. You should not present them as if you did. (For the record, I have no idea whether message length matters or, if it does, whether either of these explanations is correct. My ignorance is deliberate.)

In this case, it would be inappropriate to change your hypothesis and retitle the paper from, for example, "The Effects of Fear Messages on Behavioral Intentions to Smoke" to "The Effects of Message Length on the Relation Between Fear Messages and Behavioral Intentions to Smoke." This suggests your finding was a confirmation of a prior belief, rather than a discovery of a possible new mediating variable. Instead, you would leave the original title, report your original hypothesis as not supported or only partially supported and write in your discussion about why you might have found an interaction with message length. You can also mention this in the abstract, increasing the chances that others interested in "message length" will come across your report. The same approach is called for if you find significant results on some outcomes, such as your subjects' estimated chances of getting lung cancer, but not others, such as their intention to smoke.

This brings us to the issue of identifying primary and secondary hypotheses. The JARS suggests you label your predictions as primary and secondary. Your primary hypotheses are where your "big bets" are. These are most often your confirmatory predictions, and your characterization of them should not change after you have seen the results. Your primary hypotheses can also be exploratory if you are studying something we now know little about. Your secondary hypotheses are also of interest but less so, perhaps being (a) the exploratory hypotheses you studied in addition to the confirmatory ones, (b) analyses that are tangential to the theory driving your research, or (c) less central to your intervention (e.g., hypothesizing about the moderating effects of sex and age on subjects' reactions to the fear messages). Your post hoc explanations (like my message length example) for unanticipated findings should not become "predictions" after the fact. Post hoc explanations are more likely to have occurred by chance. Although we cannot precisely calculate the odds, in the aggregate, they are less likely to be replicable.

Method

The most important questions for you to answer as you write your Method section are

- What information will readers need to evaluate the validity of my study's conclusions and interpret its findings?
- What information would readers need to know if they wish to replicate my research?

SUBJECT CHARACTERISTICS

Clearly, a complete and transparent description of who took part in your study and how they were sampled and recruited (e.g., sign-up websites for class credit, clinical referral, over the Internet) will be critical to the ability of others to evaluate your findings and replicate your results. You are ethically obligated to reveal all the characteristics of your sample and recruitment procedures that might influence the interpretation of your results. "Might" is the operative word here. You cannot possibly know what all the contingencies could be, what characteristics of subjects might interact with your findings. But you can be confident if you describe sample characteristics that are relatively low on your probability estimates. In the study of attitudes and smoking, such characteristics as whether or not subjects were already smokers and their current health status would be obvious choices to be added to the more typically reported characteristics (such as the average and range of ages, percentages of the sexes, ethnic and educational background) that you would detail in nearly all research reports.

SUBJECT ATTRITION

It is also critical to report the number of subjects who refused to participate (are smokers less willing to take part in studies about smoking?) and the number who withdrew after the experiment began, the *attrition rate*. There is a flowchart that is part of the JARS that can help you report this information (see Appendix C, Figure C.1). If either subject refusal or withdrawal was a problem with your study, not reporting such information is an ethical breach. It might lead your readers to think your study is more generalizable than is warranted and might lead to a failure to replicate your results with the cause of the failure more difficult to identify.

POWER ANALYSIS

Brown and Hedges (2009) suggested that reporting the results of an a priori power analysis is also an ethical obligation. Knowing whether or not you included enough subjects to ensure that your study had sufficient power to uncover meaningful effects is critical knowledge for your readers and you. Brown and Hedges wrote, "Underpowered studies still involve financial and human costs but carry a high risk of producing results that are difficult to interpret, thus not fulfilling our intended purpose of moving knowledge forward" (p. 380). For example, if you included only a small number of subjects, how realistic was it for you to expect your manipulation of message content to have a large enough effect on behavioral intentions and subsequent behavior so that these analyses could reject the null hypothesis? If you expect the effect to be small, did you run enough subjects to give your manipulation a chance to reveal "success": that is, estimate its effect accurately and perhaps reject the hypothesis that it had no effect at all? Power analyses can also help you decide whether a study might be overpowered, which means you are running many more subjects than you need to uncover a significant effect with sufficient confidence (a low probability of Type I error).

PILOT STUDIES, ABANDONED METHODS, AND FAILED EXPERIMENTS

Sometimes the effects of a manipulation are not only subtle but also can depend on subtle aspects of what you did. Therefore, it is obligatory that you report descriptions of pilot studies, abandoned methods, and failed experiments.[2] If these occurred, it is likely that they led to changes in procedure that can be critical to understanding your results and facilitate attempts to replicate your findings (something you want to occur). For example, you might conduct a pilot study and find, using a manipulation check, that the messages you thought would engender fear in subjects were actually interpreted by them as quite tepid. So you make the messages more fear arousing by adding more disturbing images of the consequences of smoking. If weak results on manipulation checks caused you to rework and strengthen your manipulations, readers should know what the abandoned manipulations were. If you went so far as to collect outcome data before changing a procedure, that information should be reported. Perhaps the next researchers will not make the same "mistake" again.

CHECKS ON THE MANIPULATION

Likewise, the details of checks on the manipulations in your studies are important to report. This includes the associated statistical results. For example, if you ran a test of the difference in how fearful subjects found your fear and no-fear messages, you should report the associated test statistics and effect size.

There is an additional scientific benefit to reporting the results of manipulation checks. It is possible to use these results, expressed as effect sizes, as moderator variables in subsequent meta-analysis. For example, if meta-analysts know how much different the fear ratings

---

[2]Some journals have page limits, which might make it difficult to provide detailed reports of these facets of your research. Still, the critical aspects of the research should be reported, along with how and why these facets of your research changed the main study you report. Details should be available to those who request them. For a growing number of online journals, these details can be made available in supplemental files.

were between your fear and no-fear conditions, they could later test whether studies with larger (or smaller) differences between messages led to more (or less) dramatic effects on attitudes. Thus, manipulation checks and their results (especially if they lead to change in manipulations) need to be reported. They not only lend credibility to your manipulation but also may help your study make contributions to subsequent research syntheses.

UNLUCKY RANDOMIZATION

Unlucky randomization also needs to be reported. This occurs when, even though you assigned subjects to conditions at random, pretests suggest that before the experimental procedures were administered, differences existed between groups on important individual characteristics of subjects. Yes, this happens. In fact, the probabilistic nature of subject assignment tells us we can be certain it happens sometimes. If we looked at enough pretests in even a single study, we would be almost certain to find some bad luck in random assignment.

The key to whether you should be concerned is how related the unluckily randomized variable is to your important outcome variables.[3] For example, suppose even though you randomly assigned people to view fear and no-fear messages, more smokers end up in your no-fear condition. Did this lead you to changes in your analytic strategy, perhaps using smoking status as a covariate? If so, you are ethically obligated to report such occurrences.

DELETED CASES

In Chapter 5, I mentioned that two reasons for deleting data were that the subject had too many missing responses or that you were concerned about the trustworthiness of responses. Manipulation checks can help you make this latter determination. For example, in your study of attitudes toward smoking, you might be concerned about whether or not subjects truly attended to the manipulations. To check this, you might ask subjects to tell you about features of the manipulation. So you might ask people to tell you some characteristics of the message they saw: for example, the sex and approximate age of the person in the message, or an occupation mentioned by the person. If subjects cannot answer these questions correctly, you could decide their data ought not to be used. For obvious reasons,

---

[3]Many researchers do not test the outcome of their randomization procedures. It is most important to do so if your sample is small and/or you use a pretest of the outcome measure as a covariate (expected to correlate with your dependent variable) in a study that involves random assignment.

you should not construct these rules after you have analyzed the data and know the results might change if certain subjects are dropped.

As I mentioned in Chapter 5, you should report the number of cases you discarded and your reasons for doing so. It is especially important that your decision rules for discarding subjects' data be determined *before* you begin your analyses. In addition, you should keep a copy of the data set that includes the subjects you deleted.

STOPPING RULES

I discussed stopping rules in Chapter 5. With regard to reporting, the key issue is that if you used a stopping rule, you need to report what the rationale was and exactly how the stopping was carried out. Again, stopping rules are rare in psychology and can make results difficult to replicate if they are done improperly because they can produce results that capitalize on chance.

Results

The previous chapter, on statistical analyses, dealt with the ethics of reporting statistical analyses interwoven with other aspects of the ethical conducting of data analysis. Here, I touch on just two additional reporting issues.

EFFECT SIZES

The reporting of effect sizes is relatively new in psychological science, but as Brown and Hedges (2009) wrote, "Undoubtedly, in the minds of many, the issue of reporting effect sizes has moved from being recommended to becoming a matter of data ethics" (p. 379). Effect sizes from complex analyses, such as interactions involving multiple variables, can be hard to interpret and typically are not reported. However, in these cases you may find yourself interpreting simpler effects within other conditions. For example, you might find an interaction between fear messages and smoking status. You conduct statistical tests within each smoker category and find the messages were effective for nonsmokers but not smokers. If you formally tested these simple effects (which you almost always should), these two effect sizes should be reported.

Because effect sizes are estimates drawn from samples, you should also report their confidence intervals and/or standard errors. It is also the case that effect size estimates do not exist for all statistical tests.

ADVERSE EFFECTS

When your experiment involves an evaluation of a treatment or intervention and you discover that it had harmful or undesirable side effects on some participants, you are obligated to disclose those effects in your research report along with how frequently they occurred.

A study's potential to have both helpful and harmful effects is something you will be asked to consider and discuss (along with what you will do if harmful effects occur) when you apply for approval from your Institutional Review Board (IRB) before your study begins. It is critical that you report adverse effects to your IRB as soon as the effects occur. Could a smoker who sees your fear message have a severe anxiety reaction? How likely is this to occur? What will you do should it happen? Those long warnings we see and hear with pharmaceutical advertisements are based, in part, on the reporting of adverse effects found in clinical trials.

Discussion

The JARS recommends that your discussion present several important elements:

- a summary of the most essential elements in your results,
- an interpretation of your findings,
- your personal evaluation of the strengths and weaknesses of your study,
- the generalizability of your findings, and
- the implications of your findings.

SUMMARY STATEMENT AND INTERPRETATION

After you restate the goals for your research, you should provide a summary statement of your principle findings. These findings will be the focus of the discussion that follows. You should say how you think your study advances knowledge on the issues it addresses. You are not obligated ethically to discuss every finding in the report, but if you do not assess the results of tests of all the principal hypotheses you mentioned in the introduction, you likely will be asked to do so by an editor or the reviewers. Likewise, important secondary hypotheses and interesting *post hoc* results need to be summarized and explained.

You should present a complete picture of the findings and an explanation for them regardless of whether or not the results supported your original predictions. Reporting all unsupportive findings, along with the supportive ones, is an ethical obligation. You should also present alternative explanations for your findings, be they based on characteristics of the method you used to generate your results (were the fear and no-fear messages of equal length?) or competing theories. These theories might be alternative explanations predicting the same result you found, or they may predict different results.

Alternative explanations should be presented in an accurate and respectful manner. It should always be the case that you evaluate only the theory or prediction at hand and not the individuals who developed the alternate explanation. Do not say critical things about people; discuss what you see as flaws in reasoning and the applicability of a theory. If you are aware of other studies that produced results dissimilar to yours, you are ethically obligated to note them, if only to state why you think they are not necessarily relevant to your findings.

In sum, the first thing you do in your discussion is summarize and

> place your work in the context of earlier work. You can cite work that yours replicates and extends but you should also include work with results or predictions at odds with your own. . . . When you do this, you should propose reasons why the contradictions may have occurred. (Cooper, 2011, p. 78)

STRENGTHS AND LIMITATIONS OF THE STUDY

An important part of the interpretation of your results will be an assessment of your own study's strengths and limitations. For example, your smoking study might have been meant to assess the causal effect of fear messages on changing attitudes toward smoking, but your research design had some limitations that call into question the strength of the causal inferences it can support; for example, noticeably more smokers in the no-fear message condition or high attrition in the fear message condition. These limitations need to be acknowledged in the discussion. No study is without some limitations; the perfect experiment has yet to be conducted.

If your research design did not allow for strong causal inferences, it is also critical that you avoid using terms in your discussion that imply your study uncovered a causal connection. For example, suppose you showed subjects an antismoking public service advertisement drawn from a magazine and asked them to tell you how fearful it made them. You then measured their attitudes toward smoking and found a negative correlation. In this study, fear was not manipulated (subjects placed themselves in fear conditions), so terms such as "caused," "produced," or "brought about" should not be used in describing such results. Instead, "related," "associated," and "linked" are most appropriate. On the bright side, this research design might have higher external validity than an experiment that constructed artificial ads just for the study.

Do not be afraid to state the limitations of your study. It is expected of you. Taking a critical posture toward your own work speaks well of you. It shows that the advancement of knowledge was your first priority. It assures readers that you understood what you were doing. In addition, your discussion should not address only your study's limitations. Methods that allow strong inferences, that build confidence in your explanation (e.g., random assignment, impactful manipulations, reliable measurement), also should be noted.

GENERALIZABILITY

Although we think first that the generalizability of a study's findings involves the kinds of people the results apply to, there are at least four different cases of generalization. Cronbach (1982) referred to these cases by using the acronym UTOS: units, treatments, outcomes and settings.

- *Units*: Are the people in the study in some way a restricted sub-sample of the target population? If they are, do the restrictions suggest that the results pertain to some, but not all, members of the target population? Be especially cautious about generalizations to more extreme populations (e.g., when the findings might be influenced by the subjects' age from adults to adolescents).
- *Treatments*: How might the way the manipulation was operationalized in your study differ from how it would be experienced in other settings, especially naturally occurring ones. For example, how might ads constructed specially for your study differ from ones you found in magazines and on television?
- *Outcomes*: Are the outcomes you used in your study a good representation of all the outcomes that might be of interest? For example, if you measured only subjects' attitudes toward smoking, does this result generalize to behavioral intentions?
- *Settings*: Was there something unique about the settings of your study that suggests similar results might or might not be obtained in other settings. For example, how might responses obtained in a laboratory setting differ from those obtained in a more everyday context, such as while the subjects are reading a magazine ad or viewing a commercial on television?

IMPLICATIONS

You are free to discuss what you think the implications of your findings are for theory, policy, practice, and/or future research. However, be careful to stay within your area of competence. Your ethical obligation is to tie your implications clearly to your results. Your implications can go beyond the results, but these should be labeled as speculation of more or less varying degrees. Do not use your research to make claims it logically does not support. Instead, use your study to propose what future research should look like in order for the field to continue to advance.

Conclusion: Using the JARS Proactively

The reporting standards that today's researchers are asked to meet can seem a bit overwhelming at first. The best advice I can give for turning what seems like a formidable amount of detail into a manageable task is that you keep good notes and records as you make decisions and carry them out (see Chapter 3). You can refer to the JARS often as you move through your research. It not only will simplify your writing of the report but also will assist you in making good decisions at the right time by reminding you of what you should be thinking about. If you do this, when you get to the task of writing, you should find that the standards serve not only as reporting obligations but also as a good writing guide, even supplying you with center, side, and paragraph heads to structure your report.

In addition, remember that the detail does not have to be all in the body of your text. You can use supplemental files for the finer descriptions of what you have done if you think the details will interfere with the flow of your narrative. You can find on the APA website (APA, 2015b) descriptions of examples of supplemental files (e.g., audio and video tapes, oversized tables, lengthy appendices, detailed methods descriptions, supplemental data sets) and how these should be formatted.

With a well-constructed manuscript in hand, you are ready to begin the process of getting your paper published.

Plagiarism 7

The Office of Research Integrity (ORI; 2013a) defines *plagiarism* "to include both the theft or misappropriation of intellectual property and the substantial unattributed textual copying of another's work" (p. 1). The American Psychological Association's (APA, 2010a) *Ethical Principles of Psychologists and Code of Conduct* (APA Ethics Code) states that "Psychologists do not present portions of another's work or data as their own, even if the other work or data source is cited occasionally" (Subsection 8.11, p. 11). *Merriam-Webster* defines the term *plagiarize* as "to steal and pass off (the ideas or words of another) as one's own: use (another's production) without crediting the source" (Plagiarize, n.d.).

There are three types of intellectual products mentioned in these definitions: ideas, writing, and data. In everyday usage, plagiarism is most closely associated with the theft of someone else's writing, which might include her or his ideas. I discussed ownership of intellectual ideas in Chapter 1 because it is relevant to ethical issues when a research problem is being formulated. I view stealing data as first and foremost an issue

http://dx.doi.org/10.1037/14859-008
Ethical Choices in Research: Managing Data, Writing Reports, and Publishing Results in the Social Sciences, by H. Cooper
Copyright © 2016 by the American Psychological Association. All rights reserved.

of who deserves authorship of a research report, so that topic was covered in Chapter 3. In this chapter, I deal with the plagiarism of text because it arises as an issue in the preparation of a report. I discuss primarily the types of text plagiarism and how they can be uncovered and avoided.

Today, committing plagiarism is easier than ever. Millions of documents are just a few clicks away on the Internet, and most software that displays these documents has a copy-and-paste feature. For example, a few years ago, I had a student who copied a paragraph from a published paper (without citing the original authors and indenting the text to show that it was quoted) but forgot to change the font. The different font was suspicious and suggested to my teaching assistant and me that we investigate. The "voice" of the paragraph also seemed different from the rest of the paper. As another example, when I was chief editorial advisor for the APA's journals, a manuscript was submitted for publication that was found to be almost entirely from an unpublished report (available on the Internet) written by others more than a decade earlier.

Pupovac and Fanelli (2014) performed a meta-analysis of surveys that queried scientists regarding whether they had committed plagiarism or admitted knowing at least one colleague who had done so. They found an average of 1.7% of scientists admitted plagiarizing, and 29.6% knew someone who had.[1]

As it has become easier to plagiarize another's work, it also has become easier to catch such thieves. Programs are available that can scan millions of documents, including web pages and scientific journals, and provide detailed accounts of how much a target document matches other works. The program provides a list of the closest matches. This will be discussed in greater detail later in this chapter.

When you are writing, you should ask yourself this question: "Have I presented someone else's writing as if it were my own?" The answer to this question should be an emphatic "no." If the answer is "yes," the consequences to your career and reputation can be devastating. These consequences include professional sanctions, such as loss of your job, inability to obtain research funds, and prohibition from publishing in certain journals. In addition, the published corrections that would follow a finding of plagiarism will be a permanent part of the scientific record. Because plagiarism is avoidable, it is never worth committing.

In the following section, I discuss the types of plagiarism with special attention given to the different forms plagiarism can take, the importance of accurately citing the work of others, tools that are used to uncover plagiarism, the theft of ideas (again, briefly), and how to avoid plagiarism.

---

[1]Remember when interpreting this statistic that more than one respondent could have been aware of the same instance of plagiarism by another.

Types of Plagiarism

Not everything that is labeled plagiarism involves copying and pasting large swathes of text without attribution. Roig (2003) provided a categorization of types of plagiarism.[2] The categories include, first and foremost, the previously mentioned unaltered copying of text. Roig also noted it is not acceptable to change a few words written by another person by replacing the original author's words with synonyms or shorter or longer phrases. Howard (1999) called this *patchwriting*.

In patchwriting, the original source is undocumented. Interestingly, Howard proposed that in some disciplines patchwriting, at least when it is committed by students, "does not belong in the category of plagiarism" (p. 4). She suggested that it is "a move toward membership in a discourse community, a means of learning unfamiliar language and ideas . . . a gesture of reverence . . . [that] recognizes the profundity of the source and strives to join the conversation in which the source participates" (p. 7). All of what Howard writes may be true, but it is hard to justify patchwriting in scientific writing, when the writer is expected to have a certain degree of expertise already, or when it occurs out of sheer laziness.

Patchwriting turns into *inappropriate paraphrasing* if the original author is cited but only minimal changes are made to the text, and the text gives no indication (such as quotation marks) that it is not original writing by the report author. Roig (2003) noted that when technical terms and language are involved, authors are given more leeway to adopt terms and short phrases of a few words, but the attribution to their original source still must be clear. It also can be deceptive to paraphrase or rephrase an entire section of another's work and then just cite the person at the end of a paragraph.

Finally, *summaries* present shortened descriptions of someone else's writing. Summaries become plagiarism when phrases are used from the original document and they are not restated in the words of the summarizer or properly documented and enclosed in quotation marks.

Obviously, when you paraphrase or summarize another's work, the distinction between plagiarism and new material can get fuzzy. The phrasing and context of what you write play a role in whether or not the original writing will be viewed by others as attributable to you. Can the original author's thoughts be conveyed in different and fewer words without losing clarity of meaning? This is where a determination of the need for technical terms and phrases enters. The key to avoiding

---

[2]Roig (2003) includes duplicate publication, generating multiple reports from a study that should be reported as one, and copyright infringement as forms of plagiarism. I treat these separately.

plagiarism when paraphrasing and summarizing, especially technical material, is to remember to cite the original source and use quotation marks when you are using phrases published elsewhere.

Things that are viewed as *common knowledge* do not need citations. Stern (2009) defined common knowledge as "widely known information about current events, famous people, geographical facts or familiar history" (p. 6). The results of a past study would almost never qualify as common knowledge, and the study should always be cited. However, as with paraphrasing technical material, what constitutes common knowledge often is difficult to pin down and can vary from context to context. For example, standard statistical approaches, such as the *t*-test, analysis of variance, and multiple regression, qualify as common knowledge. But less familiar techniques, such as structural equation modeling and hierarchical linear modeling, need a reference, not only so that readers can find more information on the techniques but also to identify the particular software you used. Stern presented five questions you can ask yourself before deciding whether a statement is common knowledge or needs documentation:

- Is this information that you know, or that you would expect others to know, without having to look it up?
- Is this information readily available in many sources without documentation?
- Is this information in a general dictionary?
- Is it a common saying or expression?
- Is this widely known information about authorship or creation? (Stern, 2009, pp. 6–7)

Clearly, judgment is still involved. Terms such as "expect others to know," "readily available," and "widely known" require you to think about your audience. What is widely known to some groups of people (e.g., you can expect that all people reading your article in a psychology journal would know that Sigmund Freud was the developer of psychotherapy) may be unfamiliar to others. In that case, it needs documentation so the less-well versed can verify your claim and learn more on the topic. Both Roig (2003) and Stern (2009) counseled, when in doubt, document.

Another categorization of plagiarism is provided by Turnitin, a plagiarism detection service. Turnitin (2012) focuses on student plagiarism and provides a 10-category scheme for classifying plagiarism. This scheme is reproduced in Exhibit 7.1. The plagiarism types are based on the results of a survey of instructors in secondary and higher education that asked the instructors to rank their level of concern about various types of plagiarism. The 879 respondents used a scale of 0 (*less concern*) to 10 (*more concern*). It is important to note that the types

EXHIBIT 7.1

Ten Types of Plagiarism Ordered From Most to Least Concern Rated by Secondary and Higher Education Instructors

1. CLONE:
   An act of submitting another's work, word-for-word, as one's own.
2. CTRL-C:
   A written piece that contains significant portions of text from a single source without alterations.
3. FIND–REPLACE:
   The act of changing key words and phrases but retaining the essential content of the source in a paper.
4. REMIX:
   An act of paraphrasing from other sources and making the content fit together seamlessly.
5. RECYCLE:
   The act of borrowing generously from one's own previous work without citation; To self plagiarize.
6. HYBRID:
   The act of combining perfectly cited sources with copied passages—without citation—in one paper.
7. MASHUP:
   A paper that represents a mix of copied material from several different sources without proper citation.
8. 404 ERROR:
   A written piece that includes citations to non-existent or inaccurate information about sources.
9. AGGREGATOR:
   The "Aggregator" includes proper citation, but the paper contains almost no original work.
10. RETWEET:
    This paper includes proper citation, but relies too closely on the text's original wording and/or structure.

Note. From *Turnitin White Paper: The Plagiarism Spectrum*, http://turnitin.com/assets/en_us/media/plagiarism_spectrum.php. Copyright 2012 by Paradigms, LLC. Reprinted with permission.

ranked below "mashup" had average survey responses below 3 on the scale, with the final two, "remix" and "retweet," being hardly concerning at all (average scores of .5). The survey also found that the frequency of occurrence of the plagiarism types closely, but not perfectly, mirrored the educators' concern.

Barnett and Campbell (2012) took a different approach to distinguishing between types of plagiarism. They based their categorization on the motivations of the offending author. *Intentional plagiarism* involves the conscious use of another's words or ideas without attribution. *Unintentional plagiarism* occurs when an author hears or reads words, phrases, or ideas from another and then forgets the sources, perhaps thinking they were original. *Inadvertent plagiarism* is similar to unintentional plagiarism, but instead of being a cognitive lapse, it occurs when someone omits the source of a thought or quotation in the act of note taking. All of these are plagiarism (by definition) but not necessarily misconduct because misconduct involves knowledge of the act and intentionality.

A NOTE ON INTERNATIONAL AUTHORS

The shades of plagiarism involve the text that is reproduced but also may take into consideration characteristics of the reproducers and the context in which they are writing. This is especially relevant to authors who are writing in a language other than their native one. For example, if English is the authors' second language and they are writing for a journal published in English, the temptation to copy and paste may be greater. Paraphrasing and summarizing may be more difficult because it is harder to come up with the needed words and phrases. All the same, the change in "voice" (from the author to the plagiarized text) will be more apparent to those who read the work.

Also, different cultures have different norms. Howard (1999) suggested that,

> Not all cultures today endorse the autonomous, originary author. . . . In some Asian countries, for example, textual values approximating those of the ancient or medieval West prevail, insofar as a writer's work is valued for its use of authoritative sources. To cite those sources would be a crass insult to the reader's erudition. (p. 119)

In other words cultures can differ in where to draw the line between what needs a citation and what can (and should) be considered common knowledge. Cultures more generally also differ in their individualistic versus collectivist orientation: "Do I need a citation here, or is this common knowledge"? My feeling is that authors and editors should take these issues into account. Authors should be aware of the norms for writing of the journals to which they submit papers. Editors need to work with authors from other cultures to revise manuscripts before they are published so as to avoid allegations of intentional plagiarism.

Self-Plagiarism

Without careful consideration, *self-plagiarism* can be viewed as no different from plagiarism of any other source except that in this instance, you are "stealing" from yourself. If that sounds absurd, Roig (2003; citing Hexham, 1999) pointed out that the key determinant of self-plagiarism rests in whether the author is attempting to deceive the reader into thinking that the text is original to the new document. Barnett and Campbell (2012) suggested that self-plagiarism is the result of causes such as "laziness, a feeling that rules do not apply to oneself, poor time management, the pressure to be published, and others" (p. 318). These are the same causes that may be cited for plagiarism in general.

Text recycling occurs when a researcher who is systematically working on a topic uses some of her or his previously written text for a new purpose. Many forms of text recycling are accepted practice. In fact, the difference between self-plagiarism and text recycling has more to do with normative practices than anything else. For example, Roig (2003) noted that institutional review board (IRB) submissions, which are often the first time ideas for a study are shared on paper, can contain material that can be reused in the manuscript when the study is complete and the results are reported. Grant applications also fall into this category. Brief papers that summarize presentations at conferences also can contain text acceptable for use for other purposes. In these instances, self-plagiarism becomes text recycling because the original documents were for a different purpose and a smaller audience.

Less clear is when an author recycles material from an earlier published article. In this instance, the purpose and audience for the two documents can be quite similar. It is fairly common practice for the same researchers to use descriptions of the same methods multiple times. For example, your study of loneliness and depression may use the same measures you used in an earlier published article. The descriptions can be quite similar from one report to the next. Often, when you have worked and reworked a description of a method in an earlier report, it is difficult and not necessarily possible to improve on it for your next paper. The most frequently occurring accepted text recycling involves descriptions of measures and data analysis techniques that a researcher uses repeatedly. If procedures are replicated from study to study, it is important to reference the earlier research in the method description. As a rule, reuse of previously published material in introductions and discussion sections, even if it is your own writing, should be kept to a minimum, rephrased, and referenced to its original appearance, just as if it were written by someone else.

Citing the Work of Others

When you refer to the work of others, be sure to provide an accurate citation. Accuracy means not only getting the citation in your reference section correct but also ensuring that what you say another has said or done is, in fact, correct. Ask the question: "Does the cited source actually say what I am citing it for?"

This means you need to read the source and not simply rely on what someone else has said about the source, unless the original source is unavailable to you. For example, in this chapter, I cite a web page attributed to Hexham (1999), as cited in Roig (2003). I first read about Hexham's work in Roig's work, but when I went to retrieve the original, the web page was gone.

Roig (2003) suggested that cited sources should be the first time the idea or phenomenon was reported. The *Publication Manual* (APA, 2010b) suggested that when writing a research report you cite "one or two of the most representative sources for each key point" (p. 169). I will add that you should cite the most recent, directly relevant work(s) of which you are aware. In most instances, choosing among the first, the most representative, and/or the most recent sources will not be an issue because the best referent of your assertion will be clear. When the reference is to a more general assertion on your part, consider using more than one reference. When using representative references, be sure to preface your citation with "for example" (or "e.g." for parenthetical text). You should balance your desire to be helpful to your readers (who may want to follow up by reading original sources) with historical accuracy.

There are other reasons that in and of themselves are not sufficient cause to cite a work. First, you should not cite work simply because it is yours, unless it is clearly relevant to the study being described. There is temptation to do this type of citation padding. Self-citations can be used to impress editors and reviewers with your credentials for conducting the study (if your study is to undergo anonymous review, self-citations typically are replaced by reference to "author," but the hoped-for effect can be the same). Self-citations can also increase the overall citation count for your articles.[3] This may later assist you in job promotion and other professional rewards, if the person counting your citations is not careful to discount self-citations. The advantage to self-citation is lost if the citation is not directly relevant to the assertion being made, and editors, reviewers, and readers discover the citation padding. In that situation, your reputation is damaged, not enhanced.

Finally, as noted in Chapter 6, citations should present a balanced picture of past research. It is not scientifically legitimate to knowingly ignore research that stands in opposition to your own hypothesizing or

---

[3]Astoundingly, I have heard of journal editors who have asked authors of accepted papers to add references to works that previously appeared in the journal that accepted the paper. This increases the journal's citation count and impact factor (roughly, citations per article published).

findings. Often, you can use the conflicting conclusions of past work to justify your research and its importance. Ask yourself: Have I cited work I know of that both supports and refutes my contentions?

QUOTATIONS

Not surprisingly, material quoted from others should always be in quotation marks and accompanied by the cited authors' names, publication year, and page number(s) upon which the quoted matter appears. This is a major protection against an accusation of plagiarism. Further, if the quotation is long or if you reproduce a table or figure, you will need to obtain the permission of the publisher. APA has produced guidelines to help you decide whether such permission is needed. The guidelines are reproduced in Exhibit 7.2. Note that your paper, if it is accepted, will not go to print without completed documentation that you have received these permissions.

EXHIBIT 7.2

APA Guidelines and Assurance That Permission Has Been Received for Reprinted Material

PERMISSIONS ALERT FORM FOR APA JOURNAL AUTHORS

Does your paper include material borrowed from another source? If so, you must cite the original source in your paper. In addition, you may need to secure permission to reuse the material. Below are listed the types of material that may require permission.

1. Figures and tables:
   This includes both figures and tables that are directly reprinted and those that have been adapted from previously published figures and tables.
2. Data:
   This applies only to data that are directly reproduced from another source; data that have been reanalyzed do not require permission.
3. Test items, questionnaires, vignettes, etc.:
   This applies mainly to items that are from copyrighted and commercially available tests (e.g., MMPI, Wechsler Adult Intelligence Scale, Stanford-Binet). Obtaining these permissions can be difficult and time-consuming, and a preferable alternative may be to reword or paraphrase those items so as not to duplicate the exact wording.
4. Long quotations:
   Each copyright holder has its own definition of fair use. It is your responsibility to determine whether the copyright holder requires permission for long quotations.
5. Photographs (and other images):
   Photos and other images not created by the author as part of the study may be subject to permission requirements. Copyright ownership and permission status can be particularly difficult to establish for images downloaded from the Internet, but we cannot publish them without full documentation. There is no need to seek permission for images taken from a database whose purpose is the open dissemination of stimuli for academic research (e.g., the International Affective Picture System).

(continued)

EXHIBIT 7.2 (Continued)

6. Photo releases:
   The subjects of photographs (if other than the authors) must give permission for publication if they are recognizable. This is done through a release letter. This is not an issue of permission to use copyrighted material, but permission to use someone's likeness. If images have been taken from research databases, there is no need to seek a release.

   Does your article contain material that has been reproduced or adapted from an APA publication? If it does not exceed APA's fair use criteria, then you do not need to request permission from APA. (Per APA, fair use constitutes reprinting or adapting up to three tables and/or figures, a text extract of fewer than 400 words, or a series of text extracts totaling fewer than 800 words.) Most other scholarly journals have adopted the same fair use guidelines as APA; however, it is the author's responsibility to obtain the fair use guidelines for the relevant copyright holder to determine whether you need to secure permission. The use of a figure, table, test item, appendix, abstract, or similar work that was commercially copyrighted or published in a book requires permission.

   If permission is required, contact the copyright holder (usually the publisher) and request permission to reproduce or adapt the material in all formats (online as well as in print). When permission has been secured, forward the copyright holder's letter with your manuscript. Permission can be secured via fax, mail, e-mail, or the publisher's website (e.g., see http:// www.apa.org/pubs/journals and click on Copyright & Permissions for permission to reproduce material published by APA). Start this process early, as it may take several weeks.

   Your article cannot go into production until all permissions are secured for reproduced and adapted items. For more information regarding permissions policies, see pp. 231–236 of the sixth edition of the APA *Publication Manual*. Regardless of whether permission is required, you must acknowledge the original source in your paper. Please include a full citation for each item that is reproduced or adapted from another source, including the page(s) on which is it found.

The following items in my article are reproduced or adapted from another source:

_____

_____

_____

_____

Author Signature _____

Tools for Uncovering Plagiarism

Aside from the discovery of plagiarism by readers, probably the most frequently used tool for uncovering plagiarism in scientific writing is the iThenticate (2014) software program. iThenticate uses the Crosscheck database (Crossref.org, 2015), which includes millions of scientific articles, magazine articles, conference papers, books, and encyclopedias and billions of current and archived web pages. The major publishers of social science and health journals and books subscribe to iThenticate. For an increasing number of journals published by APA, manuscripts newly submitted for publication are routinely run through iThenticate before they are sent for review. The publisher of the journal sets parameters for what it will consider duplication (for example, the number of identical words strung together), and the journal editor gets a report that identifies the documents, if any, that share the most text with the target article. If the amount of duplication appears worth investigating, the editor can examine the documents side by side to see what they share.

The ORI provides a plagiarism detection tool called eTBLAST (2012). Like a search engine, it matches submitted keywords from the target document with a document database. The keywords can be any length, including an entire document, but the optimum length for searching is between 50 and 500 words. eTBLAST focuses primarily on medical journals but has been expanding to other disciplines. It can be used free of charge.

Avoiding Plagiarism

I found two excellent guides to avoiding plagiarism. Roig (2003), a work I have cited frequently in this chapter, prepared such a guide for the ORI; it is available online free of charge. It also covers issues in authorship assignment. Stern (2009) wrote *What Every Student Should Know About Avoiding Plagiarism*; it is available at minimal cost. Both guides provide numerous examples of plagiarism, some in gray areas, and how it can be avoided. Roig (2003) also provided numerous guidelines for avoiding plagiarism. I have reproduced the guidelines related to theft of text in Exhibit 7.3. The material in Exhibit 7.3 is quoted without change but has been truncated, grouped, and reordered to follow the outline of this chapter.

Perhaps the final step you should consider to avoid charges of plagiarism is to submit your own paper to one of the plagiarism detection services and see whether you have unconsciously included other peoples' work without attribution or simply forgot to include quotation marks and a reference. As mentioned, this is likely the first action that will be taken on your paper after it has been submitted for publication. If you do this yourself, you will be able to see what the journal editor will see.

HAVE I COMMITTED PLAGIARISM?

To provide an example, I submitted the penultimate draft of this chapter to iThenticate. The report I received back began with a "similarity index" that gauged the similarity of my paper to all other papers in the CrossCheck database and on the Internet. The algorithm iThenticate uses to generate this index is proprietary, so I cannot tell you exactly

EXHIBIT 7.3

Selected Guidelines for Avoiding Plagiarism

General Advice

An ethical writer ALWAYS acknowledges the contributions of others and the source of his/her ideas.

Any verbatim text taken from another author must be enclosed in quotation marks.

We must always acknowledge every source that we use in our writing; whether we paraphrase it, summarize it, or enclose it [in] quotations.

A responsible writer has an ethical responsibility to readers, and to the author/s from whom s/he is borrowing, to respect others' ideas and words, to credit those from whom we borrow, and whenever possible, to use one's own words when paraphrasing.

When borrowing heavily from a source, authors should always craft their writing in a way that makes clear to readers which ideas are their own and which are derived from the source being consulted.

Because some instances of plagiarism, self-plagiarism, and even some writing practices that might otherwise be acceptable (e.g., extensive paraphrasing or quoting of key elements of a book) can constitute copyright infringement, authors are strongly encouraged to become familiar with basic elements of copyright law.

Paraphrasing and Summarizing

When we summarize, we condense, in our own words, a substantial amount of material into a short paragraph or perhaps even into a sentence.

Whether we are paraphrasing or summarizing we must always identify the source of our information.

When paraphrasing and/or summarizing others' work we must reproduce the exact meaning of the other author's ideas or facts using our words and sentence structure.

In order to make substantial modifications to the original text that result in a proper paraphrase, the author must have a thorough understanding of the ideas and terminology being used.

Common Knowledge

When in doubt as to whether a concept or fact is common knowledge, provide a citation.

Self-Plagiarism

While there are some situations where text recycling is an acceptable practice, it may not be so in other situations. Authors are urged to adhere to the spirit of ethical writing and avoid reusing their own previously published text, unless it is done in a manner consistent with standard scholarly conventions (e.g., by using of quotations and proper paraphrasing).

Citing the Work of Others

Authors who submit a manuscript for publication containing data, reviews, conclusions, etc., that have already been disseminated in some significant manner (e.g., published as an article in another journal, presented at a conference, posted on the internet) must clearly indicate to the editors and readers the nature of the previous dissemination.

Authors are strongly urged to double-check their citations. Specifically, authors should always ensure that each reference notation appearing in the body of the manuscript corresponds to the correct citation listed in the reference section and that each source listed in the reference section has been cited at some point in the manuscript. In addition, authors should also ensure that all elements of a citation (e.g., spelling of authors' names, volume number of

(continued)

EXHIBIT 7.3 (*Continued*)

journal, pagination) are derived directly from the original paper, rather than from a citation that appears on a secondary source. Finally, authors should ensure that credit is given to those authors who first reported the phenomenon being studied.

The references used in a paper should only be those that are directly related to its contents. The intentional inclusion of references of questionable relevance for purposes of manipulating a journal's or a paper's impact factor or a paper's chances of acceptance is an unacceptable practice.

Authors should follow a simple rule: Strive to obtain the actual published paper. When the published paper cannot be obtained, cite the specific version of the material being used, whether it is a conference presentation, an abstract, or an unpublished manuscript.

Generally, when describing others' work, do not rely on a secondary summary of that work. It is a deceptive practice, reflects poor scholarly standards, and can lead to a flawed description of the work described.

If an author must rely on a secondary source (e.g., textbook) to describe the contents of a primary source (e.g., an empirical journal article), s/he should consult writing manuals used in her discipline to follow the proper convention to do so. Above all, always indicate the actual source of the information being reported.

Note: From *Avoiding Plagiarism, Self-Plagiarism, and Other Questionable Writing Practices*, by M. Roig, 2003, http://ori.hhs.gov/avoiding-plagiarism-self-plagiarism-and-other-questionable-writing-practices-guide-ethical-writing. The material is quoted without change but has been grouped and reordered. Reprinted with permission.

how it is determined. I can tell you it compared a "fingerprint" of my chapter to the documents in the databases.

My chapter had a similarity index of 27%, suggesting it would be a good idea for me to take a closer look at where and with what documents it overlapped. The report also listed for me 10 documents with which my draft shared 30 or more words (in a string of at least six words) and 10 more documents sharing six to 22 words in strings (less than 1% of the words in my chapter). In addition, iThenticate provided me with a copy of my paper that was coded numerically and by color, so I could see exactly which phrases, sentences, and paragraphs matched writing in which documents that were written by someone else. To my relief, when I examined the annotated copy of the returned draft, my reproduced and attributed material in Exhibit 7.3 accounted for 14% of the similarity and Exhibit 7.1 accounted for 4% of the similarity index. These are sources I had permission to reproduce. The other similarities were quotations from sources, bibliographic entries (which I could have asked iThenticate to exclude), and the titles of the Roig (2003) and Stern (2009) books.

I also ran the draft chapter through the eTBLAST (2012) search engine. This allowed me to check for similarity using only medical research databases. It also provided a similarity score and ratio. These were all low, but it was reassuring to see that nine of the top 10 matches were to writings on plagiarism in the medical literature. A nice feature of eTBLAST is that it also provides suggestions for scholars you could ask for feedback (based on having published similar works) and journals that have published similar papers.

There was one additional benefit to conducting the plagiarism checks I had not anticipated: iThenticate alerted me to mistakes I had made in quotations. For example, in copying a quotation, I had accidentally typed "there" instead of "their." My returned document had color coded all the words surrounding my mistake but not the mistake itself, making it clear to me that I needed to check the quotation.

I found the plagiarism checking process interesting and informative. But most of all, I felt I could proceed with submitting my chapter with a high degree of confidence that I had not unconsciously made an egregious error.

Conclusion

In this chapter I have defined the plagiarism of text, delineated types of plagiarism, and described how it can be uncovered and corrected. Checking for inadvertent or unintentional plagiarism likely will be your last action before you submit your paper for publication, the topic I turn to next.

THE PUBLICATION PROCESS IV

Before Submitting the Manuscript for Publication

8

ith your manuscript complete, you should be excited about sharing it with others and getting it published. In doing so there are protocols to follow, issues of professional etiquette to consider, and unethical actions to avoid. These ethical breaches include submitting your manuscript to more than one journal at a time, getting it published more than once, and writing more than one paper from your data with the knowledge that all of the results could have been presented in one manuscript. I discuss these matters in this chapter. I also present advice on how to choose a journal and how to construct the cover letter that will accompany your submitted manuscript so that it is professional and reveals the information the editor needs to know to put your work in proper context.

http://dx.doi.org/10.1037/14859-009
Ethical Choices in Research: Managing Data, Writing Reports, and Publishing Results in the Social Sciences, by H. Cooper
Copyright © 2016 by the American Psychological Association. All rights reserved.

Sharing Reports Before Submission

It is not unusual for authors to share their manuscripts with other researchers once the papers are completed. In fact, it is a good idea to have people knowledgeable and whose opinion you respect provide you with reactions to your paper. This is best done before the paper is submitted if you might revise the manuscript based on the comments you receive. You can ask your colleagues to give you an honest review, similar to what you might receive as part of the journal review process.

The reason to do this before, not after, you submit the manuscript for journal review is simple. Reviewers for the journal will be reacting to a manuscript that is different from the one you ultimately want to publish if you substantively revise the manuscript after submission. If your manuscript is rejected and you then ask to make the revisions suggested by your colleagues and have the paper reviewed again, the journal editor is unlikely to agree. If your manuscript receives initially positive reviews, additional changes based on comments from outside the journal's review process may be frowned upon by the editor and reduce the chances your manuscript is ultimately accepted.

Commenters should be acknowledged in your Author Note when you submit the manuscript. Not only does this reward your colleague, but it also alerts the editor to who has seen the manuscript. Editors take this information into consideration when choosing reviewers. It speeds the process if the editor does not have to learn this from the reviewer. Having seen the paper does not necessarily disqualify a scholar from being a reviewer, but it gives the editor the proper context in considering who should review your manuscript and how to interpret reviewers' reactions.

Remember that once you have shared a manuscript before publication, that person cannot provide a review without knowledge of who the authors are, although the person may still provide a review that is anonymous to you. The reviewer is likely to alert the editor to this. In addition, it is not unheard of for scholars to decline to review an article because it is not anonymous to them or for which they have provided comments to the authors directly.

You might consider whether or not to make a manuscript available on your personal or institutional website while it is under review. Typically, doing so will not be considered prior publication by journals, so it should not jeopardize your chances of getting the paper into print (this is discussed in greater detail later). However, before posting your manuscript you should consider that you will not have control over who sees it before it is in final form. The review process often involves revisions, sometimes substantial ones. Making substantial changes before the manuscript is published might lead to confusion about what you did or found. As an alternative to web posting, you can post an abstract and tell your website visitors that the manuscript is available on request. This gives you more control over who sees the paper, allows you to emphasize that the paper is still in draft form, and request that it not be cited without permission (you can even make this clear by using a watermark).

Finally, your results might be timely, and you are interested in getting media coverage so your work can contribute to a pressing public debate. For example, your findings about loneliness might suggest an improved way to identify adolescents who are prone to depression. Generally, this should be done with great caution before a completed review process by a scientific journal. Until your research has undergone review and been accepted for publication, it is open to revisions that might lead to significant changes in analyses and interpretation, as well as the discovery of mistakes or clarifications that you might want to correct before "going public." I know of one instance in which a researcher shared results of a study with a national newspaper before the report was written. The media description was incomplete out of necessity, and the précis of the work the authors provided when the newspaper article appeared included a request that the information not be shared with others until the complete manuscript was available. This reversed the proper order of events and is to be avoided.

Simultaneous Submission

You cannot submit your manuscript to more than one journal at a time. Simultaneous submission is not allowed in science for the publication of research reports. It is tempting to submit a manuscript to more than one journal at a time because it will increase your chances of getting your work published quickly. However, remember that if your manuscript is rejected by one journal, you can submit it to the next journal on your list.

The reason scientific journals disallow simultaneous submissions of the same manuscript to more than one journal is simple. If you submit your paper to three journals at one time, for example, you are tripling the amount of work for editors and reviewers. The American Psychological Association's (APA's) journals processed approximately 8,400 submissions in 2013 (American Psychological Association, 2014b), probably two-thirds of which went out to two or more reviewers. Imagine the burden if this load tripled. Most reviews for journals are performed as a service to the profession. Scholars agree to do reviews because they accept the *norm of reciprocity.* That is, they understand that other scholars will be asked to review their manuscripts (and have agreed to do so in the past), so agreeing to review manuscripts is their in-kind contribution to their field.

In addition, if your manuscript were accepted by more than one journal, you would be in the position of having to choose publication venues. This might seem like an enviable decision to have to make, but it is not. Telling one editor that you submitted it simultaneously to multiple journals and have chosen another outlet can have negative consequences for you. It could lead the editor of the journal you declined to refuse to review your future manuscripts and communicate with the editor of the other journal. Based on your simultaneous submissions, they might both refuse to publish the report. In fact, this might happen before your manuscript is accepted if two editors send the manuscript to the same reviewer and that person informs the editors of the simultaneous submission.

What will an editor do if he or she suspects that a manuscript has been simultaneously submitted to two journals? The Committee on Publication Ethics (2006) has developed a flowchart that describes how the process proceeds. The flowchart is reproduced in Figure 8.1.

Unlike submissions to scientific research journals, it is permissible to submit a grant or book proposal to more than one funding agency or publisher. Still, it is important to let publishers and funders know you are doing this. In fact, some will ask you this question as part of the submission process.

Duplicate and Redundant Publication

In some instances researchers have been known not only to submit manuscripts to be reviewed simultaneously but also to have published the same research results more than once. The Office of Research Integrity (ORI, 2013b) calls this *duplicate publication,* when researchers submit a manuscript that has been published and get it published again (it has also been called *prior publication* and *repetitive publication*). The new publication differs only slightly from the first, perhaps in the title, abstract, and/or order of authorship. *Redundant publication*

> occurs when researchers publish the same data, with somewhat different textual slant within the body of the paper. For example, redundant papers may contain a slightly different interpretation of the data or the introduction to the paper may be described in a somewhat different theoretical or empirical context. (Office of Research Integrity, 2013b, p. 1)

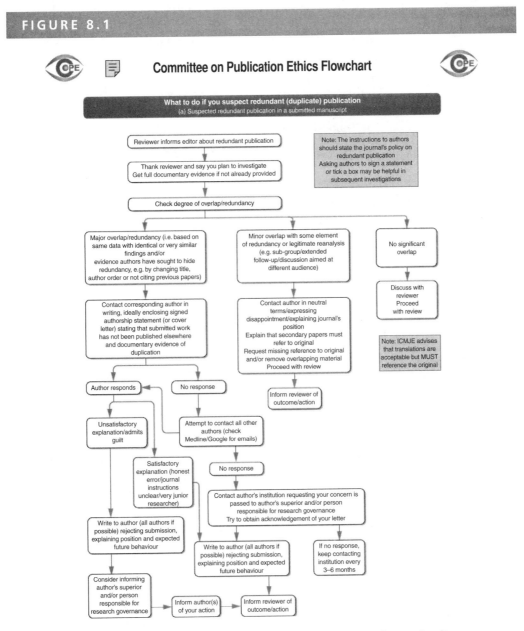

FIGURE 8.1

Committee on Publication Ethics flowchart of editor actions when a simultaneous submission is suspected. From *Committee on Publication Ethics Flowchart.* Copyright 2006 by the Committee on Publication Ethics. Reprinted with permission. Retrieved from http://publicationethics.org/resources/flowcharts

This could happen, for example, if your article on loneliness and depression in adolescents was submitted simultaneously to one journal that focuses on developmental psychology and one that focuses on counseling psychology. The methods, data, and results are the same, but slight variations can be made to the introduction and discussion based on the audience.

For the National Institutes of Health, Steneck (2000) reviewed five studies in medical research that examined the rates at which the same article was published twice without the second article referencing the first. The reported rates of duplicate publication ranged from 4% to 12% (I know of no similar effort in the social sciences).

The principle motivation for duplicate and redundant publications is to make the researcher's productivity look better than it actually is. A "padded" curriculum vitae can improve one's chances of professional promotion and make one's future research more competitive for funding.

NEGATIVE EFFECTS OF DUPLICATE PUBLICATION

Duplicate publication is frowned upon for numerous reasons other than that it distorts the author's record of productivity. Most critically, it can distort the scientific record. For example, if a reviewer of the literature on loneliness and depression does not detect that two articles are reporting the same data, he or she might conclude that there is more evidence about a hypothesis or relationship (supporting the direction of the duplicated results) than actually exists. As a real example, Tramèr, Reynolds, Moore, and McQuay (1997) found that including duplicate publications uncovered while they were performing a meta-analysis of a drug treatment to prevent postoperative nausea caused the treatment's effectiveness to be overestimated by 23%.

Duplicate publication, like duplication submission, is wasteful of the time and resources of journal editors and reviewers as well as journal space. It also can lead to conflicts over copyright; it is not clear who holds the copyright to the same article published separately by different publishers. In fact, it is likely that the authors have violated their copyright agreement with both publishers. APA journals require that cover letters to submissions state the manuscript has not been published or submitted elsewhere. It also requires that authors transfer copyright for the material to the publisher. A copy of this form, which you will sign when your manuscript is accepted but before it appears in print, is reproduced in Exhibit 8.1.

As with simultaneous submissions, discovery of duplicate publications may lead to the authors being prohibited from submitting to the offended journals in the future. In addition, the publisher may contact

EXHIBIT 8.1

Guidelines and Forms for Transfer of Copyright and Author Verification for APA Journals

APA PUBLICATIONS RIGHTS FORM

Instructions: Complete and sign Sections 1 and 2 of this form.

Accepted manuscripts cannot be published unless this form is completed, signed, and returned to the Editor. For information on APA copyright policies, please see the reverse side of this form. This form and the terms contained herein may not be amended without the express written consent of the American Psychological Association.

Manuscript title _____

Author names (in order of authorship)

_____

_____

Corresponding author _____ **Phone number** _____

Email address _____

APA publication _____

1. Copyright Transfer

A. AUTHORIZED CORRESPONDING AUTHOR: The undersigned, desiring to publish the above manuscript in a print publication and/or electronic information service of the American Psychological Association (APA), hereby assigns to APA on behalf of all authors, all rights, title, and interest in the above manuscript and any supplemental materials. (If the majority of authors or primary authors are U.S. government employees, a signature is required in Section C and not in this section.) All proprietary rights other than copyright, such as patent rights, shall remain with the author(s). In return for copyright, APA hereby grants to the authors listed in Section 2 of this form, and the employers for whom the work was performed (if applicable), royalty-free, nonexclusive, limited licenses to:

1. Reproduce, or have reproduced, the above manuscript for the author(s)' personal use or for the author(s)' intracompany use provided that (a) the source and APA copyright notice are indicated and (b) the copies are not used in a way that implies APA endorsement of a product or service of an employer. This license does not include the right for the author(s) to transfer, offer for sale, or sell the manuscript to any third party.

2. Distribute or post all or portions of the above manuscript, after final acceptance for publication by APA, to the repository at the author(s) institution in compliance with APA's Prior Publication Policy and Internet Posting Policy (available at www.apa.org/pubs/authors/posting.aspx and incorporated herein by reference).

3. In the case of work performed under U.S. Government contract, APA grants the U.S. Government royalty-free permission to reproduce all or portions of the above manuscript and to authorize others to do so for U.S. Government purposes.

For manuscripts arising from National Institutes of Health (NIH) funded investigations, APA will send the final peer-reviewed and accepted manuscript file to the NIH manuscript submission system on your behalf, in a manner consistent with federal law. Please complete the form "Statement of Eligibility for NIH Deposit" in order for APA to identify relevant manuscripts.

(continued)

EXHIBIT 8.1 (*Continued*)

Through signature below, the undersigned author (a) signifies acceptance of the terms and conditions listed above; (b) affirms that written permission has been obtained for all previously published and/or copyrighted material contained in this manuscript and any supplemental materials for online publication, as well as any other requisite permissions or releases; (c) affirms that the manuscript is an original work of authorship that has not been previously published, does not infringe any third party's intellectual property rights, and does not contain any material that is obscene, defamatory, or libelous; (d) has read and agrees to APA's internet posting policy; and (e) affirms that he/she is authorized to sign this form on behalf of all authors.

_____   _____
Authorized signature and title   **Date**

B. AUTHORS OF WORK FOR HIRE: In addition to the author signature in Section A above, authors whose work was performed within the scope of their employment must provide the signature of an authorized representative of the employer, and the employer's signature below affirms its acceptance and grant of the assignment and rights set forth herein to APA.

_____   _____
Authorized signature and title   **Date**

C. U.S. GOVERNMENT EMPLOYEES: In lieu of the author signature in Section A above, author(s) whose work was performed within the scope of their employment with the U.S. Government must provide the signature of an authorized representative, certifying that the work is in the public domain. (If the work was performed under Government contract but the author is not a Government employee, no signature is required in this section—please see Section A.3 above.)

     I certify that the majority of the authors or the primary authors of the manuscript cited above are employees of the U.S. Government and performed this work as part of their employment and that the paper is therefore not subject to the U.S. copyright protection.

_____   _____
Authorized signature and title   **Date**

2. Authorship Certification (all authors must sign this section)
Note: Faxed signatures, digital signatures, or photocopies are acceptable for all authors. By signing below, the undersigned author(s) agrees to indemnify, defend, and hold harmless APA for third party claims of copyright infringement based on APA's use of the manuscript and to approve the order of authorship as listed at the top of this form.

Name	Date	Name	Date
Name	Date	Name	Date
Name	Date	Name	Date
Name	Date	Name	Date

EXHIBIT 8.1 (*Continued*)

APA Permission Policy Governing the Secondary Use of Copyrighted Material

It is the policy of APA to own the copyrights to its publications, and to the contributions contained therein, in order to protect the interests of the Association, its authors, and their employers, and at the same time to facilitate the appropriate reuse of this material by others.

In exercising its rights under U.S. copyright law, APA requires authors to obtain APA's permission and/or pay APA a fee to republish or reuse the author(s)' manuscript under certain circumstances.

Circumstances in which no permission or fees will be required:

- Authors seeking to reproduce their own manuscript for personal use
- Photocopying of isolated articles for noncommercial classroom and/or library reserve use

Circumstances in which permission is required, but no fee will be charged:

- Authors seeking to use their own material commercially (but for use in edited book compilations, fees are waived for the author only if he or she is serving as the editor of that book compilation)

Circumstances in which permission and a fee will be charged:

- Photocopying of materials for classroom use in which students are charged for the copies
- Photocopying of two or more articles, regardless of classroom use
- Photocopying of materials for course packs and other large-scale copying, regardless of whether a fee is charged to the students
- Commercial organizations seeking to reprint APA materials

Fees are normally charged to all commercial organizations that secure permission to reprint APA-copyrighted material. This fee, after an appropriate deduction to cover APA's costs associated with administering the permission function, is turned over to the American Psychological Foundation, a charitable nonprofit 501(c)(3) organization, incorporated independently of APA. For more information on permissions and fees, please see the APA Permissions Policy available at http://www.apa.org/about/contact/copyright/index.aspx and incorporated herein by reference.

the authors' institutions, who may impose punishments of their own. Duplicate publication also could lead to retraction of one of the articles. The attempt to enhance one's professional record now results in a professional embarrassment.

WHEN DUPLICATE PUBLICATION IS PERMITTED

Sometimes, redundant publication of the same data is permitted. The *Publication Manual* (APA, 2010b) describes the criteria to apply when making this decision:

1. The amount of duplicated material must be small relative to the total length of the text.
2. The text must clearly acknowledge in the author note and other relevant sections of the article (i.e., methods and/or results sections)

that the information was reported previously, and the citation to the previous work must be given.

3. Any republished tables and figures must be clearly marked as reprinted or adapted, and the original source is provided both in the text and in a footnote to the table or figure.

4. The original publication venue must be clearly and accurately cited in the reference list.

When the original publication has multiple authors and the authorship is not identical on both publications, it is important that all authors receive agreed-upon credit (e.g., in an author note) for their contributions in the later publication. (p. 14)

The APA guidelines mention that previous publication in abstract form, such as the proceedings of a professional meeting, is permitted. Presenting your paper on loneliness at the APA annual meeting does not constitute prior publication. However, disciplines and scientific organizations vary with regard to how they view the publication status of meeting presentations. If your talk or a report you prepare of it will be published in the proceedings of the meeting, either in a printed book or online, this may constitute publication. In this case, you may be asked to complete a copyright transfer. You should check with the meeting organizers and the editor of the journal you want to submit to so you can be certain about whether they view this as publication.

Appearance in a periodical with limited circulation, for example, a report listed in the products of a research center or a report to a government agency, does not preclude publication in a scientific journal. If the study was your dissertation project or master's thesis, it is not considered prior publication. In most of these cases, the data may be the same, but the text would be substantially revised for publication in the new venue.

The Office of Research Integrity (2013b) adds to this list of permissible rationales that the "paper would be of interest to each set of readers who would probably not otherwise be aware of the other publication" (p. 1). Thus, although your paper on loneliness in adolescents ought not to be published in both a developmental and counseling psychology journal, it might be permissible to publish it in one of these journals and then write a separate piece about your study for a journal with an audience of practicing school psychologists. The ORI guideline might also permit articles that appear in one language to be translated for publication into a different language. Republication of an article as a book chapter is also permitted. In all these instances, of course, the prior publication must be fully disclosed to the editor upon submission, permission must be obtained from the publisher holding the copyright, and the earlier publication must be acknowledged in the subsequent one.

Data and results from a prior wave of a longitudinal study or as part of a follow-up study can be used and reported again in a new publication.

The new manuscript clearly will be different, and citation to the original report of the prior wave of data collection will limit the amount of space needed to explain the first set of analyses and results.

Finally, reanalysis of the same data with new techniques may or may not be publishable. In this instance, the new manuscript should cite and summarize the results of the prior analyses and the case be made for why the new analyses contribute something unique and important to understanding the topic.

Piecemeal Publication

Drotar (2010), following the *Publication Manual* (APA, 2010b), defined *piecemeal publication* as "the unnecessary submission of findings from the same study, in piece by piece fashion, rather than as an integrated single report or a smaller number of integrated reports" (p. 225). This practice also has been called *fragmented publication* and, perhaps humorously but not to diminish the seriousness of the practice, *salami science, least publishable units (LPUs),* and *minimal publishable units (MPUs).*

Sometimes, it may be legitimate to publish more than one report that contains different data and analyses performed on the same data set. This can happen if a data set contains many variables and a single publication would become so lengthy and unwieldy that the message of the work would be lost. The audience for different variables in a data set might be different as well. For example, you might think that your results regarding loneliness and depression and those regarding loneliness and social activity will interest different audiences (the first clinical psychologists, the second developmental psychologists). Your predictions and results might be based on and relevant to distinct theoretical formulations. This rationale for piecemeal publication has lost some credibility as electronic retrieval of articles has replaced printed reference databases (so that a search on "loneliness" captures both clinical and developmental psychology journals). Still, covering all your results in one report may be difficult and require a manuscript that exceeds the page limits of the journals (and the attention span of readers) you are considering.

Finally, it generally is frowned upon to publish separately the same variables and analyses conducted on different subsamples from the same study. Again, if you think this approach is called for, you are obligated to disclose your multiple submissions or publications along with a cogent rationale for doing so in your cover letter to the editor and in the manuscripts. Thus, if you decide to prepare separate manuscripts on your loneliness data for your samples of adolescents and young adults, you need a strong rationale, similar to the criteria you would use for dividing manuscripts by measured variables.

Website Posting

The *Publication Manual* (APA, 2010b) guidelines for how to post manuscripts on the Internet before and after they are published are reproduced in Exhibit 8.2. Web posting will not be considered prior publication if you follow these rules. They are consistent with the recommendation of ORI (2013b):

> Authors who submit a manuscript for publication containing data, reviews, conclusions, etc., that have already been disseminated in some significant manner (e.g., published as an article in another journal, presented at a conference, posted on the internet) must clearly indicate to the editors and readers the nature of the previous dissemination. (p. 1)

Before you post a manuscript, review the rules for the journals to which you are interested in submitting your report.

EXHIBIT 8.2

APA *Publication Manual* Guidelines for Posting Articles on the Internet

Certain rights are linked to copyright ownership, including the exclusive right to reproduce and distribute the copyrighted work. Journals are committed to publishing original scholarship and distributing peer-reviewed articles, in both print and electronic formats, that serve as the version of record. Thus, many publishers have policies delineating the terms under which an article may be posted on the Internet by the author.

If a paper is unpublished, the author may distribute it on the Internet or post it on a website but should label the paper with the date and with a statement that the paper has not (yet) been published. (Example: Draft version 1.3, 1/5/99. This paper has not been peer reviewed. Please do not copy or cite without author's permission.)

Upon submitting the paper for publication, the author is obligated to inform the editor if the paper has been or is posted on a website. Some editors may consider such a Web posting to be prior publication and may not review the paper.

Authors of articles published in APA journals may post a copy of the final manuscript, as a word processing, PDF, or other type file, on their website or their employer's server after it is accepted for publication. The following conditions would prevail:

- The posted article must carry an APA copyright notice and include a link to the APA journal home page.
- The posted article must include the following statement: "This article may not exactly replicate the final version published in the APA journal. It is not the copy of record."
- APA does not permit archiving with any other non-APA repositories.

APA does not provide electronic copies of the APA published version for this purpose, and authors are not permitted to scan in the APA published version.

Note. Reprinted from *Publication Manual of the American Psychological Association* (6th ed., pp. 237–239), by the American Psychological Association, 2010, Washington, DC: American Psychological Association. Copyright 2010 by the American Psychological Association.

Choosing a Journal

When you consider what journal to submit your manuscript to, you will first consider what journals reach the audience you wish to know about your research. For this reason, you should consider where you intend to submit your paper before you begin writing it. Different journals will have different criteria for the preparation of submitted manuscripts. Day and Gastel (2011) suggested the submission guidelines of most journals cover the following issues:

- the types of articles the journal publishes (e.g., primary studies, reviews of the literature);
- the maximum length of articles;
- what writing style and manuscript format should be used (e.g., sections of the article, placement of footnotes and tables, how references should be formatted);
- whether supplemental material is permitted and, if so, how it should be formatted and where it will be made available (e.g., on the journal's website);
- whether there is a limit to the number of tables and figures that can be included;
- how to submit the manuscript (typically, through an online portal accessed from the journal's website).

APA journals mostly follow a common set of formatting conventions, described in the *Publication Manual* (APA, 2010b). Specific APA journals often have additional reporting guidelines that address issues specific to the journal. For example, an abbreviated copy of the instructions to authors for the *Journal of Experimental Psychology: General* (*JEP General*; APA, 2015c) is reproduced in Exhibit 8.3. Note that much of the requested material relates to formatting issues of particular pertinence to the type of research that might appear in that journal, for example, presentation of tables, graphs, figures (and the costs to authors for color figures), displays, equations, computer code, and references. Some of these instructions appear in the *Publication Manual* (APA, 2010b), but they are restated in the journal because many authors who submit papers to it may not be psychologists who are familiar with the guidelines. The website also notes that other APA journals that publish experimental research might have different manuscript submission guidelines. Authors should use the *Publication Manual* as a reference for matters pertaining to formatting and reporting rules not mentioned on the website.

A good first clue to which journals might be best for your paper are those you intend to cite as references: what journals published the articles

EXHIBIT 8.3

Submission Instructions to Authors: *Journal of Experimental Psychology: General*

Manuscripts should be submitted electronically through the Manuscript Submission Portal.

**Submission
Portal Entrance**

The file format should be Microsoft Word Format (.doc or .docx), or PDF (.pdf).

If authors wish to do so for review, to facilitate readability, they can include tables, figures and figure legends as appropriate in the manuscript close to where they would appear in the published article. Note however that when a paper is accepted, a file will need to be promptly submitted that must exactly copy, in all respects and in a single Word file, the complete APA-style printed version of the manuscript.

In a cover letter, provide the following information:

- a brief paragraph summarizing how the work might appeal to more than one traditional area of psychology
- a list of 3–5 appropriate reviewers with no conflict of interest, explaining what their relevant expertise is
- a list of non-preferred reviewers (no explanation is necessary but is welcomed)

On the first page of the manuscript, provide a word count for the text excluding title, references, author affiliations, acknowledgments, figures and figure legends, but including the abstract.

Articles in the Journal will be evaluated for the quality of the research designs, in particular their ability to provide strong tests of broadly important theoretical hypotheses.

Articles will also be evaluated for the soundness of their statistical claims. Authors are urged to consider reporting effect sizes (and confidence intervals around them) and to discuss their practical and theoretical implications. The editorial team believes precision of estimation can at times be more important than the dichotomous statistical decisions of null hypothesis significance testing.

We also encourage authors to explain their sample sizes, ideally using power analyses based on effect sizes calculated from their own prior studies, other prior work, or when available, meta-analyses. This is particularly important when samples sizes are relatively small, or vary greatly from one experiment to the next, in which case the stopping rule for data collection should be clearly stated.

Graphs and tables should include error bars that are clearly labeled in the figure legend, and tables should also provide clearly labeled measures of variability (the use of confidence intervals is encouraged, and ranges may be more appropriate for small samples). . . .

In addition to mailing addresses and phone numbers, please supply email addresses and fax numbers for potential use by the editorial office and later by the production office.

Keep a copy of the manuscript as a guard against loss.

General correspondence may be directed to Editor's Office.

Masked Review Policy

Masked reviews are optional. If you want a masked review, indicate that in the cover letter. Do not include authors' names and affiliations on the title page. Instead, place this information in the cover letter, which is not seen by reviewers.

Footnotes that identify the authors should also be removed from the manuscript and can be included in the cover letter. Authors should make every effort to see that the manuscript itself contains no clues to their identities.

If your manuscript was mask reviewed, please ensure that the final version for production includes a byline and full author note for typesetting.

EXHIBIT 8.3 (*Continued*)

Related Journals of Experimental Psychology

For the other JEP journals, authors should submit manuscripts according to the manuscript submission guidelines for each individual journal . . .

Manuscript Preparation

Prepare manuscripts according to the *Publication Manual of the American Psychological Association (6th edition)*. Manuscripts may be copyedited for bias-free language (see Chapter 3 of the *Publication Manual*).

Review APA's Checklist for Manuscript Submission before submitting your article.

Double-space all copy. Other formatting instructions, as well as instructions on preparing tables, figures, references, metrics, and abstracts, appear in the Manual.

Below are additional instructions regarding the preparation of display equations, computer code, and tables.

Display Equations

We strongly encourage you to use . . .

Computer Code

Because altering computer code in any way (e.g., indents, line spacing, line breaks, page breaks) during the typesetting process could alter its meaning, we treat computer code differently from the rest of your article in our production process. To that end, we request separate files for computer code . . .

Tables

Use Word's Insert Table function when you create tables. Using spaces or tabs in your table will create problems when the table is typeset and may result in errors.

Submitting Supplemental Materials

APA can place supplemental materials online, available via the published article in the PsycARTICLES® database. Please see Supplementing Your Article With Online Material for more details.

Abstract and Keywords

All manuscripts must include an abstract containing a maximum of 250 words typed on a separate page. After the abstract, please supply up to five keywords or brief phrases.

References

List references in alphabetical order. Each listed reference should be cited in text, and each text citation should be listed in the References section.

Examples of basic reference formats . . .

Figures

Graphics files are welcome if supplied as . . .

For authors who prefer their figures to be published in color both in print and online, original color figures can be printed in color at the editor's and publisher's discretion provided the author agrees to pay:

- $900 for one figure
- An additional $600 for the second figure
- An additional $450 for each subsequent figure

(continued)

EXHIBIT 8.3 *(Continued)*

Permissions

Authors of accepted papers must obtain and provide to the editor on final acceptance all necessary permissions to reproduce in print and electronic form any copyrighted work, including test materials (or portions thereof), photographs, and other graphic images (including those used as stimuli in experiments).

On advice of counsel, APA may decline to publish any image whose copyright status is unknown.

▪ Download Permissions Alert Form (PDF, 13KB)

Publication Policies

APA policy prohibits an author from submitting the same manuscript for concurrent consideration by two or more publications.

See also APA Journals® Internet Posting Guidelines.

APA requires authors to reveal any possible conflict of interest in the conduct and reporting of research (e.g., financial interests in a test or procedure, funding by pharmaceutical companies for drug research).

▪ Download Disclosure of Interests Form (PDF, 38KB)

Authors of accepted manuscripts are required to transfer the copyright to APA.

▪ For manuscripts **not** funded by the Wellcome Trust or the Research Councils UK Publication Rights (Copyright Transfer) Form (PDF, 83KB)
▪ For manuscripts funded by the Wellcome Trust or the Research Councils UK Wellcome Trust or Research Councils UK Publication Rights Form (PDF, 34KB)

Ethical Principles

It is a violation of APA Ethical Principles to publish "as original data, data that have been previously published" (Standard 8.13).

In addition, APA Ethical Principles specify that "after research results are published, psychologists do not withhold the data on which their conclusions are based from other competent professionals who seek to verify the substantive claims through reanalysis and who intend to use such data only for that purpose, provided that the confidentiality of the participants can be protected and unless legal rights concerning proprietary data preclude their release" (Standard 8.14).

APA expects authors to adhere to these standards. Specifically, APA expects authors to have their data available throughout the editorial review process and for at least 5 years after the date of publication.

Authors are required to state in writing that they have complied with APA ethical standards in the treatment of their sample, human or animal, or to describe the details of treatment.

▪ Download Certification of Compliance With APA Ethical Principles Form (PDF, 26KB)

The APA Ethics Office provides the full Ethical Principles of Psychologists and Code of Conduct electronically on its website in HTML, PDF, and Word format. You may also request a copy by emailing or calling the APA Ethics Office (202-336-5930). You may also read "Ethical Principles," December 1992, *American Psychologist*, Vol. 47, pp. 1597–1611.

Other Information

▪ Appeals Process for Manuscript Submissions
▪ Preparing Auxiliary Files for Production
▪ Document Deposit Procedures for APA Journals

Note. Reprinted from the Manuscript Submission section of the *Journal of Experimental Psychology: General,* web page. Retrieved from http://www.apa.org/pubs/journals/xge/index.aspx?tab=4. Copyright 2015 by the American Psychological Association.

you will reference in your manuscript? You might also consider journals based on your sample's characteristics. If your loneliness and depression study was conducted on a college campus, journals focusing on higher education might be good outlets. You will also consider your chances of having this work accepted at each of the journals you think might be appropriate. Here, you will need to realistically assess the strength of your research against the criteria the journal will use to assess how it stacks up relative to the articles it typically publishes. These criteria will include the following:

- how appropriate it is to its audience (the same determination you made);
- the significance of the topic;
- the clarity of the presentation;
- the correspondence of the methods to your desired inferences and argumentation.

Each journal might have additional criteria, but these are the major dimensions on which most editors will ask reviewers to judge your paper. Often, you can gain insight into what criteria will be used by a journal in its statement of scope, instructions to authors, and most recent editorial.

You will find that journals differ in their acceptance rates of submitted manuscripts. This will be related to the prestige of the journal in the field, which is related to the size of the journal's audience and the frequency with which the articles published in it are cited by other authors in the field. Often, you can find out about a journal's acceptance and citation rates on its web page or in the Web of Science reference database (Thomas Reuters, n.d.).

Open Access Journals

Open access journals make their articles available to readers on the Internet free of charge and typically with a reduced set of copyright restrictions. You may be attracted to publishing in open access journals because you hold to the principle that wide access to your work is your important responsibility as a scientist. Open access journals may reach a wider audience and be more likely to be cited in the works of others (OpCit Project, 2012).

The arguments in favor of open access journals were persuasively presented by the Budapest Open Access Initiative (2012). It argued that removing barriers to accessing the scientific literature can speed discoveries, facilitate education, reduce economic barriers inhibiting the access of people in poor countries, and "lay the foundation for uniting humanity in a common intellectual conversation and quest for knowledge" (p. 1). The Harvard Open Access Initiative (Berkman Center for Internet and Society, 2012) added that open access "maximizes the return on our investment in research, and speeds the development of all the benefits that depend on research, from new medicines and useful technologies to informed decisions, solved problems, and improved public policies" (p. 1).

The expense of distributing the material in open-access journals is borne by the author or an institution supportive of open access. If you are interested in publishing in an open access journal, you can consult your institutional librarian, who should know (or know who should know) how you can obtain these funds. In addition, it is not unusual today for principal investigators to include journal fees in their grant budgets. The fees may be for submitting the article, publishing it, or a combination of both. The fees vary greatly from journal to journal. Some journals have sliding fee schedules, charging students less than faculty members or other submitters.

The Cover Letter

The cover letter of your manuscript should contain important information about your study and report, much of which has been mentioned already. Along with your cover letter you will submit several forms that attest to your ethical behavior in conducting the study and preparing the manuscript. For submissions to APA journals (APA, 2010b), the cover letter should include

- details about the manuscript, including its title, length (sometimes in pages, sometimes in words), and number of tables and figures;
- whether you wish to have your manuscript treated as anonymous or have your identity disclosed, if your choice is different from the default option of the journal (covered in the next chapter);
- recommendations for potential reviewers or individuals you wish not to review;
- information about previous presentations of the paper;
- information about closely related manuscripts that have been simultaneously submitted to other journals;
- disclosure of potential conflicts of interest (e.g., your own or your relatives' financial interests if procedures or tests are evaluated);
- verification that subjects were treated in accordance with ethical standards (this typically means that you state your protocol was approved by an Institutional Review Board [IRB]);
- copies of permissions to reproduce or adapt materials that are copyrighted by others or assurance that such permission is not

necessary (e.g., the material is in the public domain) or is pending (a guide is provided to help you decide which materials need permission and to provide a list of your permissions; American Psychological Association, 2014a);

■ assurance that all authors are in agreement with the content of the manuscript and the order of authorship; and

■ contact information for the corresponding author.

The form that APA journals use to request certification by all authors is reproduced in Exhibit 8.1. The corresponding author takes responsibility for keeping other authors up to date as the manuscript moves through the review process and is revised.

The cover letter for each journal might have additional specifications. For example, *JEP General* requests that the cover letter contain "a brief paragraph summarizing how the work appeals to more than one traditional area of psychology" (APA, 2015c, p. 1). The editor is expressing a desire to use as one evaluation criteria for the manuscript whether it crosses boundaries in psychology. *JEP General* also asks for a list of three to five potential reviewers and asks explicitly that they have no conflict of interest and why their expertise is relevant.

Conclusion

Submitting a manuscript for publication may involve more decision points with ethical implications than you realized. These include when and how to submit and what to disclose to editors at the time of submission. Even the decision about which journal to submit to can have ethical implications. In addition, for some decisions, what is acceptable or improper behavior is not always clear. Your actions will fall on a continuum from the always unethical—submitting the same manuscript at the same time to multiple related journals—to the perfectly appropriate—using the first wave of published data again as part of a later report of a longitudinal study.

The best way to avoid accusations of misconduct in the submission process is to be open about what you have done in the manuscript and transparent in your cover letter to the editor. In fact, you can communicate your intentions to the journal editor before a manuscript is submitted. Journal editors should respond quickly, perhaps saving you the time and effort required to make a formal submission (and them the time to respond formally). The key is that you be guided by your desire to maintain the integrity of the scientific record and your own reputation.

The Manuscript Review Process 9

T he *peer review* process is the central mechanism used to ensure the quality of reports that appear in the scientific record. Peer review can be described as "a formal system whereby a piece of academic work is scrutinized by people who were not involved in its creation but are considered knowledgeable about the subject" (Wager, Godlee, & Jefferson, 2002, p. 3). According to Shamoo and Resnik (2009),

> peer review is regarded by many philosophers of
> science as a key pillar of the scientific method
> because it promotes objectivity and repeatability. . . .
> Science is "self-correcting" because scientists review
> and criticize research methods, designs, and conclu-
> sions and repeat experiments and tests. (p. 117)

Peer review is used in science to evaluate all sorts of work, including the quality of reports submitted for journal publication, proposals to present at professional meetings, grant applications and reports, and book proposals and manuscripts. Universities also use peer review to make assessments of the entire body of work by faculty members being considered for

http://dx.doi.org/10.1037/14859-010
Ethical Choices in Research: Managing Data, Writing Reports, and Publishing Results in the Social Sciences, by H. Cooper
Copyright © 2016 by the American Psychological Association. All rights reserved.

job promotion and/or tenure as well as for distinguished chairs in an academic department. Professional societies and universities may use peer review when considering scholars for awards.

In this chapter, I focus on the peer review process by scientific journals. Again, I use the American Psychological Association's (APA's) guidelines as the template, but the process will be roughly similar throughout the social sciences. Because APA publishes so many journals, its process is carefully detailed and has a fine division of labor. If you understand it, you should understand other publishers' processes. There are journals that do not employ a rigorous peer review process, but they will have little credibility in your field. I begin with a description of the different actors in the peer review process and the roles they play.

Actors in the Review Process

When a manuscript is submitted to an APA journal, the first person to see it is usually the *managing editor* or *manuscript coordinator*. This person is part of the journal's administrative staff. She or he will check the manuscript to make sure everything needed for the review process is in order and the formatting rules have been followed. The managing editor will log your manuscript electronically, and you will receive an e-mail that informs you of the manuscript's identification number. The e-mail may also contain a link that allows you to track your manuscript as it moves through the review process: for example, it may tell you when your manuscript has been assigned to an editor, when reviews have been requested, and when they have been returned (but not what the reviews say).

The journal editor, or *editor-in-chief*, is a recognized scholar in the field covered by the journal. In addition, this person usually has considerable editorial experience, typically having worked his or her way up through the lower ranks of editorial responsibility with an exemplary record. The editor of the journal will read your manuscript and make a judgment about its appropriateness for the journal. The editor also will look to see if the submission and manuscript guidelines have been followed. He or she will make a broad judgment about the significance and quality of the work. If the editor thinks the manuscript has little or no chance of acceptance for publication, he or she may reject it before it goes out for review. This is called a *desk reject*; it saves work for editors and reviewers and time for the authors. It typically is based on the judgment that the research is inappropriate for the journal or has a glaring methodological flaw, such as a sample size that is too small.

Next, the editor will decide whether she or he will serve as *action editor* or send the paper to an *associate editor* to guide the review process and make a decision about its fate at the journal. In many cases, editors could not possibly process all the journal's submissions themselves; editors typically hold their journal positions in addition to their other professional responsibilities. For example, some APA journals, such as *Journal of Experimental Psychology: General*, *Journal of Consulting and Clinical Psychology*, and *Journal of Applied Psychology*, process hundreds of manuscripts every year and serve broad subfields of psychology. Each has about a dozen associate editors. The editor will choose associate editors with areas of expertise that complement one another so the field is covered. It is likely that your manuscript will be acted upon by the associate editor with expertise closest to the topic of your study, although this is not guaranteed. Also taken into consideration is the associate editor's workload at the time you submit and any potential conflict of interest, such as whether the manuscript contains a criticism of her or his past work.

The action editor chooses reviewers for the manuscript. These can be chosen from a list of *consulting editors* who have agreed to review a certain number of manuscripts for the journal each year. For example, *Journal of Experimental Psychology: General* has about 80 consulting editors. They are listed on the journal's editorial board, along with the editor and associate editors. Consulting editors are chosen for their expertise and because they have provided cogent and timely reviews in the past. Doing a consistently good job as a consulting editor is an excellent credential for moving on to become an associate editor. (Yes, editor's reviews are subject to evaluation. In fact, some review forms contain scales at the bottom for editors to rate the review.)

The action editor also may request *ad hoc reviewers* to assess your manuscript because of their specialized knowledge of the topic. The action editor can choose these persons because the editor knows of their expertise. However, some journals maintain databases of past ad hoc reviewers that can be searched by keywords to find reviewers with a particular expertise. In many instances, consulting editors and ad hoc reviewers will be used on the same manuscript. When a reviewer accepts an assignment, he or she typically is asked to disclose any real or potentially perceived conflicts of interest with regard to the paper (e.g., the reviewer is aware the paper was prepared by a past student) or content of the manuscript (e.g., it competes with the reviewer's own work). These potential conflicts of interest might not disqualify the reviewer, but the editor needs to know if they exist.

As mentioned in Chapter 8, submission materials may allow you to request that certain reviewers be used or not used. Wager, Parkin, and Tamber (2006) found that the source of the reviewer recommendation was not associated with the quality of the review, but author-nominated reviewers were more likely to rate a manuscript favorably. Countervailing this possible positive effect is that the editor will know you nominated the reviewer, so his or her review may be given slightly less weight than are those of reviewers chosen by the editor. The action editor also will examine your acknowledgments and consider the previous works you reference, along with her or his own knowledge of the field, when making a decision about who to select as reviewers.

Typically, once the reviews are completed, the action editor will write the *action letter*. The letter is then approved and/or revised by the editor-in-chief before it is sent to you. If you are fortunate enough to have your paper accepted, you will then interact with the manuscript coordinator again, who will make sure all assurances (e.g., copyright transfers, author agreements, approvals to reprint material) are up to date. The final stop will be the *copyeditor*, who will help you prepare your manuscript for typesetting.

INAPPROPRIATE MANIPULATION OF THE PEER REVIEW PROCESS

You may become aware of agencies that offer services that help you prepare your manuscript for review. These services can range from preview of your completed manuscript to nonjudgmental assistance with formatting and writing. This step may be especially useful if you have no colleagues to review your work or if you are submitting your manuscript to a journal published in a language in which you are less fluent.

However, some disreputable agencies sell authorships to prewritten manuscripts. Obviously, this is an ethical violation with dire consequences if the "author" and agency are caught. Other agency misbehaviors include providing authors with fabricated contact details for peer reviewers (e.g., bogus e-mail addresses) and then supplying fabricated comments when the "reviewer" is contacted. The Committee on Publication Ethics (n.d.-a) works with publishers and journals to identify these agencies. If you contact an agency for help with a manuscript, be certain that the agency is reputable, and check the accuracy of any suggestions it makes for potential reviewers of your work. If you find something is amiss, contact the Committee on Publication Ethics.

PROPOSALS TO PROFESSIONAL MEETINGS

Proposals to present your work at professional meetings will undergo a similar review process but with less specialization, and all the reviewers will be ad hoc. You will submit your proposal to the program chairs. Typically, they will have asked in advance a number of scholars to serve as reviewers, before they know the topics of papers that will be submitted. The program chairs then divide up the submissions as best they can, based on the expertise of the available reviewers. Reviewers rank proposals on a common scale. Chairs choose submissions to accept primarily using a cutoff dictated by the time available for presentations. Depending on the size of the meeting, the number of submissions and reviewers, and the time available for review, you may get little feedback on your proposal, perhaps a paragraph or two from each reviewer. In addition you will have no opportunity to revise and resubmit if your work is rejected. Typically, acceptance rates for conference presentations are higher than those for prestigious journals. Acceptance rates also vary by the type of presentation you propose. A poster presentation has a better chance of acceptance (it takes less time on the meeting program) than does a paper or a proposed symposium.

Anonymous Review

Although there is consensus among scientists about the value of peer review, there is considerable debate about the value and effects of *anonymous* or *masked review*. Anonymous review occurs when the identity of the authors and/or reviewers are kept from the other parties. For example, you may be asked to submit your manuscript with all information that could be used to identify you and your co-authors removed from the title page. You will submit a separate title page with this information and the Author Note on it, and the reviewers will not see this page. You also may be asked to prepare the manuscript with any references to your previous work removed and replaced with "Author (date)" in the text and the references removed from the Reference section.

Keeping the authors of a manuscript anonymous is difficult, especially if the authors are well known in the line of work or many references are made to their own previous work. Reviewers can actively seek out authors' identities, which is all the easier if authors have placed the manuscript on a website or given a presentation with a similar title at a professional conference. However, a good reviewer will not attempt to uncover the author's identity.

Some journals do not use masked review of authors, and others allow authors to decide whether they wish to be anonymous or have their names revealed. When submitting your paper, you should check the submission guidelines for the journal. Make your case in your cover letter. In most journals, the reviewers will be anonymous to the authors, but reviewers can sign their reviews if they wish. Some reviewers are ethically opposed to anonymous review.

Pros and Cons of Anonymous Review

Arguments have been made about the positive and negative effects of anonymous review. There is general agreement and some evidence that the peer review process improves the quality of published articles (cf. Jefferson, Wager, & Davidoff, 2002). However, Godlee (2002) noted that if peer review led to perfect decisions, reviewers would never disagree, strong and creative manuscripts would never be rejected, and cases of data misconduct would never appear in print. This expectation, of course, is unrealistic.

Disagreements among reviewers are to be expected. You should not take this to mean the process has failed you. Some of the determinations that reviewers are asked to make are inherently subjective (e.g., the importance of a contribution) or require different types of expertise (e.g., substantive or methodological), and good editors will pick reviewers whose skills and perspective are meant to complement, not mirror, one another.

But other factors that can affect the peer review process are not justifiable, including the theoretical, conceptual, and methodological preferences of the reviewers. Such biases may lead to rejection of manuscripts, and this can stifle debate and innovation. Professional rivalries, institutional favoritism, and personal feuds also can corrupt the peer review process (cf. Shamoo & Resnik, 2009). Exacerbating the problem is that because the competition is high for journal space, especially in the most prestigious journals, one reviewer offering a negative review based on personal biases may be enough to scuttle a submission.

The anonymous review process is meant to alleviate some of the potential biases. By keeping reviewers unaware of the name and affiliation of authors, it is hoped that there will be less chance for bias based on factors such as the sex and seniority of the authors and the prestige of their institution. However, a study in medicine revealed that reviewers were able to identify the authors of nearly half (42%) of masked manuscripts (van Rooyen, Godlee, Evans, Smith, & Black, 1998), and Godlee (2002) suggested that the rate of successful masking ranged from 50% to 76%.

Keeping the reviewers' identities masked also has its supporters and distractors (Shamoo & Resnik, 2009). Supporters argue that anonymous reviewing allows the reviewers to be more truthful about their assessment, without fear of retribution from the authors. This is especially important when the reviewer is an early professional. Detractors argue that reviewers will be more conscientious and careful in their criticisms if their identity is revealed. They also contend that there is less likelihood that reviewers will steal ideas from submitted manuscripts, not that this happens often (see LaFollette, 1992; and my later discussion on confidentiality).

The debate over the value of anonymous review remains unresolved, which is reflected in the different rules about anonymous review at different journals. That is why it is important to read the journal's rules. If you disagree with them, contact the editor and make your case. If your arguments are rejected, you can acquiesce or you can submit to another journal, one with a review process more in tune with your beliefs.

Undue Editorial Lag

The length of time it will take for you to receive a decision about your manuscript will vary from journal to journal, depending on the length and complexity of your manuscript and the number of reviewers asked to examine it. If your manuscript gets rejected without review, you should quickly receive a letter from the editor with a short explanation for why the manuscript will not be reviewed.

The *Publication Manual* (APA, 2010b) states that you can expect a decision within 3 months of submission. After that, it would be appropriate for you to contact the editor. You can assume this is true for any non-APA journals that use the *Publication Manual* unless they explicitly state otherwise. Again, you may be able to track the progress of your manuscript by looking at the manuscript history page with the link sent to you in the acknowledgment of submission. After 3 months, a brief, polite note to the editor asking for information on the status of the manuscript will alert the editor to your concern.

In many instances, the causes of undue editorial delays are understandable. For example, the action editor may have a large number of manuscripts to handle. The editor may have difficulty finding scholars to agree to review the manuscript. This is becoming more common as the rewards for this type of professional service have diminished in comparison with the rewards for publishing one's own work. In addition, your paper might be complex and need extra reviews after the initial reviews have come in so that the action editor can get a complete picture of its value.

Still, simple neglect does happen. It can happen on the part of reviewers who agree to review and then forget or become swamped by other responsibilities. Action editors may become overwhelmed with other responsibilities and let editing take a back seat. This should not happen; editing and reviewing manuscripts are central to the scientific process and should not be taken on by individuals unless they intend to give the tasks high priority. You can assume this is true. They should treat your manuscript the same way they hope their manuscripts will be treated when they enter the review process. Contacting the editor in a nonconfrontational manner almost always results in an explanation and an expedited conclusion to the review process.[1]

Confidentiality of the Review Process

Regardless of whether or not you and the reviewers have revealed your identities, all participants in the review process have agreed to keep confidential the manuscript and all correspondence related to it. Reviewers have agreed not to share the manuscript, seek assistance with the review from others, or talk about it with others without the permission of the journal editor. The editor will not share the manuscript or allow action editors to share it without your permission.

Occasionally, reviewers will ask the editor to ask you if you are willing to share your identity with them. This typically happens so they can seek clarifications during the review process or after they have written their review. Typically, this sharing is not done; all communication between you and reviewers will be mediated by the editor. If you are contacted directly by a reviewer, you should let the editor know this has happened. Reviewers might also ask the editor if they can share the manuscript with a graduate student or postdoctoral fellow and have that person write the review under their tutelage. This can be a good method of training the next generation of reviewers. The decision to allow this is up to the editor.

Once the review has been written, reviewers are asked to destroy their copy of the manuscript by shredding any paper copies or deleting the electronic copy. Not to do so is an ethical violation. If you become aware of unauthorized sharing, you should report this to the editor.

COMMENTS TO THE EDITOR ONLY

On the reviewer's comment sheet is a section labeled "for the editor only." These comments will not be shared with you when your decision letter arrives. If reviewers have concerns about misconduct (e.g., evi-

---

[1]Once, I submitted a manuscript and waited many months for reviews. I finally contacted the editor, who told me he thought the action letter had been sent. He discovered he had written the letter while traveling and misplaced it. If I had not contacted him, I might still be waiting.

dence they find of data tampering, plagiarism, or previous publication), they can notify the editor without accusing the authors in the review. The "editor only" section of the review often contains harsher assessments about the quality of the manuscript that the reviewer does not wish to convey directly to the authors. The editor may include some of these concerns in the action letter.

EXCEPTIONS TO CONFIDENTIALITY

There are a few exceptions to the rules of confidentiality. When the review is complete, the action letter, with reviews attached, may be shared with the reviewers, although the identities of the reviewers will remain anonymous. Some journals reveal the name of the corresponding author as it appears on the action letter. Other journals redact this from the correspondence. If you are asked about sharing your name at this point, the decision is yours. Authors of rejected manuscripts may wish to remain anonymous, perhaps because of a negative review or because they want to remain anonymous for purposes of future review by a different journal. The publisher of the journal will have access to your manuscript file and may examine it should some question arise about the review process.

Typically, you are not to share the reviews except with your coauthors. That said, I have seen instances in which disgruntled authors have posted reviews on the Internet along with an attempt to refute them. This may be done as a principled attempt to open the review process. It also may be done to cast doubt on the credibility of the journal and its editors (the reviewers will still be anonymous). Although there is little professional recourse should this be done, the process has risks for the web poster as well as the journal. It may open the authors' work to scrutiny by others who may or may not share their perspective on the validity of the reviews. It also may make the editor (and other editors) leery of the authors. It may lead potential reviewers, regardless of how they might evaluate your work, to refuse to review your future manuscripts.

Reviewers are also not allowed to act on what they have read until they have your permission or your manuscript has become public (perhaps another reason to not post it before it has been reviewed and revised in ways that strengthen the contribution). I am aware of one instance in which authors who had submitted a paper that was accepted became aware of a failure to replicate their work before the work was published. The authors knew who the reviewer was and said the reviewer had breached confidentiality. However, it turned out the authors had presented the results at a conference. The authors then said the reviewer had not had time to conduct the replication study between the date of the public presentation of the original study and the appearance of the failure to replicate. Investigation revealed that the reviewer's institutional review board (IRB) protocol was submitted after the date of the work's first public presentation.

ACKNOWLEDGING REVIEWERS

You may find that reviewers' comments are so instructive that you wish to acknowledge their help when the article is published. You can ask the editor to ask the reviewers to reveal themselves to you for this purpose. However, acknowledging reviewers' contributions is unnecessary, and you likely will be discouraged from doing so. You occasionally see a "Thanks to anonymous reviewers for their helpful comments" in an Author Note (I did this in the Acknowledgments for this book), but reviewers understand they are "giving" you their suggestions anonymously. Many journals publish a list of ad hoc reviewers who helped with manuscripts in the final issue of a journal volume without listing the articles they reviewed.

The Decision Letter

Let us assume you have conducted a study meant to test whether anxiety affects people's performance of a public speech. You submit the manuscript to a journal of experimental psychology. The letter you receive from the action editor likely will contain one of five decisions:

- accept the manuscript as is;
- accept the manuscript with minor revisions;
- conditionally accept the manuscript with significant revisions needed;
- reject the manuscript but allow it to be resubmitted after significant revision; or
- reject the manuscript.

When you submit your manuscript for the first time, it is rare in psychology to have it accepted as is. Receiving such an acceptance is quite an achievement. The vast majority of manuscripts that eventually are accepted for publication receive decisions falling into the middle three categories.

Manuscript Revisions

If the manuscript is accepted with minor revision, your course of action will be clear. You can follow the suggestions of the editor and resubmit your manuscript. The minor revisions often involve simple clarification of things you wrote. For example, you might have forgotten to say precisely how long before the speech the measure of anxiety was taken. This disposition of your manuscript on first submission is also rare but not as rare as outright acceptance.

If significant revisions are requested, the action letter typically will detail what needs to be done for the manuscript to be reconsidered. The editor will describe suggestions for what needs to be revised. She or he will also highlight the comments of reviewers that are most important for you to consider or are required for resubmission to be successful. It is up to you to decide whether you think the required changes are needed and/or worth the effort.

Many editors favor the "reject but allow revision" decision rather than "accept with significant revision" because they do not know how the resubmitted manuscript will change. They do not want to be committed to accepting the manuscript until they have seen how it has been revised. Acceptance with significant revisions can lead to an awkward situation if the revisions are not satisfactory or reveal weaknesses in your design, analysis, and interpretation that were not obvious in the first submission. For example, if you are asked for more details and reveal your measure of anxiety was a state measure, not a trait measure, the measures may have been administered too far in advance of the speech. The editor might think this disqualifies your study from publication. If you studied trait anxiety, the editor may request that this be made clearer in the manuscript and perhaps even included in the title. Typically, if the editor is optimistic about your paper, he or she will encourage you to pursue publication in the journal but will not guarantee that your paper ultimately will be published.

Significant revisions can vary greatly, from requesting reanalysis or reinterpretation of your data to asking you to conduct additional studies or additional conditions within your study. For example, you may be asked to include a new control group to rule out alternative explanations for the effect of anxiety, perhaps varying the instructions subjects are given about the speech they are supposed to give.

COVER LETTER ACCOMPANYING THE REVISED MANUSCRIPT

Often, you will be asked to provide a detailed cover letter describing how you dealt with each of the requested changes. You should write this letter in a respectful and professional tone. Many authors provide a list of all the requested changes (even the simple ones, such as word changes) as bullet points in their cover letter and describe under each bullet what they did to address the comment. I have found that creating such a list also helps me organize my revisions; I write the cover letter explanations as I complete each revision in the manuscript, which helps me keep track of my progress.

You might find that reviewers suggest opposing revisions. For example, one review might say you should expand in your introduction a section on the definition of anxiety, whereas another says this should be removed and replaced by just a few references to articles that cover the topic. Point this out to the editor in your cover letter and describe why you chose to follow the directive you did. Of course, do not assume that because one reviewer made a suggestion and the others omitted the point entirely it means the point need not be addressed. It does. Reviewers focus on different things. They were chosen to do this.

You may think that following a suggestion would not strengthen the manuscript: for example, a lengthy discussion of the definition of anxiety would distract from the main purpose of your manuscript. In your letter, make your strongest case for why you did not follow a reviewer's advice. If you disagree with any recommended revisions, be sure not to respond emotionally. Just stick to the facts. Your manuscript might be sent back to the reviewer, and you do not want her or him to become personally defensive.

It is good strategy to recognize that a suggested change will occur to readers as well as the reviewer. For this reason, it might be good to put directly into the manuscript your rationale for not conducting your study or interpreting it in the manner proposed by the reviewer. This should be done without reference to the review itself. It may anticipate and forestall future (unwarranted) criticisms of your work. Editors will take this into account when they reconsider your manuscript, with no guarantee they will agree with you. Still, do not do things you disagree with just to get published. You, the author, not the editor or reviewers, will live with the consequences of your actions.

TIMELINES

Many editors will tell you whether the manuscript will have to undergo additional review upon resubmission and whether new or the same reviewers, or a combination of both, will be asked to reconsider it. It is a good sign if the editor writes that only she or he will examine your revision. At this point you will need to consider whether the revisions are feasible given their level of complexity and whether the time needed for revision fits into your other commitments. For example, do you have time to run another condition that includes the measure of anxiety at a different time? Perhaps you have moved on and are now studying how anxiety influences working memory as a mediator of anxiety's effect on performance.

Editors will ask you to let them know your intentions and when you anticipate being able to resubmit. It is good professional behavior to respond, even if you decide to submit the manuscript elsewhere. Editors may also give you a deadline for resubmission. If you need more time, you can correspond with the editor to find a resubmission date that you agree upon. In addition, it is not uncommon for a manuscript to undergo more than one round of revisions before it is accepted for publication.

Remember that, similar to conducting the study itself, manuscript revision is a team effort. You can divide the work between yourself and your coauthors, often along the same partitioning of responsibilities that guided data collection. Who wrote the introduction, and can the writer expand on the definition of anxiety? The corresponding author need not be responsible for all revisions. Once the revised manuscript is complete, all authors need to sign off again on its content and the order of authorship. Authorship orders rarely change during the revision process, but you should explicitly address this issue with your coauthors again to ensure no misunderstanding arises.

Disputes With Editors and Reviewers

If your manuscript is rejected outright, it probably is best to move on. As Wager, Godlee, and Jefferson (2002) wrote

> Resubmitting to the same journal is not usually worthwhile. However, if you feel that your paper has been completely misunderstood, or if you are able to answer major criticisms, for example by including additional data, it might be worthwhile appealing against a decision in a well-argued letter to the editor. In most cases, however, it is better to swallow your pride and submit somewhere else. Don't be too disheartened—with perseverance most work will be published somewhere! (p. 28)

You should consider the reason for rejection before you appeal the editor's decision. Rejections based on the manuscript being inappropriate for the journal or the research not meeting the standards of the journal with regard to the significance of the contribution are harder to counter than arguments made on how you substantively interpreted the findings, especially if you think reviewers misunderstood what you wrote.

DISAGREEMENTS BETWEEN REVIEWERS

You may discover that reviewers have disagreed about the disposition of your manuscript. Perhaps one reviewer appears to recommend acceptance with minor revisions, one recommends you be allowed to resubmit after major revisions, and one recommends outright rejection. Remember that the decision to publish your manuscript is not a counting game; the reviews are advisory to the action editor, who can weight them as she or he sees fit. Editors may seek additional reviews if they cannot decide what to do based on the first set of reviews they receive (this will slow the review process).

The editor will make a global assessment about your manuscript considering who the reviewers are, the type of articles published previously in the journal and that the journal wishes to publish in the future, and the editor's evaluation of the manuscript. I have seen papers that received predominantly negative reviews given an opportunity for revision and papers with predominantly positive reviews turned away. These latter decisions are especially difficult for editors. For this reason, editors ask reviewers to focus their comments on both the positive and negative aspects of the manuscript and not come to a global decision about its disposition in the comments that are shared with you. The reviewers are asked to save their recommendation for that particular question on the review form that is shared only with the editor. I have read reviewer comments that were quite positive but accompanied by recommendations to reject the manuscript. The reviewer was trying to be polite, but the positive comments leave the editor in an awkward position. Such reviewers are less likely to be asked to review again or to be consulting editors.

EDITOR AND REVIEWER CONFLICT OF INTEREST

You should share with the editor if you think a particular reviewer has revealed a conflict of interest. This might be based on your belief that the reviewer is trying to keep a competitor's work out of print. For example, your paper may cast doubt on a finding that has already appeared in print (such as that anxiety does not diminish short-term memory) or on the validity of a theory with which another researcher is closely associated. This is a serious allegation and should not be made lightly. Before you make this charge, you need to know with certainty the identity of the reviewer and have good evidence of reviewer misconduct.

I have also seen this allegation made against editors. Typically, if a journal has more than one editor, the editor-in-chief will take the possibility of a conflict of interest into consideration when she or he chooses the action editor.

The Appeal Process

Before you initiate an appeal of a rejection, ask a colleague to give you an honest assessment of the legitimacy of your concerns. In this case, it is permissible to share your manuscript and a verbal description of what was in the reviews with a trusted colleague, with the understanding that she or he will keep your exchange confidential. In addition, although the Committee on Publication Ethics does not weigh in on individual cases, it does maintain a database of publishing conundrums submitted by editors and others that are presented in generic terms (I return to this resource in the final chapter). You can use this resource to help you decide whether there is a case similar to yours and possible resolutions.

If you decide to appeal an editor's decision, you should first appeal to the action editor. If you are still unconvinced about a negative decision, you can appeal to the editor-in-chief if your manuscript was handled by an associate editor. What recourse you have after these appeals will depend on the journal. For independent journals or journals published under the auspices of a small professional groups, you may have no further recourse. Larger organizations may have an ombudsperson who considers appeals.

APA has a chief editorial advisor. Other publishers of journals or professional organizations (likely the larger ones) also may have a person who serves in this role. If so, this person will provide an independent and impartial opinion. She or he does not have jurisdiction to overturn a decision and will examine appeals based only on an alleged aberrant review process or conflict of interest, not on substantive grounds. I served in this role for APA for 6 years. My responsibility was to tell the authors I found their argument without merit or suggest to the editor that the manuscript deserved reconsideration. The final decision was still up to the editor. Authors who remained unsatisfied could take the complaint about the review process or conflict of interest to the APA Publications and Communications Board. This process is open to you if you think something was amiss in the review process, but remember that the manuscript cannot be submitted to a different journal while the decision is appealed.

Conclusion

The peer review process serves as a safeguard that improves the quality of the scientific record. It can also be long and complex, involving many actors coming to the process from different perspectives with different mandates on their actions. The process will confront you with many decisions that involve not only ethics (e.g., confidentiality) but also professional etiquette (e.g., how you write your correspondence with editors). If you can traverse this terrain successfully, you will be appropriately rewarded.

After the Manuscript Is Accepted and the Article Is Published

10

Let us assume the best: your manuscript has been reviewed, revised, and accepted for publication. But your work and ethical obligations are not done yet. There are still a few steps to the publication process and even some things that might happen after your article is published that might require you to make some ethics-related decisions.

Page Proofs

After you have submitted the final draft of your accepted paper, the next person in the publication chain you will hear from is the copyeditor. Journals vary with regard to whether the next version of your paper you see will be your copy edited manuscript or the *page* or *galley proof.* Either way, this is your last opportunity to make changes to the manuscript, and they will have to be minor. You cannot change anything

http://dx.doi.org/10.1037/14859-011
Ethical Choices in Research: Managing Data, Writing Reports, and Publishing Results in the Social Sciences, by H. Cooper
Copyright © 2016 by the American Psychological Association. All rights reserved.

of substance. From an ethical point of view, if you check your numbers one last time and find an error, the copyeditor will have to confirm these changes with the editor. That said, you should not wait until this point to make your final check.

The copyeditor will query you on matters of formatting and errors he or she finds in your submitted manuscript. A few of these have ethical and etiquette implications. For example, if you added mention of a study in the text late in the editorial process, you may have forgotten to add it to the reference section. The copyeditor will ask for the source publication information. Or the date of a citation in the text may not correspond to the date provided in the references. Errors in references, especially names and dates, can have implications for others who want to retrieve the document or gauge the impact of the referenced article on the field. For example, suppose your reference to "Cooper (2016)" appears in the references as "Cooper (2061)." Someone conducting a citation search on "Cooper (2016)" will not find that your paper refers to the source. In addition, if someone is doing a count of the number of times an author is cited (something that is done for tenure and promotion reviews at a research-intensive universities), misspelled names will lead to missed citations of authors. "Cooper" will not get credit for citations of "Copper (2016)."

The copyeditor, trained to find such inconsistencies, also points to mathematical copy errors or a sentence here and there that is unclear or uses poor grammar. These can be no small matter. As Day and Gastel (2011) said, "The damage can be real in that many errors can destroy comprehension. Something as minor as a misplaced decimal point can sometimes make a published paper almost useless" (p. 136). You should take seriously your own proofreading of your papers and not rely on the copyeditor to find errors.

You will be given only a few days to return the page proof along with your responses to any queries. Once the proof is returned, you will not be able to change your article again. The next time you see your article is when it is published.

ONLINE PUBLICATION

Some journals now publish articles online before they appear in print. For example, the American Psychological Association (APA) uses Online First Publication. Your article can appear online within 2 weeks of when you return your proofs. Once your article appears in Online First, it will also appear in the PsycARTICLES database. You will not be notified when online publication has occurred, but you can check PsycARTICLES for your paper's appearance and the correct way to reference it until it appears in print. Online appearance constitutes publication, and the article cannot be altered again before it appears in print. If you find a mistake in the Online First version, any change will have to appear as an erratum, or correction notice. I know of at least one instance in which a reader of an online publication informed the authors of a potential error in their data. It was too late to withdraw the manuscript before it appeared in "print." If your article is not published in an APA journal, you should check your journal's website to see if it has a similar mechanism for rapid online publication.

Public Access to the Manuscript

In addition to posting the final version of your manuscript on your website or that of your employer (see Chapter 8), once the article is published you may have obligations to your funders with regard to making the final manuscript publicly accessible. For example, the National Institutes of Health (2014) require that funded research be deposited in the National Library of Medicine's PubMed Central when it is accepted for publication and must be made publicly available no later than 1 year after the printed publication date. Other funders may also have requirements for public access. These will be spelled out in the agreement you (and your institution) signed when you accept funding support.

Errors Found After Publication: Erratum, Corrigendum, and Retractions

What should you do if you discover an error in your paper after it has been published? The APA's *Ethical Principles of Psychologists and Code of Conduct* (APA Ethics Code; APA, 2010a) states that "If psychologists discover significant errors in their published data, they take reasonable steps to correct such errors in a correction, retraction, erratum, or other appropriate publication means" (p. 11, Subsection 8.10(b)). The APA Ethics Code makes specific mention of errors in data, but other types of errors appear in journal articles. First among these are errors in data analysis. Typically, the term *erratum* is used to label corrections of errors that occurred during the production of the article caused by the publisher. For example, if a figure is mislabeled or if your table of means and standard deviations is misaligned so the column headings do not have the proper information listed under them, this might have been caused by a computer error in setting the journal type. The term *corrigendum*, or more simply *correction notice*, is used when the error is the fault of the authors. *Retraction notice* is used when an entire article needs to be treated as though it was never part of the scientific record.

Articles that are being retracted do not disappear from the electronic versions of journals, nor does someone remove the pages from printed journals (this would be quite a task!). Instead, the electronic journal version of the article is amended to contain a prominently displayed notice that the article is no longer viewed as scientifically sound. The article itself is not changed; the notice typically appears at the end of the electronic version of the article. For the printed version of articles, a similar notice will be published in a later issue of the journal. Obviously, the link between the printed version and retraction notice will be less immediate and proximal. This is also how errata and correction notices are handled.

There is one other type of notice that you may see appear with an article; it is called an *expression of concern*. Expressions of concern typically appear when a charge of misconduct has been made against the author(s) of an article. Following the guidelines of the Committee on Publication Ethics (2009), an expression of concern is published when journal editors and publishers

- have evidence that misconduct by the authors has occurred but the evidence is inconclusive;
- have evidence that the findings in the article are unreliable but the authors' institution will not investigate the case;
- believe that an investigation has not been, or would not be, fair, impartial or conclusive; or
- know an investigation is under way, but a judgment will not be available for some time.

Expressions of concern appear at the discretion of the editor and publisher, typically after considerable discussion. They are meant to be temporary notices and can cast a shadow over researchers' work when they have done nothing wrong. Once the issue of misconduct is resolved, the expression of concern will be accompanied by another notice that either exonerates the authors or retracts the article. Like other notices, an expression of concern is not itself removed from the scientific record.

DIFFERENCE BETWEEN CORRECTIONS AND RETRACTIONS

Correction notices are most likely to appear when an article has only a small flaw, and the flaw is an honest mistake (there is no such thing as a small intentional flaw). This might be an error as simple as the accidental misreporting of the degrees of freedom or the means and standard deviations associated with an analysis. For example, this might happen if you transposed the numbers as you copied them from the results of the data analysis. Or you might have accidentally reported standard errors but labeled them as standard deviations (a mistake I have seen occur more than once). Or it might be that you find an analysis of your anxiety and performance data was conducted improperly. Somehow, this eluded both you and the reviewers but was noticed by a reader who brought it to your attention.

If you find a small error in your article, you should contact the editor and ask that a correction be published; everything else in the article is as it should be. You would propose to the editor what the changes might be, such as how the text needs to be altered or a table substituted. You might also state how, if at all, the correction changes the conclusions of your study.

FREQUENCY AND TYPE OF RETRACTIONS AND ERROR NOTICES

In a study of articles in the Medline database, Wager and Williams (2011) found that between 2005 and 2009, approximately 2 in 1,000 medicine-related articles had been retracted for any reason. This was about a 10-fold increase since the early 1980s. About 1 in 10 retractions could be classified as being attributable to misconduct with data on the part of the researchers, but by far the largest portion of retractions was honest error. About 1 in 6 retractions was attributable to plagiarism and a similar portion to duplicate publication. About 1 in 10 retractions occurred because the authors of the original article were not able to replicate their own findings.

Grieneisen and Zhang (2012) also analyzed retraction notices included in 42 databases covering a variety of areas of scholarship. They found results similar to those of Wager and Williams (2011). They also discovered that a small number of repeat offenders who had committed data fraud (it is likely the fraud contains both falsification and fabrication, but the authors do not define the category precisely) accounted for a large portion of all retractions. In other words, they had committed fraud multiple times.

Fanelli (2013) found little change since the 1950s in the annual ratio of correction notices to all records in the Web of Science, but she did find an increase in the number of retraction notices and the number of journals that issued retraction notices The lower frequency of retraction in the Web of Science than in Medline probably is attributable to the smaller portion of empirical research in the former.

Furman, Jensen, and Murray (2012) found that in medicine the median time to retraction of an article was less than 24 months. It probably takes longer for retractions to appear in the social sciences, but this is my impression, not an empirically established fact. Trikalinos, Evangelou, and Ioannidis (2008) found that retraction takes longer for articles in medical journals if a more senior researcher was implicated in misconduct than if the author was a junior researcher. Finally, retraction notices led to a precipitous drop in the number of times an article was cited. That is good. They should never be cited again, except in the context of what not to do.

NOTIFYING THE JOURNAL

The *Publication Manual* (APA, 2010b) tells authors how to proceed if they discover an error. It states that it is the authors' responsibility to make the error public. First, they should inform the editor. According to Wager and Williams (2011) about two thirds (63%) of the retractions in Medline were instigated by one or all of the authors, and about three fourths of these were signed by all authors. About 1 in 5 retractions were attributed to the editor. In about 1 in 14 cases, it was unclear who had retracted the article.

When retractions are initiated and signed by parties other than authors or editors, it is more difficult to classify whom the responsible parties were or what the process might have been that led to retraction. Retraction notices are notoriously unclear about this. Sometimes the ambiguity occurs because the involved parties wish to protect the innocent, the institution, the publisher and journal, or any and all of these parties from legal entanglements.

CONTENT OF NOTICES

Retractions and correction notices are meant to correct erroneous information. They are intended to bring errors to the attention of future users of the scientific record. That said, other than a statement of retraction and a specific reference to the article being retracted, it is hard to find consistency in how retraction notices are worded and what information they contain. The Committee on Publication Ethics (2009) guidelines recommend that a notice of retraction should

- be linked to the retracted article wherever possible (i.e., in all electronic versions),
- clearly identify the retracted article (e.g., by including the title and authors in the retraction heading),
- be clearly identified as a retraction (i.e., distinct from other types of correction or comment),
- be published promptly to minimize harmful effects from misleading publications,

- be freely available to all readers (i.e., not behind access barriers or available only to subscribers),
- state who is retracting the article,
- state the reason(s) for retraction (to distinguish misconduct from honest error), and
- avoid statements that are potentially defamatory or libelous. (pp. 1–2)

The guidelines for constructing erratum and correction notices are the same.

Some other elements of retraction and correction notices have been suggested. These include a statement of who among the authors was and was not responsible for the errors that led to the notice. If there are multiple authors on a paper, it might be that the cause of the retraction was the responsibility of one, some, or all of the authors, and that only some authors were aware that misconduct or large errors occurred. If misconduct is involved, this information can protect the innocent.

It is also the case that authors can disagree about whether an error found in a paper requires that it be retracted or just corrected. This probably happens infrequently, but it can reveal deeper disagreements about how the research was conducted and interpreted. It may not be possible for the editor to resolve these issues, so the authors' institution(s) become involved. The notice in such a case might inform readers that a disagreement persists.

The retraction or correction notice might also include an indication of whether other research by the author(s) was also examined for errors or misconduct. Remember that surveys suggest a significant portion of all retractions is caused by the misbehavior of a few individuals. Being aware of a retraction will lead the scientific community to question the entire body of research conducted by a researcher found guilty of misconduct in a single case. In some instances, the group that investigates the misconduct may examine more research than just the study that brought the possible misconduct to their attention. Of course, when this occurs, all of the articles found to be erroneous should be retracted. But if the retraction notice says nothing about whether such a broad examination of the researcher's work occurred, other work may remain under a cloud of suspicion, rightly or wrongly. This may leave future researchers in a quandary about whether to believe or cite other work by an author who had a work retracted because of misconduct.

CONSEQUENCES

The consequences of correction notices will vary as a function of the magnitude of the error and the length of time until the error is corrected. For example, the error scenario described earlier, an honest miscalculation that does not influence the conclusions of a study, will have little effect on the researchers or on the scientific record if (a) the error is reported by the parties who made it and (b) it is found quickly. At the opposite extreme, instances of intentional misconduct can be devastating to the researcher's career, as they should be.

The length of time the error goes undetected will be the length of time the scientific record is distorted, sometimes longer. Greitemeyer (2014) conducted an experimental study in which some subjects (undergraduates) read scientific articles about the relationship between height and prosocial behavior. Some subjects were then told that the article had subsequently been retracted. Although subjects readjusted their belief toward that held before they read the article, their belief did not readjust fully. The subjects who had generated more explanations for the (erroneous) findings readjusted their beliefs least.

Errors in research that go undetected (or take a long time to be corrected) might also lead to mischaracterizations of the literature as a whole. For example, in Chapter 9, I note the effect of duplicate publication on the findings of meta-analyses. Erroneous results could have the same effect on statistical combinations of the literature.

Finally, there are economic costs associated with retracted articles. Stern, Casadevall, Steen, and Fang (2014) examined the cost of 291 retracted articles cataloged between 1992 and 2012 by the Office of Research Integrity. Most (95.9%) were retracted because of data falsification or fabrication. Stern et al. (2014) found that the median attributable cost in grant funds from all sources was nearly $240,000, with a total cost of approximately $58 million.

Sharing Data With Others

Digital storage has made retention of data easier. In addition, the issue of how long to keep data (discussed in Chapter 3) may become moot as the sciences move toward an ethic that promotes (and requires) the sharing of data after it has been published (National Institutes of Health, 2014). Currently, the *Publication Manual* (APA, 2010b) states that,

> Researchers must make their data available to the editor at any time during the review and publication process if questions arise with respect to the accuracy of the report. Refusal to do so can lead to rejection of the submitted manuscript without further consideration. In a similar vein, once an article is published, researchers must make their data available to permit other qualified professionals to confirm the analyses and results. (p. 12)

Similarly, the APA Ethics Code (American Psychological Association, 2010a) states that

(a) After research results are published, psychologists do not withhold the data on which their conclusions are based from other competent professionals who seek to verify the substantive claims through reanalysis and who intend to use such data only for that purpose, provided that the confidentiality of the participants can be protected and unless legal rights concerning proprietary data preclude their release. This does not preclude psychologists from requiring that such individuals or groups be responsible for costs associated with the provision of such information.

(b) Psychologists who request data from other psychologists to verify the substantive claims through reanalysis may use shared data only for the declared purpose. Requesting psychologists obtain prior written agreement for all other uses of the data. (p. 12, Substandard 8.14)

As I note in Chapter 3, before sharing data you are responsible for ensuring that the data are not proprietary and the data files contain no information that might allow the people you share it with to be able to identify participants. The *Publication Manual* (APA, 2010b) also states that it is important for you to have a written agreement about the conditions under which the data are to be shared. This agreement should state explicitly

- how the shared data may be used (e.g., to verify already published results, for secondary analysis);
- limits on the distribution of the shared data, for example, whether it may be used only by the requestors and individuals the requestor supervises or with no limitations;
- limits on the dissemination of the results of any reanalyses of the data;
- who will be the authors of any work that results from reanalysis; and
- "proper consideration of copyright restrictions, consent provided by subjects, requirements of funding agencies, and rules promulgated by the employer of the holder of the data." (p. 13)

This may seem like a lot of legal information to know and understand. It is. However, there are a growing number of data repositories in which you can store your data. Many of these have standard agreements covering issues of data sharing. For example, APA maintains a repository under the auspices of the Inter-university Consortium for Political and Social Research (n.d.-a). This repository accepts data sets directly from the data generators and provides excellent advice on how to manage data sharing and curating (Inter-university Consortium for Political and Social Research, n.d.-b).

The APA Ethics Code (American Psychological Association, 2010a) also indicates that you have the right to deny access to your data if you think the requestor does not possess the competence required to carry out the purposes for which she or he is requesting the data. For example, denying such a request might be legitimate if a high school student asks for your data to fulfill a science project requirement. Few such requests will be this clearly deniable based on the competence of the requestor. You must use your judgment, but remember that the requestor may disagree with you and could then ask your institution, funder, or publisher to adjudicate. It is also not unheard of for data to be requested for educational purposes, such as for use in college or graduate-level courses that teach statistics. In this case, the purpose is an admirable one, and you can word the written agreement so that the data are used for that purpose and that purpose only. It is also likely the case that such reanalyses of you data will verify the results you obtained.

RECENT DEVELOPMENTS IN DATA SHARING

Requirements for data sharing have begun to expand beyond the purpose of verification of results. In particular, a plan for sharing data is now required by many agencies that fund psychological research, including the National Institutes of Health (for grant proposals of $500,000 or more in any one year; National Institutes of Health, 2007), the National Science Foundation (2011), the Wellcome Trust (2012), and the European Union (Times Higher Education, 2012).

An APA Publications and Communications Board task force (Replications and Data Sharing Task Force, memo dated October 6, 2013) concluded that data sharing had many positive benefits for psychological science beyond simply verifying past analyses and conclusions. Data sharing promotes new hypothesis generation and testing, can help establish the generalizability of particular results, allows the data to be analyzed using new techniques, and encourages openness and accountability in scientific research. It also can help prevent data misconduct and make it easier to detect. Finally, as the interest in sharing data by funding agencies suggests, it is a cost-effective use of a scarce resource. The task force proposed that APA adopt five principles regarding the sharing of data. These are as follows:

- Sharing data promotes good science.
- APA journals require authors to share the data on which articles are based.
- An author must find and deposit data on a hosting site in a usable and interpretable form.
- The generator and the next user of the data both are responsible for individual subject privacy protection and confidentiality.
- The next user of data must acknowledge the original source of the data.

CONCERNS ABOUT SHARING DATA

You will likely have at least three concerns if you are asked to share your data or put it in a public archive. The first is that the next users of the data will not be as committed to protecting the rights and privacy of your subjects as you are. This concern can be lessened through your deidentification procedures before the data are archived or shared. In addition, more and more Institutional Review Boards (IRBs) are becoming sensitive to researchers using informed consent agreements that explicitly inform subjects that, after deidentification, the data may be shared with others. You should check whether your IRB has suggested language for how to communicate this to subjects. As noted, your agreement to share the data should make explicit the next user's commitment to keep the data confidential.

Your second concern will involve the time it takes to prepare data for sharing in a manner that it is usable by others. I discuss this in Chapter 3. The best strategy is to collect and document your data from the get-go as if it were to be used by others and you are not there to help them understand its characteristics. Having to backtrack on documentation after the study is complete can cost you much time with no guarantee of success. In addition, as the APA Ethics Code (American Psychological Association, 2010a) states, it is perfectly appropriate to ask requestors to assume the additional expense required for sharing.

Finally, you may worry that other researchers requesting your data will use it to publish analyses you had thought of but had not yet got around to conducting. There are two protections against this. First, when you publish a study, you are obligated to share only the data on which the article is based, although sharing more is certainly permitted, and sponsored data collections may require sharing after a certain period of time. For example, if you publish an article on how anxiety affects performance but also collected data on its effects on short-term memory, you are obligated to share only the data that went into the article on performance. If you are storing your data in a repository, it may also be possible for you to store the entire data set (for its integrity and your convenience) but embargo (restrict) access to, portions of the data file for a prespecified period of time.

Second, if you have worked it out in your data sharing agreement with the next users, you can be listed as an author of any papers they may produce. In this way, you will be able to be an author on papers using the data you collected but based on ideas contributed by the next users. In a sense, you are treating the next users as if you and they were members of the same laboratory. This fosters the collaborative spirit that serves science best. That said, data sharing does not always *entitle* the data generator to future authorships; being denied such authorship is not an excuse for not sharing data.

Being a Published Author

Now that your article has been published, if your research receives the attention of the general public and the community of scholars, some additional opportunities and obligations will come your way. Two of these will involve (a) interactions with the media and (b) being asked to be a peer reviewer of manuscripts submitted by others. Each of these entails some additional ethical considerations on your part as well as general behaviors that should be consistent with professional norms of behavior.

INTERACTING WITH THE MEDIA

In Chapter 8, I briefly discuss the media coverage of research. In particular, I point out that it can create problems to discuss research with the media before it has undergone peer review. Research that has not been formally vetted is open to revisions that might lead to significant changes, as well as the discovery of needed clarifications or mistakes. If your research has been widely disseminated before peer review and mistakes are found, it could be a source of public embarrassment to you, your institution, and your supporters. Premature media coverage can also undermine the credibility of science and research in your field. It can lead to wasted resources if others attempt to replicate what you have done, only to discover that the original findings were not as they were reported. Generally speaking, publicly communicating your results before they have undergone peer review is not a good idea.

However, once your research has been published, things change. In fact, many scientists believe that they have a responsibility to inform the public about their work. Think about the running examples I have used in this book. Two are related to the impact of psychological factors on health: interventions to improve eating habits and attitudes toward smoking. One relates to the determinants of depression. Two relate to well-being in the general population: parents' involvement in their children's afterschool activities and the effects of anxiety on performance.

> Shamoo and Resnik (2009) wrote: We believe that scientists have a social responsibility to report their findings to the media because these finding are often useful to the public. Scientists also have an obligation to educate and inform the public. Research findings can help prevent harm to individuals or to society and can promote general welfare. Reporting discoveries and results in the press can also enhance the public's understanding of science. (p. 132)

Add to this list of reasons the investment that funders have made to support your work, if you did it under a grant or contract. Media coverage is another step in ensuring your funder gets paid back for the investment.

Communicating effectively with the media is not always an easy task. First and foremost, your results may lead to complex conclusions that are not easy to translate into the brief messages that interest most media. For example, if you discover that your intervention to change eating habits works but only for people within a particular range of weights and only if they attend meetings regularly, you may be distressed when a newspaper article appears with the headline "Miracle cure found for obesity." It may also be that the concepts and operationalizations you use in your study are complex and need careful translation into more everyday language. For example, you may have used body mass index as the dependent variable in your study. Translating this to simply "weight" is inaccurate, and "overweight" has a specific criterion on the body mass index. It may be a struggle to describe your measures in ways that are understandable to an audience without research expertise.

Some people argue that knowledge is value neutral; how research findings are used by other people is not the responsibility of researchers. APA, on the other hand, endorses a more active role for researchers. Thus, while you cannot be held responsible for others who may distort your findings and use them in ways that contravene the ethical principles, you need not passively accept your work being used for malfeasance. If you see your work being used improperly, speak up. If you wish to promote its use to enhance human welfare and social justice, speak up but speak accurately.

Working With Media Specialists

Although you may not be able to control precisely what a media outlet reports about your work, you should follow the APA Ethics Code (American Psychological Association, 2010a) principle that states, "Psychologists do not knowingly make public statements that are false, deceptive or fraudulent concerning their research" (p. 8, Subsection 5.01). The best way to help ensure you do not violate this guideline is to work with a professional who has experience translating research for public dissemination. Take this step before you speak with the media.

Most universities have a communications office that not only will help you fashion a press release that is accurate and to your liking but also disseminate the release to media outlets they work with on a regular basis. Trying to circulate a press release on your own will be far less successful and far more time consuming. In fact, some university communications offices behave proactively. You may receive a general message from time to time asking, "Have you done anything interesting lately?"

The publisher of your work may also have staff devoted to this task. For instance, APA maintains a media relations office. If you publish in an APA journal, the media relations office may be able to assist you. A representative from the office may contact you about fashioning a press release when your article appears. The representative may have contacted the editors of journals to inquire about recently published articles that might be of interest to the general public. Or the journal editors may contact them. Your funder also may have an office that performs these media-related tasks.

The American Association for the Advancement of Science (2014) maintains a Center for Public Engagement with Science and Technology. The Center supports workshops and provides other resources meant to enhance the meaningful interaction of scientists and scientific institutions with the public. Your university also may conduct workshops in which you can learn the best strategies for interacting with the media and who on your campus can help you. If you have little experience working with the media, it is in your best interest to take advantage of these resources.

SERVING AS A REVIEWER

In Chapter 9, I discuss the role of a peer reviewer from the point of view of the person who has submitted the manuscript. Once you have published in a particular research area and if your work has garnered some attention, you may find that an editor requests that *you* serve as a peer reviewer for someone else's work. This is a sign that you are becoming visible in your field.

Doing reviews is good professional behavior because it reciprocates your colleagues for the time they spend reviewing your articles. If you do a good job, it may also lead to more requests and eventually to a request that you become a consulting editor for a journal that frequently asks you to provide reviews. The editor wants to count on your help, as well as acknowledge it on the journal's cover every issue of the journal rather than once a year in the final issue of the volume. (When the journal's editorship changes, the new editor will choose her or his own consulting editors and will renew the request for you to continue as a consulting editor if that is her or his wish.) If you are a junior professor, your report of activities should include details regarding what journals you reviewed for and how often. This service to the profession will be viewed by your colleagues as a sign of your growing recognition in the field.

I have discussed your obligations as a reviewer to keep all of your correspondence about a manuscript confidential, to communicate with authors solely through the editor, and to not act on anything you learned from the manuscript until it is published or otherwise made public or the author has given you permission. In addition, you do not act on the manuscript based on your biases, be they theoretical, methodological, empirical (you do not like the results), or personal. If you think this will be a problem, you should return the manuscript to the editor and explain briefly why you cannot do the review. If you think you can act without bias but others may perceive bias or a conflict of interest, explain this to the editor and discuss together how you might proceed.

There are two other questions you should ask yourself before making a decision to review a manuscript. The first is whether you have the requisite expertise to do a competent job. If you think you do not, turn down the request. In some cases, you may find you have expertise in some areas of the manuscript but not others. For example, you may be asked to review a meta-analysis of studies on the effects of anxiety on performance. You may know the substantive literature well but not the meta-analysis techniques or vice versa. In this case, you can contact the editor and explain the situation. You can also say in the review that your remarks are restricted in the main to one or another area of expertise.

The other question to ask is whether you can perform the review in a timely fashion. Decide whether you can complete the review in the time requested. Remember that delayed reviews can have negative consequences for the authors, especially if they are new to the profession.

Once you begin writing the review, you should keep several other prescriptions in mind. Wager, Godlee, and Jefferson (2002, pp. 37–40) provided a good list of principles for what should be contained in a peer review. These included the following:

- Begin with a brief paragraph that states the title of the paper, its methods, intention, and results. This will be much like a short abstract, but it should be in your own words.
- Find both positive and negative things to say about the manuscript. All scientific research has strengths and limitations. Explicitly stating both will enhance your credibility with the authors and editor and increase the likelihood that your suggestions will be carefully considered.
- Refrain from personal criticisms. There is nothing to be gained by being nasty. It might even hurt your credibility with both the author and the editor. It will diminish the chances you will be asked to review again.
- If you think something in the manuscript is wrong, say how so and suggest how it can be fixed, if at all. For example, a vague mention that, "The measure of anxiety was taken at a nonoptimal interval before performance" is not helpful. It should be accompanied by a description of why this is the case and what would have been more appropriate timing.

- Stick to the facts. Do not make guesses about what you thought were the motives or intentions of the authors. A statement such as, "The authors might have erroneously been thinking . . ." can always be rephrased to something like, "This procedure leaves open the alternative explanation that . . ."
- Be sure you can substantiate the claims you make in a review.
- Set reasonable goals and expectations for what can be done to improve the manuscript. If you truly believe the manuscript is not salvageable, say so in the comments to the editor only.
- Remember that you are the reviewer not the author. There is a difference between what you would *like* to see in the manuscript and what you think must be done for the manuscript to keep moving through the review process.

As a peer reviewer you are not expected to serve as the copyeditor. Pointing out typos and minor grammatical errors is not needed, although many reviewers include a section of "minor points," in which they list such issues. Your job is to evaluate the science of the research, it soundness, its ability to make the inferences the authors claim, and the significance of the contribution.

Barnett and Campbell (2012; pp. 326–331) also presented a nice summary of the role of reviewer. They proposed (following from Gelso's work as editor of the journal *Psychotherapy: Theory, Research, Practice, Training* in 2009) that five guidelines be followed for reviews: educational value, clarity, objectivity, thoroughness, and tact.

Robert Sternberg (2002) expounded on the negative effects of tactless reviews. As mentioned, a lack of tact on the part of the reviewer will diminish the credibility of the review and reduce its ability to affect change in the manuscript. It will create animosities. Further, if the author is junior in the field, it may discourage her or him from pursuing research (even though the problem may reside more in the reviewer's lack of tact and empathy than with the author's shortcomings). Barnett and Campbell (2012) emphasized the importance of mentoring in the peer review process, by both the editor for the reviewer and the reviewer for the author. Finally, guidelines for being a reviewer are provided by the APA (2015d). These guidelines, first developed for the *Journal of Counseling Psychology*, are applicable for any scientific journal.

In sum, in addition to understanding that you are acting as a gatekeeper to the scientific record, the most ethical position to take when you are a peer reviewer is to follow the oldest ethical principle of them all: "Do unto others as you would have others do unto you."

Epilogue

T hroughout this book, I refer frequently to specific sections of the American Psychological Association's (APA) *Ethical Principles of Psychologists and Code of Conduct* (APA, 2010a; APA Ethics Code). Perhaps it is fitting that the last topic brings us to the general principles that begin these guidelines. The five principles are

- beneficence and nonmaleficence: Do no harm. Safeguard the welfare and rights of those you interact with professionally and other affected persons. Do not misuse your influence.
- fidelity and responsibility: Establish trusting relationships with coworkers. Remain aware of your professional and scientific responsibilities.
- integrity: Promote accuracy, honesty, and truthfulness in the science, teaching, and practice of psychology.
- justice: Recognize that all persons are entitled to fair and just access to and benefit from the contributions of psychology.

http://dx.doi.org/10.1037/14859-012
Ethical Choices in Research: Managing Data, Writing Reports, and Publishing Results in the Social Sciences, by H. Cooper
Copyright © 2016 by the American Psychological Association. All rights reserved.

■ respect for people's rights and dignity: Respect the dignity and worth of all people and their rights to privacy, confidentiality, and self-determination.

These principles say that you have responsibilities not just for conducting your research in an ethical manner but also after it is complete. You are expected to take actions that help ensure your research is used in a manner that promotes human welfare, justice, and the respect for people's rights and dignity.

Further Assistance With Ethical Concerns

One service that the Committee on Publication Ethics (n.d.-b) provides is a searchable database of summaries of the ethical cases it has discussed at its forums. Its membership comprises primarily editors of journals across the scientific disciplines, and the summaries are written from an editor's perspective, although the database is available to all. You may find its contents instructive as an author and peer reviewer as well as an editor, should you become one.

The case summaries in the database do not allow identification of the specific instances that brought the issue to attention. Rather, the summaries give a broad outline of the ethical issues involved in the case, the advice that was given to the person who brought the case forward, and the follow-up or resolution of the case. The database has about 500 cases. In Exhibit 1, I reproduce a case example. This case involves an instance of duplicate publication. After the articles in question were compared, it was noticed that the authors on the two publications were different.

Another product of the ethical cases is a taxonomy of the issues brought to the forum's attention (Committee on Publication Ethics, n.d.-c). This taxonomy provides a nice catalog of the ethical topics I discuss in this book. For that purpose, I reproduce the complete taxonomy in Appendix D. Applying the taxonomy to the case example in Exhibit 1, the Committee on Publication Ethics classified the case as an example of two different types of misbehavior: "authorship/questionable authorship practice" and "redundant/duplicate publication and multiple submissions." You can find this and similar cases in the database using either of these taxonomy categories as search terms. In addition, you can find this case by searching the term "whistleblower" because this case was brought to the editors' attention by a third party.

The Office of Research Integrity (n.d.-b) also maintains a database available to the public that contains cases "in which administrative actions were imposed due to findings of research misconduct." All of these cases involve research and research training that was supported

EXHIBIT 1

An Example Case From the Committee on Publication Ethics Database

Case number:
98-21
Case text (Anonymized)

Two articles were published in two different journals. The articles had been submitted within days of each other, and were subsequently peer reviewed, revised, and published within a month of each other. The authors failed to reference the closely related article as submitted or in press, and the editors of the two journals were unaware of the other article.

After publication the editors viewed this as duplicate publication because of the considerable overlap of material and failure of the authors to disclose the existence of the other paper. Both editors issued a notice in their journals of duplicate publication. It was also noticed that two of the authors were only mentioned on one paper and another author indicated that he had been unaware of the submission of the article at all.

The editors have been asked by a third party to formally withdraw both articles on the grounds of fraudulent behavior by the authors.

Advice:
The editors should write to the third party who has made the allegations of fraud and ask for the evidence.

If this is forthcoming, the editors should write to the head of the institution involved.

If a subsequent investigation proves the fraud, then the editors should take appropriate action.

Follow up:
The editors of the two journals felt very strongly that they should not be involved in investigating allegations of fraud, and that this should be the responsibility of the institutions involved, with the third party actioning this. They therefore decided to take no further action.

Note. From *Case 98-21*. Copyright by the Committee on Publication Ethics. Retrieved from http://publicationethics. org/cases. Reproduced with permission.

by the Public Health Service. The Office of Research Integrity does not conduct investigations, but it does provide technical assistance to institutions that do. This database includes only cases involving individuals who have had administrative actions imposed against them. Individuals whose actions have expired are not included. These cases do identify the individuals involved. Closed investigations and ones that found no evidence of wrongdoing are also included in the database. By visiting the Office of Research Integrity website, you can find numerous resources (under "RCR resources") relating to the various topics I cover in this book.

A Final Note

We have come a long way from my initial discussion of your assessment of whether you are competent and motivated enough to undertake a project. We have traversed intellectual property, data collection and management, statistical issues, authorship issues, reporting requirements, how to navigate the review process, how to handle errors, and finally, how to behave professionally once your article is published.

I hope the number of issues I have discussed has not left you with the impression that the obstacles to conducting and publishing scientific research are insurmountable. They are not. Thousands of articles are published every year that have met the challenge. The rewards are great for doing research both well and ethically. The rewards are personal and professional, and the challenges make the effort that much more rewarding.

If there is a theme running through this book, it is that openness and transparency along with a desire to receive and act on critical feedback are the hallmarks of good scientific research and reporting. Remember that no research is perfect, nor is it expected to be.

You can do it.

Appendix A

Selected APA Principles and Codes of Conduct

Standard 2: Competence
2.01 Boundaries of Competence

(a) Psychologists provide services, teach and conduct research with populations and in areas only within the boundaries of their competence, based on their education, training, supervised experience, consultation, study or professional experience.

(b) Where scientific or professional knowledge in the discipline of psychology establishes that an understanding of factors associated with age, gender, gender identity, race, ethnicity, culture, national origin, religion, sexual orientation, disability, language or socioeconomic status is essential for effective implementation of their services or research, psychologists have or obtain the training, experience, consultation or supervision necessary to ensure the competence of their services, or they make appropriate referrals, except as provided in Standard 2.02, Providing Services in Emergencies.

Reprinted from *Ethical Principles of Psychologists and Code of Conduct (2002, Amended June 1, 2010)*, by the American Psychological Association, Washington, DC. Copyright 2010 by the American Psychological Association.

(c) Psychologists planning to provide services, teach or conduct research involving populations, areas, techniques or technologies new to them undertake relevant education, training, supervised experience, consultation or study.

(d) In those emerging areas in which generally recognized standards for preparatory training do not yet exist, psychologists nevertheless take reasonable steps to ensure the competence of their work and to protect clients/patients, students, supervisees, research participants, organizational clients and others from harm.

2.03 Maintaining Competence

Psychologists undertake ongoing efforts to develop and maintain their competence.

2.04 Bases for Scientific and Professional Judgments

Psychologists' work is based upon established scientific and professional knowledge of the discipline.

2.05 Delegation of Work to Others

Psychologists who delegate work to employees, supervisees or research or teaching assistants or who use the services of others, such as interpreters, take reasonable steps to (1) avoid delegating such work to persons who have a multiple relationship with those being served that would likely lead to exploitation or loss of objectivity; (2) authorize only those responsibilities that such persons can be expected to perform competently on the basis of their education, training or experience, either independently or with the level of supervision being provided; and (3) see that such persons perform these services competently.

2.06 Personal Problems and Conflicts

(a) Psychologists refrain from initiating an activity when they know or should know that there is a substantial likelihood that their personal problems will prevent them from performing their work-related activities in a competent manner.

(b) When psychologists become aware of personal problems that may interfere with their performing work-related duties adequately, they take appropriate measures, such as obtaining professional consultation or assistance and determine whether they should limit, suspend or terminate their work-related duties.

Standard 3: Human Relations
3.06 Conflict of Interest

Psychologists refrain from taking on a professional role when personal, scientific, professional, legal, financial or other interests or relationships could reasonably be expected to (1) impair their objectivity, competence or effectiveness in performing their functions as psychologists or (2) expose the person or organization with whom the professional relationship exists to harm or exploitation.

Standard 4: Privacy and Confidentiality
4.01 Maintaining Confidentiality

Psychologists have a primary obligation and take reasonable precautions to protect confidential information obtained through or stored in any medium, recognizing that the extent and limits of confidentiality may be regulated by law or established by institutional rules or professional or scientific relationship. (See also Standard 2.05, Delegation of Work to Others.)

4.02 Discussing the Limits of Confidentiality

(a) Psychologists discuss with persons (including, to the extent feasible, persons who are legally incapable of giving informed consent and their legal representatives) and organizations with whom they establish a scientific or professional relationship (1) the relevant limits of confidentiality and (2) the foreseeable uses of the information generated through their psychological activities. (See also Standard 3.10, Informed Consent.)

(b) Unless it is not feasible or is contraindicated, the discussion of confidentiality occurs at the outset of the relationship and thereafter as new circumstances may warrant.

(c) Psychologists who offer services, products, or information via electronic transmission inform clients/patients of the risks to privacy and limits of confidentiality.

4.03 Recording

Before recording the voices or images of individuals to whom they provide services, psychologists obtain permission from all such persons or their legal representatives. (See also Standards 8.03, Informed Consent for Recording Voices and Images in Research; 8.05, Dispensing with Informed Consent for Research; and 8.07, Deception in Research.)

4.04 Minimizing Intrusions on Privacy

(a) Psychologists include in written and oral reports and consultations, only information germane to the purpose for which the communication is made.

(b) Psychologists discuss confidential information obtained in their work only for appropriate scientific or professional purposes and only with persons clearly concerned with such matters.

4.05 Disclosures

(a) Psychologists may disclose confidential information with the appropriate consent of the organizational client, the individual client/

patient or another legally authorized person on behalf of the client/ patient unless prohibited by law.

(b) Psychologists disclose confidential information without the consent of the individual only as mandated by law, or where permitted by law for a valid purpose such as to (1) provide needed professional services; (2) obtain appropriate professional consultations; (3) protect the client/patient, psychologist, or others from harm; or (4) obtain payment for services from a client/patient, in which instance disclosure is limited to the minimum that is necessary to achieve the purpose. (See also Standard 6.04e, Fees and Financial Arrangements.)

4.06 Consultations

When consulting with colleagues, (1) psychologists do not disclose confidential information that reasonably could lead to the identification of a client/patient, research participant or other person or organization with whom they have a confidential relationship unless they have obtained the prior consent of the person or organization or the disclosure cannot be avoided, and (2) they disclose information only to the extent necessary to achieve the purposes of the consultation. (See also Standard 4.01, Maintaining Confidentiality.)

4.07 Use of Confidential Information for Didactic or Other Purposes

Psychologists do not disclose in their writings, lectures or other public media, confidential, personally identifiable information concerning their clients/patients, students, research participants, organizational clients or other recipients of their services that they obtained during the course of their work, unless (1) they take reasonable steps to disguise the person or organization, (2) the person or organization has consented in writing, or (3) there is legal authorization for doing so.

Standard 8: Research and Publication
8.06 Offering Inducements for Research Participation

(a) Psychologists make reasonable efforts to avoid offering excessive or inappropriate financial or other inducements for research participation when such inducements are likely to coerce participation.

(b) When offering professional services as an inducement for research participation, psychologists clarify the nature of the services, as well as the risks, obligations and limitations.

8.08 Debriefing

(a) Psychologists provide a prompt opportunity for participants to obtain appropriate information about the nature, results, and conclusions of the research, and they take reasonable steps to correct any misconceptions that participants may have of which the psychologists are aware.

(b) If scientific or humane values justify delaying or withholding this information, psychologists take reasonable measures to reduce the risk of harm.

(c) When psychologists become aware that research procedures have harmed a participant, they take reasonable steps to minimize the harm.

8.10 Reporting Research Results

(a) Psychologists do not fabricate data.

(b) If psychologists discover significant errors in their published data, they take reasonable steps to correct such errors in a correction, retraction, erratum or other appropriate publication means.

8.11 Plagiarism

Psychologists do not present portions of another's work or data as their own, even if the other work or data source is cited occasionally.

8.12 Publication Credit

(a) Psychologists take responsibility and credit, including authorship credit, only for work they have actually performed or to which they have substantially contributed.

(b) Principal authorship and other publication credits accurately reflect the relative scientific or professional contributions of the individuals involved, regardless of their relative status. Mere possession of an institutional position, such as department chair, does not justify authorship credit. Minor contributions to the research or to the writing for publications are acknowledged appropriately, such as in footnotes or in an introductory statement.

(c) Except under exceptional circumstances, a student is listed as principal author on any multiple-authored article that is substantially based on the student's doctoral dissertation. Faculty advisors discuss publication credit with students as early as feasible and throughout the research and publication process as appropriate.

8.13 Duplicate Publication of Data

Psychologists do not publish, as original data, data that have been previously published. This does not preclude republishing data when they are accompanied by proper acknowledgment.

8.14 Sharing Research Data for Verification

(a) After research results are published, psychologists do not withhold the data on which their conclusions are based from other competent professionals who seek to verify the substantive claims through reanalysis and who intend to use such data only for that purpose, provided that the confidentiality of the participants can be protected and unless legal rights concerning proprietary data preclude their release. This does not preclude psychologists from requiring that such individuals or groups be responsible for costs associated with the provision of such information.

(b) Psychologists who request data from other psychologists to verify the substantive claims through reanalysis may use shared data only for the declared purpose. Requesting psychologists obtain prior written agreement for all other uses of the data.

8.15 Reviewers

Psychologists who review material submitted for presentation, publication, grant or research proposal review respect the confidentiality of and the proprietary rights in such information of those who submitted it.

Appendix B

Ethical Guidelines for Statistical Practice

Prepared by the Committee on Professional Ethics
Approved by the American Statistical Association
Board of Directors, August 7, 1999

Executive Summary

This document contains two parts: I. Preamble and II. Ethical Guidelines. The Preamble addresses **A. Purpose of the Guidelines, B. Statistics and Society,** and **C. Shared Values**. The purpose of the document is to encourage ethical and effective statistical work in morally conducive working environments. It is also intended to assist students in learning to perform statistical work responsibly. Statistics plays a vital role in many aspects of science, the economy, governance, and even entertainment. It is important that all statistical practitioners recognize their potential impact on the broader society and the attendant ethical obligations to perform their work responsibly. Furthermore, practitioners are encouraged to exercise "good professional citizenship" in order to improve the public climate for, understanding of, and respect for the use of statistics throughout its range of applications.

Note. From *Ethical Guidelines for Statistical Practice,* by the American Statistical Association. Copyright 1999 by the American Statistical Association. Retrieved from http://www.amstat.org/about/ethicalguidelines.cfm. Reprinted with permission of the author.

The **Ethical Guidelines** address eight general topic areas and specify important ethical considerations under each topic.

A. **Professionalism** points out the need for competence, judgment, diligence, self-respect, and worthiness of the respect of other people.

B. **Responsibilities** to Funders, Clients, and Employers discusses the practitioner's responsibility for assuring that statistical work is suitable to the needs and resources of those who are paying for it, that funders understand the capabilities and limitations of statistics in addressing their problem, and that the funder's confidential information is protected.

C. **Responsibilities in Publications and Testimony** addresses the need to report sufficient information to give readers, including other practitioners, a clear understanding of the intent of the work, how and by whom it was performed, and any limitations on its validity.

D. **Responsibilities to Research Subjects** describes requirements for protecting the interests of human and animal subjects of research—not only during data collection but also in the analysis, interpretation, and publication of the resulting findings.

E. **Responsibilities to Research Team Colleagues** addresses the mutual responsibilities of professionals participating in multidisciplinary research teams.

F. **Responsibilities to Other Statisticians or Statistical Practitioners** notes the interdependence of professionals doing similar work, whether in the same or different organizations. Basically, they must contribute to the strength of their professions overall by sharing nonproprietary data and methods, participating in peer review, and respecting differing professional opinions.

G. **Responsibilities Regarding Allegations of Misconduct** addresses the sometimes painful process of investigating potential ethical violations and treating those involved with both justice and respect.

H. **Responsibilities of Employers**, Including Organizations, Individuals, Attorneys, or Other Clients Employing Statistical Practitioners encourages employers and clients to recognize the highly interdependent nature of statistical ethics and statistical validity. Employers and clients must not pressure practitioners to produce a particular "result," regardless of its statistical validity. They must avoid the potential social harm that can result from the dissemination of false or misleading statistical work.

I. Preamble

A. PURPOSE OF THE GUIDELINES

The American Statistical Association's Ethical Guidelines for Statistical Practice are intended to help statistics practitioners make and communicate ethical decisions. Clients, employers, researchers, policymakers, journalists, and the public should be urged to expect statistical practice to be conducted in accordance with these guidelines and to object when it is not. While learning how to apply statistical theory to problems, students should be encouraged to use these guidelines, regardless of whether their target professional specialty will be "statistician." Employers, attorneys, and other clients of statistics practitioners have a responsibility to provide a moral environment that fosters the use of these ethical guidelines.

Application of these or any other ethical guidelines generally requires good judgment and common sense. The guidelines may be partially conflicting in specific cases. The application of these guidelines in any given case can depend on issues of law and shared values; work-group politics; the status and power of the individuals involved; and the extent to which the ethical lapses pose a threat to the public, to one's profession, or to one's organization. The individuals and institutions responsible for making such ethical decisions can receive valuable assistance by discussion and consultation with others, particularly persons with divergent interests with respect to the ethical issues under consideration.

B. STATISTICS AND SOCIETY

The professional performance of statistical analyses is essential to many aspects of society. The use of statistics in medical diagnoses and biomedical research may affect whether individuals live or die, whether their health is protected or jeopardized, and whether medical science advances or gets sidetracked. Life, death, and health, as well as efficiency, may be at stake in statistical analyses of occupational, environmental, or transportation safety. Early detection and control of new or recurrent infectious diseases depend on sound epidemiological statistics. Mental and social health may be at stake in psychological and sociological applications of statistical analysis.

Effective functioning of the economy depends on the availability of reliable, timely, and properly interpreted economic data. The profitability of individual firms depends in part on their quality control and market research, both of which should rely on statistical methods. Agricultural productivity benefits greatly from statistically sound applications to research and output reporting. Governmental policy decisions regarding public health, criminal justice, social equity, education, the environment, the citing of critical facilities, and other matters depend in part on sound statistics.

Scientific and engineering research in all disciplines requires the careful design and analysis of experiments and observations. To the extent that uncertainty and measurement error are involved—as they are in most research—research design, data quality management, analysis, and interpretation are all crucially dependent on statistical concepts and methods. Even in theory, much of science and engineering involves natural variability. Variability, whether great or small, must be carefully examined for both random error and possible researcher bias or wishful thinking.

Statistical tools and methods, as with many other technologies, can be employed either for social good or evil. The professionalism encouraged by these guidelines is predicated on their use in socially responsible pursuits by morally responsible societies, governments, and employers. Where the end purpose of a statistical application is itself morally reprehensible, statistical professionalism ceases to have ethical worth.

C. SHARED VALUES

Because society depends on sound statistical practice, all practitioners of statistics, whatever their training and occupation, have social obligations to perform their work in a professional, competent, and ethical manner. This document is directed to those whose primary occupation is statistics. Still, the principles expressed here should also guide the statistical work of professionals in all other disciplines that use statistical methods. All statistical practitioners are obliged to conduct their professional activities with responsible attention to the following:

1. The social value of their work and the consequences of how well or poorly it is performed. This includes respect for the life, liberty, dignity, and property of other people.
2. The avoidance of any tendency to slant statistical work toward predetermined outcomes. (It is acceptable to advocate a position; it is not acceptable to misapply statistical methods in doing so.)
3. Statistics as a science. (As in any science, understanding evolves. Statisticians have a body of established knowledge, but also many unresolved issues that deserve frank discussion.)
4. The maintenance and upgrading of competence in their work.
5. Adherence to all applicable laws and regulations, as well as applicable international covenants, while also seeking to change any of those that are ethically inappropriate.

6. Preservation of data archives in a manner consistent with responsible protection of the safety and confidentiality of any human being or organization involved.

In addition to ethical obligations, good professional citizenship encourages the following:

7. Collegiality and civility with fellow professionals.
8. Support for improved public understanding of and respect for statistics.
9. Support for sound statistical practice, especially when it is unfairly criticized.
10. Exposure of dishonest or incompetent uses of statistics.
11. Service to one's profession as a statistical editor, reviewer, or association official and service as an active participant in (formal or informal) ethical review panels.

II. *Ethical Guidelines*

A. PROFESSIONALISM

1. Strive for relevance in statistical analyses. Typically, each study should be based on a competent understanding of the subject-matter issues, statistical protocols that are clearly defined for the stage (exploratory, intermediate, or final) of analysis before looking at those data that will be decisive for that stage, and technical criteria to justify both the practical relevance of the study and the amount of data to be used.
2. Guard against the possibility that a predisposition by investigators or data providers might predetermine the analytic result. Employ data selection or sampling methods and analytic approaches that are designed to ensure valid analyses in either frequentist or Bayesian approaches.
3. Remain current in dynamically evolving statistical methodology; yesterday's preferred methods may be barely acceptable today and totally obsolete tomorrow.
4. Ensure that adequate statistical and subject-matter expertise are both applied to any planned study. If this criterion is not met initially, it is important to add the missing expertise before completing the study design.
5. Use only statistical methodologies suitable to the data and to obtaining valid results. For example, address the multiple

potentially confounding factors in observational studies and use due caution in drawing causal inferences.

6. Do not join a research project unless you can expect to achieve valid results and you are confident that your name will not be associated with the project or resulting publications without your explicit consent.

7. The fact that a procedure is automated does not ensure its correctness or appropriateness; it is also necessary to understand the theory, data, and methods used in each statistical study. This goal is served best when a competent statistical practitioner is included early in the research design, preferably in the planning stage.

8. Recognize that any frequentist statistical test has a random chance of indicating significance when it is not really present. Running multiple tests on the same data set at the same stage of an analysis increases the chance of obtaining at least one invalid result. Selecting the one "significant" result from a multiplicity of parallel tests poses a grave risk of an incorrect conclusion. Failure to disclose the full extent of tests and their results in such a case would be highly misleading.

9. Respect and acknowledge the contributions and intellectual property of others.

10. Disclose conflicts of interest, financial and otherwise, and resolve them. This may sometimes require divestiture of the conflicting personal interest or withdrawal from the professional activity. Examples where conflict of interest may be problematic include grant reviews, other peer reviews, and tensions between scholarship and personal or family financial interests.

11. Provide only such expert testimony as you would be willing to have peer reviewed.

B. RESPONSIBILITIES TO FUNDERS, CLIENTS, AND EMPLOYERS

1. Where appropriate, present a client or employer with choices among valid alternative statistical approaches that may vary in scope, cost, or precision.

2. Clearly state your statistical qualifications and experience relevant to your work.

3. Clarify the respective roles of different participants in studies to be undertaken.

4. Explain any expected adverse consequences of failure to follow through on an agreed-upon sampling or analytic plan.

5. Apply statistical sampling and analysis procedures scientifically, without predetermining the outcome.

6. Make new statistical knowledge widely available to provide benefits to society at large and beyond your own scope of applications. Statistical methods may be broadly applicable to many classes of problem or application. (Statistical innovators may well be entitled to monetary or other rewards for their writings, software, or research results.)
7. Guard privileged information of the employer, client, or funder.
8. Fulfill all commitments.
9. Accept full responsibility for your professional performance.

C. RESPONSIBILITIES IN PUBLICATIONS AND TESTIMONY

1. Maintain personal responsibility for all work bearing your name; avoid undertaking work or coauthoring publications for which you would not want to acknowledge responsibility. Conversely, accept (or insist upon) appropriate authorship or acknowledgment for professional statistical contributions to research and the resulting publications or testimony.
2. Report statistical and substantive assumptions made in the study.
3. In publications or testimony, identify who is responsible for the statistical work if it would not otherwise be apparent.
4. Make clear the basis for authorship order, if determined on grounds other than intellectual contribution. Preferably, authorship order in statistical publications should be by degree of intellectual contribution to the study and material to be published, to the extent that such ordering can feasibly be determined. When some other rule of authorship order is used in a statistical publication, the rule should be disclosed in a footnote or endnote. (Where authorship order by contribution is assumed by those making decisions about hiring, promotion, or tenure, for example, failure to disclose an alternative rule may improperly damage or advance careers.)
5. Account for all data considered in a study and explain the sample(s) actually used.
6. Report the sources and assessed adequacy of the data.
7. Report the data cleaning and screening procedures used, including any imputation.
8. Clearly and fully report the steps taken to guard validity. Address the suitability of the analytic methods and their inherent assumptions relative to the circumstances of the specific study. Identify the computer routines used to implement the analytic methods.
9. Where appropriate, address potential confounding variables not included in the study.

10. In publications or testimony, identify the ultimate financial sponsor of the study, the stated purpose, and the intended use of the study results.

11. When reporting analyses of volunteer data or other data not representative of a defined population, include appropriate disclaimers.

12. Report the limits of statistical inference of the study and possible sources of error. For example, disclose any significant failure to follow through fully on an agreed sampling or analytic plan and explain any resulting adverse consequences.

13. Share data used in published studies to aid peer review and replication, but exercise due caution to protect proprietary and confidential data, including all data that might inappropriately reveal respondent identities.

14. As appropriate, promptly and publicly correct any errors discovered after publication.

15. Write with consideration of the intended audience. (For the general public, convey the scope, relevance, and conclusions of a study without technical distractions. For the professional literature, strive to answer the questions likely to occur to your peers.)

D. RESPONSIBILITIES TO RESEARCH SUBJECTS (INCLUDING CENSUS OR SURVEY RESPONDENTS AND PERSONS AND ORGANIZATIONS SUPPLYING DATA FROM ADMINISTRATIVE RECORDS, AS WELL AS SUBJECTS OF PHYSICALLY OR PSYCHOLOGICALLY INVASIVE RESEARCH)

1. Know about and adhere to appropriate rules for the protection of human subjects, including particularly vulnerable or other special populations that may be subject to special risks or may not be fully able to protect their own interests. Ensure adequate planning to support the practical value of the research, validity of expected results, ability to provide the protection promised, and consideration of all other ethical issues involved.

2. Avoid the use of excessive or inadequate numbers of research subjects by making informed recommendations for study size. These recommendations may be based on prospective power analysis, the planned precision of the study endpoint(s), or other methods to ensure appropriate scope to either frequentist or Bayesian approaches. Study scope also should take into consideration the feasibility of obtaining research subjects and the value of the data elements to be collected.

3. Avoid excessive risk to research subjects and excessive imposition on their time and privacy.

4. Protect the privacy and confidentiality of research subjects and data concerning them, whether obtained directly from the subjects, other persons, or administrative records. Anticipate secondary and indirect uses of the data when obtaining approvals from research subjects; obtain approvals appropriate for peer review and independent replication of analyses.

5. Be aware of legal limitations on privacy and confidentiality assurances. Do not, for example, imply protection of privacy and confidentiality from legal processes of discovery unless explicitly authorized to do so.

6. Before participating in a study involving human beings or organizations, analyzing data from such a study, or accepting resulting manuscripts for review, consider whether appropriate research subject approvals were obtained. (This safeguard will lower your risk of learning only after the fact that you have collaborated on an unethical study.) Consider also what assurances of privacy and confidentiality were given and abide by those assurances.

7. Avoid or minimize the use of deception. Where it is necessary and provides significant knowledge—as in some psychological, sociological, and other research—ensure prior independent ethical review of the protocol and continued monitoring of the research.

8. Where full disclosure of study parameters to subjects or other investigators is not advisable, as in some randomized clinical trials, generally inform them of the nature of the information withheld and the reason for withholding it. As with deception, ensure independent ethical review of the protocol and continued monitoring of the research.

9. Know about and adhere to appropriate animal welfare guidelines in research involving animals. Ensure that a competent understanding of the subject matter is combined with credible statistical validity.

E. RESPONSIBILITIES TO RESEARCH TEAM COLLEAGUES

1. Inform colleagues from other disciplines about relevant aspects of statistical ethics.

2. Promote effective and efficient use of statistics by the research team.

3. Respect the ethical obligations of members of other disciplines, as well as your own.

4. Ensure professional reporting of the statistical design and analysis.

5. Avoid compromising statistical validity for expediency, but use reasonable approximations as appropriate.

F. RESPONSIBILITIES TO OTHER STATISTICIANS OR STATISTICS PRACTITIONERS

1. Promote sharing of (nonproprietary) data and methods. As appropriate, make suitably documented data available for replicate analyses, metadata studies, and other suitable research by qualified investigators.

2. Be willing to help strengthen the work of others through appropriate peer review. When doing so, complete the review promptly and well.

3. Assess methods, not individuals.

4. Respect differences of opinion.

5. Instill in students an appreciation for the practical value of the concepts and methods they are learning.

6. Use professional qualifications and the contributions of the individual as an important basis for decisions regarding statistical practitioners' hiring, firing, promotion, work assignments, publications and presentations, candidacy for offices and awards, funding or approval of research, and other professional matters. Avoid as best you can harassment of or discrimination against statistical practitioners (or anyone else) on professionally irrelevant bases such as race, color, ethnicity, sex, sexual orientation, national origin, age, religion, nationality, or disability.

G. RESPONSIBILITIES REGARDING ALLEGATIONS OF MISCONDUCT

1. Avoid condoning or appearing to condone careless, incompetent, or unethical practices in statistical studies conducted in your working environment or elsewhere.

2. Deplore all types of professional misconduct, not just plagiarism and data fabrication or falsification. Misconduct more broadly includes all professional dishonesty, by commission or omission, and, within the realm of professional activities and expression, all harmful disrespect for people, unauthorized use of their intellectual and physical property, and unjustified detraction from their reputations.

3. Recognize that differences of opinion and honest error do not constitute misconduct; they warrant discussion, but not accu-

sation. Questionable scientific practices may or may not constitute misconduct, depending on their nature and the definition of misconduct used.

4. If involved in a misconduct investigation, know and follow prescribed procedures. Maintain confidentiality during an investigation, but disclose the results honestly after the investigation has been completed.

5. Following a misconduct investigation, support the appropriate efforts of the accused, the witnesses, and those reporting the possible scientific error or misconduct to resume their careers in as normal a manner as possible.

6. Do not condone retaliation against or damage to the employability of those who responsibly call attention to possible scientific error or misconduct.

H. RESPONSIBILITIES OF EMPLOYERS, INCLUDING ORGANIZATIONS, INDIVIDUALS, ATTORNEYS, OR OTHER CLIENTS EMPLOYING STATISTICAL PRACTITIONERS

1. Recognize that the results of valid statistical studies cannot be guaranteed to conform to the expectations or desires of those commissioning the study or the statistical practitioner(s). Any measures taken to ensure a particular outcome will lessen the validity of the analysis.

2. Valid findings result from competent work in a moral environment. Pressure on a statistical practitioner to deviate from these guidelines is likely to damage both the validity of study results and the professional credibility of the practitioner.

3. Make new statistical knowledge widely available in order to benefit society at large. (Those who have funded the development of statistical innovations are entitled to monetary and other rewards for their resulting products, software, or research results.)

4. Support sound statistical analysis and expose incompetent or corrupt statistical practice. In cases of conflict, statistical practitioners and those employing them are encouraged to resolve issues of ethical practice privately. If private resolution is not possible, recognize that statistical practitioners have an ethical obligation to expose incompetent or corrupt practice before it can cause harm to research subjects or society at large.

5. Recognize that within organizations and within professions using statistical methods generally, statistics practitioners with greater prestige, power, or status have a responsibility to protect

the professional freedom and responsibility of more subordinate statistical practitioners who comply with these guidelines.

6. Do not include statistical practitioners in authorship or acknowledge their contributions to projects or publications without their explicit permission.

KEY REFERENCE

1. U.S. federal regulations regarding human subjects protection are contained in *Title 45* of the Code of Federal Regulations, Chapter 46 (45 CFR 46).

2. *The Belmont Report: Ethical Principles and Guidelines for the Protection of Human Subjects of Research* is available through the Office of Human Research Protections.

3. Title 13, U.S. Code, Chapter 5—Censuses, Subchapter II—Population, housing, and unemployment, Sec. 141 restricts uses of U.S. population census information. Similar restrictions may apply in other countries.

4. The International Statistical Institute's 1985 *Declaration on Professional Ethics*

5. The United Nations Statistical Commission's 1994 *Fundamental Principles of Official Statistics*

Appendix C

American Psychological Association Journal Article Reporting Standards

TABLE C.1	

Journal Article Reporting Standards (JARS): Information Recommended for Inclusion in Manuscripts That Report New Data Collections Regardless of Research Design

Paper section and topic	Description

TITLE and TITLE PAGE	___Identify variables and theoretical issues under investigation and the relationship between them
	___Author note contains acknowledgment of special circumstances:
	   ___Use of data also appearing in previous publications, dissertations, or conference papers
	   ___Sources of funding or other support
	___Relationships that may be perceived as conflicts of interest

ABSTRACT	___Problem under investigation
	___Participants or subjects; specifying pertinent characteristics, in animal research include genus and species
	___Study method, including:
	   ___Sample size
	   ___Any apparatus used
	   ___Outcome measures
	   ___Data-gathering procedures
	   ___Research design (e.g., experiment, observational study)

(continued)

TABLE C.1 (*Continued*)

Journal Article Reporting Standards (JARS): Information Recommended for Inclusion in Manuscripts That Report New Data Collections Regardless of Research Design

Paper section and topic	Description
	___Findings, including effect sizes and confidence intervals and/or statistical significance levels
	___Conclusions and the implications or applications
INTRODUCTION	
	___The importance of the problem:
	___Theoretical or practical implications
	___Review of relevant scholarship:
	___Relation to previous work
	___If other aspects of this study have been reported on previously, how the current report differs from these earlier reports
	___Specific hypotheses and objectives:
	___Theories or other means used to derive hypotheses
	___Primary and secondary hypotheses, other planned analyses
	___How hypotheses and research design relate to one another
METHOD	
Participant characteristics	___Eligibility and exclusion criteria, including any restrictions based on demographic characteristics
	___Major demographic characteristics as well as important topic-specific characteristics (e.g., achievement level in studies of educational interventions), or in the case of animal research genus and species
Sampling procedures	___Procedures for selecting participants, including:
	___The sampling method if a systematic sampling plan was implemented
	___Percentage of sample approached that participated
	___Self-selection (either by individuals or units, such as schools or clinics)
	___Settings and locations where data were collected
	___Agreements and payments made to participants
	___Institutional Review Board agreements, ethical standards met, safety monitoring
Sample size, power, and precision	___Intended sample size
	___Actual sample size, if different from intended sample size
	___How sample size was determined:
	___Power analysis, or methods used to determine precision of parameter estimates
	___Explanation of any interim analyses and stopping rules
Measures and covariates	___Definitions of all primary and secondary measures and covariates:
	___Include measures collected but not included in this report
	___Methods used to collect data

TABLE C.1 (*Continued*)

Journal Article Reporting Standards (JARS): Information Recommended for Inclusion in Manuscripts That Report New Data Collections Regardless of Research Design

Paper section and topic	Description

Research design	___Methods used to enhance the quality of measurements:
	  ___Training and reliability of data collectors
	  ___Use of multiple observations
	___Information on validated or ad hoc instruments created for individual studies, for example, psychometric and biometric properties
	___Whether conditions were manipulated or naturally observed
	___Type of research design; provided in Table C.3 are modules for:
	  ___Randomized experiments (Module 1)
	  ___Quasi-experiment (Module 2)
	Other designs would have different reporting needs associated with them

RESULTS Participant flow	___Total number of participants ___Flow of participants through each stage of the study
Recruitment	___Dates defining the periods of recruitment and repeated measures or follow-up

Statistics and data analysis	___Information concerning problems with statistical assumptions and/or data distributions that could affect the validity of findings
	___Missing data:
	  ___Frequency or percentages of missing data
	  ___Empirical evidence and/or theoretical arguments for the causes of data that are missing, for example, missing completely at random (MCAR), missing at random (MAR), or missing not at random (MNAR)
	  ___Methods for addressing missing data, if used
	___For each primary and secondary outcome and for each subgroup, a summary of:
	  ___Cases deleted from each analysis
	  ___Subgroup or cell sample sizes, cell means, standard deviations, or other estimates of precision, and other descriptive statistics
	  ___Effect sizes and confidence intervals
	___For inferential statistics (null hypothesis significance testing), information about:
	  ___The a priori Type 1 error rate adopted
	  ___Direction, magnitude, degrees of freedom, and exact *p*-level, even if no significant effect is reported
	___For multivariable analytic systems (e.g., multivariate analyses of variance, regression analyses, structural equation modeling analyses, and hierarchical linear modeling) also include the associated variance–covariance (or correlation) matrix or matrices

(continued)

TABLE C.1 (Continued)

Journal Article Reporting Standards (JARS): Information Recommended for Inclusion in Manuscripts That Report New Data Collections Regardless of Research Design

Paper section and topic	Description
	___Estimation problems (e.g., failure to converge, bad solution spaces), anomalous data points
	___Statistical software program, if specialized procedures were used
	___Report any other analyses performed, including adjusted analyses indicating those that were prespecified and those that were exploratory (though not necessarily in level of detail of primary analyses)
Ancillary analyses	___Discussion of implications of ancillary analyses for statistical error rates
DISCUSSION	
	___Statement of support or nonsupport for all original hypotheses:
	___Distinguished by primary and secondary hypotheses
	___Post hoc explanations
	___Similarities and differences between results and work of others
	___Interpretation of the results, taking into account:
	___Sources of potential bias and other threats to internal validity
	___Imprecision of measures
	___The overall number of tests or overlap among tests, and
	___Other limitations or weaknesses of the study
	___Generalizability (external validity) of the findings taking into account:
	___The target population
	___Other contextual issues
	___Discussion of implications for future research, program, or policy

TABLE C.2

Module A: Reporting Standards for Studies With an Experimental Manipulation or Intervention (in addition to material presented in Table C.1)

Methods	Description

Experimental manipulations or interventions	___Details of the interventions or experimental manipulations intended for each study condition, including control groups, and how and when manipulations or interventions were actually administered, specifically including:
	___Content of the interventions or specific experimental manipulations
	   ___Summary or paraphrasing of instructions, unless they are unusual or compose the experimental manipulation, in which case they may be presented verbatim
	___Method of intervention or manipulation delivery
	   ___Description of apparatus and materials used and their function in the experiment
	     ___Specialized equipment by model and supplier
	___Deliverer: who delivered the manipulations or interventions
	   ___Level of professional training
	   ___Level of training in specific interventions or manipulations
	   ___Number of deliverers and, in the case of interventions, the M, SD, and range of number of individuals/units treated by each
	___Setting: where the manipulations or interventions occurred
	___Exposure quantity and duration: how many sessions, episodes or events were intended to be delivered, how long they were intended to last
	___Time span: how long it took to deliver the intervention or manipulation to each unit
	___Activities to increase compliance or adherence (e.g., incentives)
	___Use of language other than English and the translation method

Units of delivery and analysis	___Unit of delivery: How participants were grouped during delivery ___Description of the smallest unit that was analyzed (and in the case of experiments, that was randomly assigned to conditions) to assess manipulation or intervention effects (e.g., individuals, work groups, classes) ___If the unit of analysis differed from the unit of delivery, description of the analytical method used to account for this (e.g., adjusting the standard error estimates by the design effect or using multilevel analysis)

(continued)

TABLE C.2 (*Continued*)

Module A: Reporting Standards for Studies With an Experimental Manipulation or Intervention (in addition to material presented in Table C.1)

Results	Description

Participant flow	___Total number of groups (if intervention was administered at the group level) and the number of participants assigned to each group:
	  ___Number of participants who did not complete the experiment or crossed over to other conditions, explain why
	  ___Number of participants used in primary analyses
	___Flow of participants through each stage or the study (see Figure C.1)

Treatment fidelity	___Evidence on whether the treatment was delivered as intended
Baseline data	___Baseline demographic and clinical characteristics of each group
Statistics and data analysis	___Whether the analysis was by intent-to-treat, complier average causal effect, other or multiple ways
Adverse events and side effects	___All important adverse events or side effects in each intervention group

Discussion	Description

	___Discussion of results taking into account the mechanism by which the manipulation or intervention was intended to work (causal pathways) or alternative mechanisms
	___If an intervention is involved, discussion of the success of and barriers to implementing the intervention, fidelity of implementation
	___Generalizability (external validity) of the findings taking into account:
	  ___The characteristics of the intervention
	  ___How, what outcomes were measured
	  ___Length of follow-up
	  ___Incentives
	  ___Compliance rates
	___The "clinical or practical significance" of outcomes and the basis for these interpretations

TABLE C.3

Reporting Standards for Studies Using Random and Nonrandom Assignment of Participants to Experimental Groups

Method	Description
	Module 1: Studies Using Random Assignment
Random assignment method	___Procedure used to generate the random assignment sequence, including details of any restriction (e.g., blocking, stratification)
Random assignment concealment	___Whether sequence was concealed until interventions were assigned
Random assignment implementation	___Who generated the assignment sequence ___Who enrolled participants ___Who assigned participants to groups
Masking	___Whether participants, those administering the interventions, and those assessing the outcomes were unaware of condition assignments ___If masking took place, statement regarding how it was accomplished and how the success of masking was evaluated
Statistical methods	___Statistical methods used to compare groups on primary outcome(s) ___Statistical methods used for additional analyses, such as subgroup analyses and adjusted analysis ___Statistical methods used for mediation analyses
	Module 2: Studies Using Nonrandom Assignment
Assignment method	___Unit of assignment (the unit being assigned to study conditions, e.g., individual, group, community) ___Method used to assign units to study conditions, including details of any restriction (e.g., blocking, stratification, minimization) ___Procedures employed to help minimize potential bias due to non-randomization (e.g., matching, propensity score matching)
Masking	___Whether participants, those administering the interventions, and those assessing the outcomes were unaware of condition assignments ___If masking took place, statement regarding how it was accomplished and how the success of masking was evaluated
Statistical methods	___Statistical methods used to compare study groups on primary outcome(s), including complex methods for correlated data ___Statistical methods used for additional analyses, such as subgroup analyses and adjusted analysis (e.g., methods for modeling pretest differences and adjusting for them) ___Statistical methods used for mediation analyses

FIGURE C.1

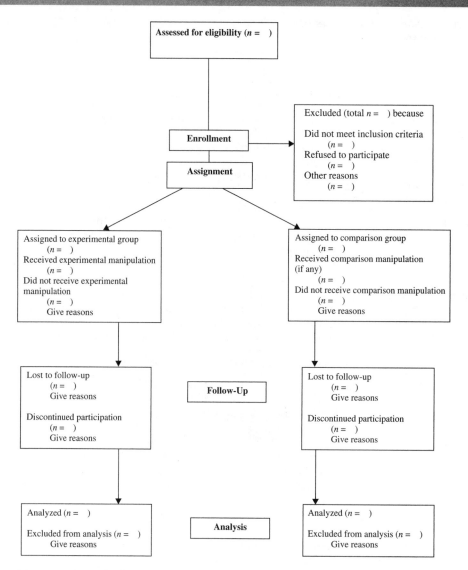

Diagram showing flow of participants through each stage of an experiment or quasi-experiment. This flowchart is an adaptation of the flowchart offered by the Consolidated Standards of Reporting Trials (CONSORT) Group (2007). Journals publishing the original CONSORT flowchart have waived copyright protection.

Appendix D

The Committee on Publication Ethics Case Taxonomy

Classifications are in capitals, keywords in lowercase, descriptions in italics.

AUTHORSHIP (Involves any aspect of authorship)

Changes in authorship: *When changes to the authorship list are requested or made, after either submission or publication.*

Disputed authorship: *When there is disagreement about any aspect of authorship, e.g., who should be listed and order of listing.*

Ghost authorship: *When someone who should/deserves to be listed as an author is omitted on a submission or publication.*

Gift authorship: *When someone who has made little/no contribution to a research project/manuscript is included as an author on a submission or publication.*

Questionable authorship practice: *Dubious behavior, e.g., making inclusion as an author dependent on something not linked to the project, depriving someone of appropriate listing.*

From *The COPE Case Taxonomy.* Copyright 2015 by the Committee on Public Ethics. Retrieved from http://publicationethics.org/wp-case-taxonomy.

CONFLICT OF INTEREST (The existence of factors, situations or relationships that might inappropriately influence (bias), positively or negatively, a person's actions)

Conflict of interest (author)

Conflict of interest (editor): *Includes any person with high-level editorial and decision-making responsibilities.*

Conflict of interest (journal): *Includes (1) journal-associated individuals and staff, and (2) when journals don't have appropriate systems for ensuring people with conflicts of interest are not included in editorial decisions.*

Conflict of interest (reviewer)

CONSENT FOR PUBLICATION (Permission/lack of to publish variety of things (personal details, other information, data, case report, article))

Consent for publication (author)

Consent for publication (institution)

Consent for publication (participant)

Consent for publication (supervisor)

CONTRIBUTORSHIP (Involves any aspect of contributorship)

Changes in contributorship: *When changes to the contributorship list or individual contributions are requested or made, after either submission or publication.*

Disputed contributorship: *When there is disagreement about any aspect of contributorship, e.g., who should be listed, actual contribution/s, order of listing.*

Ghost contributorship: *When someone who should/deserves to be listed as a contributor is omitted on a submission or publication.*

Gift contributorship: *When someone who has made little/no contribution to a research project/manuscript is included as a contributor on a submission or publication.*

Questionable contributorship practice: *Dubious behavior, e.g., making inclusion as a contributor dependent on something not linked to the project, depriving someone of appropriate listing.*

COPYRIGHT (Involves any aspect of copyright)

Copyright disputes/breaches: *When there is disagreement about copyright or breaches are involved.*

CORRECTION OF THE LITERATURE (Involves all discussion and categories of correction of the literature)

Correction of the literature, corrections

Correction of the literature, corrigenda & errata: *Corrigenda are corrections due to author errors, errata are due to journal/publisher ones.*

Correction of the literature, disputes: *When various parties can't agree on either whether a correction is needed or what kind of correction is needed; also when they refuse to correct.*

Correction of the literature, expressions of concern

Correction of the literature, retractions

DATA (Includes data, results, materials, and also submission/ publication-associated documents, e.g., consent and copyright forms)

Data fabrication: *Making up research details/findings/documents.*

Data falsification: *Altering research details/findings/documents.*

Data integrity: *When there is data falsification or fabrication, also mistakes/ problems leading to data problems.*

Data manipulation: *Issues to do with handling and changing of data.*

Data misappropriation/theft

Data ownership

Data, selective/misleading reporting/interpretation: *Data or information omitted/misreported to mislead/fit a theory, desired outcome, etc.*

Data, sharing

Data, unauthorized use

Image manipulation: *Includes all changes to original images, whether appropriate or inappropriate; also image duplication.*

EDITORIAL INDEPENDENCE (Restriction of editorial freedom/ decision making or undue influence by an outside agency)

Publisher role: *Appropriate and inappropriate intervention/influence by a publisher in editorial matters/decisions.*

Relation to society/owner: *Concerns about editor's relationship to journal owner/parent organization (e.g., incentive schemes that create conflicts of interest).*

FUNDING/SPONSORSHIP (All issues to do with funding or sponsorship of either the research/researchers or any of the individuals/practices/content of the journal)

Financial support disclosure (publication)

Financial support disclosure (research)

Funder/sponsor role: *Inappropriate involvement or intervention in any part of the research or its publication; failure to disclose role.*

Funding/sponsorship concerns

METRICS (Ways of assessing/measuring 'impact' of research output/people including but beyond just Impact Factor (e.g., altmetrics, citations, downloads, social media))

Impact Factor

Impact Factor manipulation

Metrics

Metrics (article)

Metrics (author)

Metrics (journal)

MISCELLANEOUS

Books

Social media

Legal issues

MISCONDUCT/QUESTIONABLE BEHAVIOR

Misconduct/questionable behavior (author)

Misconduct/questionable behavior (editor) *Editor acting in way that contravenes COPE Code of Conduct for Journal Editors.*

Misconduct/questionable behavior (institution)

Misconduct/questionable behavior (journal)

Misconduct/questionable behavior (publisher)

Misconduct/questionable behavior (reviewer)

Misconduct/questionable behavior (society/journal owner)

Misconduct sanctions

MISTAKES (What appear to be honest errors or where benefit of doubt has to be given)

Mistakes (author)

Mistakes (editor)

Mistakes (institution)

Mistakes (journal)

Mistakes (publisher)

Mistakes (reviewer)

Mistakes (society/journal owner)

PEER REVIEW (Involving any aspect peer review)

Editorial decisions: *Concern/complaint that decision/s not being made fairly/ ethically (e.g., editor's potential conflict of interest not being handled appropriately or decisions being unduly influenced by commercial considerations); questions regarding decisions or policy.*

Peer-review process: *Concern/complaint about a journal's peer-review process or components of that process (e.g., creates conflicts of interest, is unfair or inadequate, introduces bias, is unethical).*

Post-publication peer review

PLAGIARISM (Taking/using/presenting others' ideas, data/ results, writings and inventions without giving due or appropriate credit to the originator)

Plagiarism (published article)

Plagiarism (submitted article)

'Self-plagiarism'/text recycling (published article): *Reusing one's own previous writing without being transparent about this or appropriately referencing/quoting from the original.*

'Self-plagiarism'/text recycling (submitted article): *Reusing one's own previous writing without being transparent about this or appropriately referencing/ quoting from the original.*

QUESTIONABLE/UNETHICAL RESEARCH

Ethical review/approval: *All issues and aspects of research ethical approval, e.g., whether by appropriate and independent review bodies, with appropriate/ adequate processes.*

Participant consent: *In the research (consent for publication is in a separate classification above), failing to obtain fully informed consent or where voluntary participation/freedom to withdraw cannot be ensured.*

Participant confidentiality: *Respecting the right of individuals to have their personal details/data treated in confidence.*

Protection of subject (animal): *With respect to treatments and adherence to recognized standards.*

Protection of subject (human): *Protection of research participants from potential hazards/detriments to them of taking part in the research.*

Questionable/unethical treatments: *Administering questionable procedures (e.g., failing to inform of potential risks, that treatment experimental/ unapproved).*

Research integrity: *Of the research, materials, procedures, etc; breaches may involve ethical issues but may also result from mistakes or equipment malfunction.*

Research integrity/ethics investigations: *Involving investigations at institutions or by official bodies on the integrity/soundness/ethics of the research done.*

REDUNDANT/DUPLICATE PUBLICATION (The publication, or attempted publication, of whole or substantial parts of work/ data/analysis that have already been published (or have been submitted elsewhere), without transparency or appropriate declaration/referencing)

Multiple submissions: *Submission of identical manuscripts or those with substantial overlap to more than one journal/publication venue at a time.*

Prior publication: *Where a journal considers posting of data or a pre-print before submission as 'publication,' and which will therefore exclude those items from subsequent submission to the journal. Grey and rapidly changing area, varies greatly from journal to journal.*

Redundant/duplicate publication, translations

WHISTLEBLOWERS (Individuals who make allegations about potential research or publication misconduct, either privately or publicly, and anonymously or not)

Whistleblowers, emails
Whistleblowers, responding to

References

American Association for the Advancement of Science, Center for Public Engagement with Science & Technology. (2014). *Communicating science workshops*. Retrieved from http://www.aaas.org/page/communicating-science-workshops

American Educational Research Association. (2011). Ethical standards of the American Educational Research Association. *Educational Researcher, 40,* 145–156.

American Psychological Association. (2010a). *Ethical principles of psychologists and code of conduct (2002, Amended June 1, 2010)*. Retrieved from http://www.apa.org/ethics/code/index.aspx

American Psychological Association. (2010b). *Publication manual of the American Psychological Association* (6th ed.). Washington, DC: Author.

American Psychological Association. (2013). 2013 award winners distinguished contribution to the public interest. *American Psychologist, 68,* 685–687.

American Psychological Association. (2014a). *Permissions alert form for APA journal authors*. Retrieved from http://www.apa.org/pubs/authors/permissions-alert.pdf

American Psychological Association. (2014b). Summary of journal operations. *American Psychologist, 69,* 531–532.

American Psychological Association. (2015a). *Archives of Scientific Psychology*. Retrieved from http://www.apa.org/pubs/journals/arc/

American Psychological Association. (2015b). *Supplementing your article with online material.* Retrieved from http://www.apa.org/pubs/authors/supp-material.aspx

American Psychological Association. (2015c). *Journal of Experimental Psychology: General.* Retrieved from http://www.apa.org/pubs/journals/xge/index.aspx?tab=4

American Psychological Association. (2015d). *Guidelines for reviewing manuscripts.* Retrieved from http://www.apa.org/pubs/journals/cou/reviewer-guidelines.aspx

American Psychological Association, American Educational Research Association & National Council on Measurement in Education. (2014). *Standards for educational and psychological testing, 2014.* Washington, DC: Author

American Statistical Association. (1999). *Ethical guidelines for statistical practice.* Retrieved from: http://www.amstat.org/about/ethicalguidelines.cfm

APA Publications and Communications Board Working Group on Journal Article Reporting Standards. (2008). Reporting standards for research in psychology: Why do we need them? What might they be? *American Psychologist, 63,* 839–851. http://dx.doi.org/10.1037/0003-066X.63.9.839

Asch, S. E. (1951). Effects of group pressure on the modification and distortion of judgments. In H. Guetzkow (Ed.), *Groups, leadership and men* (pp. 177–190). Pittsburgh, PA: Carnegie Press.

Association for Psychological Science. (n.d.). *Registered replication reports.* Retrieved from http://www.psychologicalscience.org/index.php/replication

Babbage, C. (1830). *Reflections on the decline of science in England, and on some of its causes.* London, England: B. Fellowes, Ludgate Street.

Barber, T. X. (1976). *Pitfalls in human research: Ten pivotal points.* Elmsford, NY: Pergamon.

Barnett, J. E., & Campbell, L. F. (2012). Ethics issues in scholarship. In S. J. Knapp (Ed.), *APA handbook of ethics in psychology: Vol. 2. Practice, teaching, and research* (pp. 309–333). Washington, DC: American Psychological Association.

Barnett, V., & Lewis, T. (1994). *Outliers in statistical analysis* (3rd ed.). Chichester, England: Wiley.

Bartlett, T. (2010). *Document sheds light on investigation at Harvard.* Retrieved from http://chronicle.com/article/Document-Sheds-Light-on/123988/

Bartlett, T. (2011). *Marc Hauser resigns from Harvard.* Retrieved from http://chronicle.com/article/Marc-Hauser-Resigns-From/128296

Bartlett, T. (2012). *Daniel Kahneman sees 'train-wreck' looming for social psychology.* Retrieved from http://chronicle.com/blogs/percolator/daniel-kahneman-sees-train-wreck-looming-for-social-psychology/31338

Bebeau, M. J., & Monson, V. (2011). Authorship and publication practices in the social sciences: Historical reflections on current practices. *Science and Engineering Ethics, 17*, 365–388. http://dx.doi.org/10.1007/s11948-011-9280-4

Bennell, K. L., Egerton, T., Martin, J., Abbott, J. H., Metcalf, B., McManus, F., . . . Buchbinder, R. (2014). Effect of physical therapy on pain and function in patients with hip osteoarthritis: A randomized clinical trial. *Journal of the American Medical Association, 311*, 1987–1997. http://dx.doi.org/10.1001/jama.2014.4591

Berkman Center for Internet and Society. (2012). *Harvard open access project*. Retrieved from http://cyber.law.harvard.edu/research/hoap#

Bhattacharjee, Y. (2013). *The mind of a con man*. Retrieved from http://www.nytimes.com/2013/04/28/magazine/diederik-stapels-audacious-academic-fraud.html?pagewanted=all&_r=0

Bickel, P. J., Hammel, E. A., & O'Connell, J. W. (1975). Sex bias in graduate admissions: Data from Berkeley. *Science, 187*, 398–404. http://dx.doi.org/10.1126/science.187.4175.398

Borsboom, D., & Wagenmakers, E. (2013). *Derailed: The rise and fall of Diederik Stapel*. Retrieved from http://www.psychologicalscience.org/index.php/publications/observer/2013/january-13/derailed-the-rise-and-fall-of-diederik-stapel.html

Brown, A. S., & Murphy, D. R. (1989). Cryptomnesia: Delineating inadvertent plagiarism. *Journal of Experimental Psychology: Learning, Memory, and Cognition, 15*, 432–442. http://dx.doi.org/10.1037/0278-7393.15.3.432

Brown, B. L., & Hedges, D. (2009). Use and misuse of quantitative methods: Data collection, calculation, and presentation. In D. M. Mertens & P. E. Ginsberg (Eds.), *The handbook of social research ethics* (pp. 373–386). Thousand Oaks, CA: Sage. http://dx.doi.org/10.4135/9781483348971.n24

Budapest Open Access Initiative. (2012, March 17). *Budapest Open Access Initiative*. Retrieved from http://www.soros.org/openaccess/read

Burbules, N. C. (2009). Privacy and the new technologies: The limits of research ethics. In D. M. Martens & P. E. Ginsberg (Eds.), *The handbook of social research ethics* (pp. 537–549). Thousand Oaks, CA: Sage. http://dx.doi.org/10.4135/9781483348971.n34

Cizek, G. J., & Rosenberg, S. L. (2011). Psychometric methods and high-stakes assessment: Contexts and methods for ethical testing practice. In A. T. Panter & S. K. Sterba (Eds.), *Handbook of ethics in quantitative methodology* (pp. 211–240). New York, NY: Routledge.

Cohen, J. (1988). *Statistical power analysis for the behavioral sciences* (2nd ed.). Hillsdale, NJ: Erlbaum.

Committee on Professional Conduct of Harvard's Faculty of Arts & Sciences. (2010). *Report of the Investigating Committee*. Retrieved from http://cache.boston.com/news/pdfs/harvardreport.pdf?p1=Article_Related_Box_Article

Committee on Publication Ethics. (2006). *Committee on Publication Ethics flowchart.* Retrieved from http://publicationethics.org/resources/flowcharts

Committee on Publication Ethics. (2009). *Retraction guidelines.* Retrieved from http://publicationethics.org/files/retraction%20guidelines.pdf

Committee on Publication Ethics. (n.d.-a). *COPE statement on inappropriate manipulation of peer review process.* Retrieved from http://publicationethics.org/news/cope-statement-inappropriate-manipulation-peer-review-processes

Committee on Publication Ethics. (n.d.-b). COPE *cases search.* Retrieved from http://publicationethics.org/cases

Committee on Publication Ethics. (n.d.-c) *The COPE case taxonomy.* Retrieved from http://publicationethics.org/cope-case-taxonomy

Consolidated Standards of Reporting Trials. (n.d.). *CONSORT: Strength in science, sound ethics.* Retrieved from http://www.consort-statement.org/

Cooper, H. (2008). The search for meaningful ways to express the effects of interventions. *Child Development Perspectives, 2,* 181–186. http://dx.doi.org/10.1111/j.1750-8606.2008.00063.x

Cooper, H. (2011). *Reporting research in psychology: How to meet journal article reporting standards.* Washington, DC: American Psychological Association.

Cooper, H. (2012). Introduction: Objectives of psychological research and their relations to research methods. In *APA handbook of research methods in psychology* (Vol. 1, pp. xxiii–xliv. Washington, DC: American Psychological Association.

Cooper, H. (2016). *Research synthesis and meta-analysis: A step-by-step approach* (5th ed.). Thousand Oaks, CA: Sage.

Cooper, H., DeNeve, K., & Charlton, K. (1997). Finding the missing science: The fate of studies submitted for review by a human subjects committee. *Psychological Methods, 2,* 447–452. http://dx.doi.org/10.1037/1082-989X.2.4.447

Cooper, H., & Dent, A. (2011). Ethical issues in the conduct and reporting of meta-analysis. In A. T. Panter & S. K. Sterba (Eds.), *Handbook of ethics in quantitative methodology* (pp. 417–444). New York, NY: Routledge.

Copyright.gov. (2014). *Copyright in general.* Retrieved from http://www.copyright.gov/help/faq/faq-general.html#what

Coulehan, M. E., & Wells, J. F. (n.d.). *Guidelines for responsible data management in scientific research.* Washington, DC: Office of Research Integrity. Retrieved from http://ori.hhs.gov/images/ddblock/data.pdf

Cozby, P. C. (2009). *Methods of behavioral research* (10th ed.). New York, NY: McGraw-Hill.

Cronbach, L. J. (1982). *Designing evaluations of educational and social programs.* San Francisco, CA: Jossey-Bass.

Crossref.org. (2015). *Crosscheck.* Retrieved from http://www.crossref.org/crosscheck/index.html

Data (n.d.). In *Merriam-Webster's online dictinary.* Retrieved from http://www.merriam-webster.com/dictionary/data

Davidson, K. W., Goldstein, M., Kaplan, R. M., Kaufmann, P. G., Knatterud, G. L., Orleans, C. T., . . . Whitlock, E. P. (2003). Evidence-based behavioral medicine: What is it and how do we achieve it? *Annals of Behavioral Medicine, 26,* 161–171. http://dx.doi.org/10.1207/S15324796ABM2603_01

Day, R. A., & Gastel, B. (2011). *How to write and publish a scientific paper.* Santa Barbara, CA: Greenwood.

DeCoster, J., Sparks, E., Sparks, J., Sparks, G., & Sparks, C. (2014). *Opportunistic biases: Origins, prevalence, effects, and prevention.* Retrieved from https://prezi.com/xuagocsroczc/opportunistic-biases-2014-02-28/

Drotar, D. (2010). Editorial: Guidelines for submission and review of multiple publications derived from the same study. *Journal of Pediatric Psychology, 35,* 225–230. http://dx.doi.org/10.1093/jpepsy/jsp134

Enders, C. K. (2010). *Applied missing data analysis.* New York, NY: Guilford.

Epstein, R. M., & Hundert, E. M. (2002). Defining and assessing professional competence. *Journal of the American Medical Association, 287,* 226–235. http://dx.doi.org/10.1001/jama.287.2.226

Equator Network. (n.d.). *Enhancing the quality and transparency of health research.* Retrieved from http://www.equator-network.org/library/guidance-on-scientific-writing/

eTBLAST. (2012). *eTBLAST: A text-similarity based search engine.* Retrieved from http://etest.vbi.vt.edu/etblast3

Fanelli, D. (2009). How many scientists fabricate and falsify research? A systematic review and meta-analysis of survey data. *PLoS ONE, 4,* e5738. http://dx.doi.org/10.1371/journal.pone.0005738

Fanelli, D. (2013). Why growing retractions are (mostly) a good sign. *PLoS Med, 10,* e1001563. http://dx.doi.org/10.1371/journal.pmed.1001563

Fang, F. C., Bennett, J. W., & Casadevall, A. (2013). Males are over-represented among life science researchers committing scientific misconduct. *mBio, 4*(1), e00640-e12. http://dx.doi.org/10.1128/mBio.00640-12

Federal Register. (2000, December 6). Office of Science and Technology Policy: Executive Office of the President; Federal Policy on Research Misconduct; Preamble for Research Misconduct Policy, *65*(235), 76260–76264.

Fine, M. A., & Kurdek, L. A. (1993). Reflections on determining authorship credit and authorship order on faculty-student collaborations.

American Psychologist, 48, 1141–1147. http://dx.doi.org/10.1037/0003-066X.48.11.1141

Fisher, C. B. (2009). *Decoding the ethics code: A practical guide for psychologists* (2nd ed.). Los Angeles, CA: Sage.

Fisher, C. B., & Vacanti-Shova, K. (2012). The responsible conduct of psychological research: An overview of ethical principles, APA Ethics Code standards, and federal regulations. In S. J. Knapp (Ed.), *APA handbook of ethics in psychology* (Vol. 2, pp. 335–369). Washington, DC: American Psychological Association.

Foster, R. D., & Ray, D. C. (2012). An ethical decision-making model to determine authorship credit in published faculty–student collaborations. *Counseling and Values, 57,* 214–228. http://dx.doi.org/10.1002/j.2161-007X.2012.00018.x

Freelon, D. G. (2010). ReCal: Intercoder reliability calculation as a web service. *International Journal of Internet Science, 5,* 20–33.

Furman, J. L., Jensen, K., & Murray, F. (2012). Governing knowledge in the scientific community: Exploring the role of retractions in biomedicine. *Research Policy, 41,* 276–290. http://dx.doi.org/10.1016/j.respol.2011.11.001

Gardenier, J. S. (2011). Ethics in quantitative professional practice. In A. T. Panter & S. K. Sterba (Eds.), *Handbook of ethics in quantitative methodology* (pp. 15–36). New York, NY: Routledge.

Geelhoed, R. J., Phillips, J. C., Fischer, A. R., Shpungin, E., & Gong, Y. (2007). Authorship decision making: An empirical investigation. *Ethics & Behavior, 17,* 95–115. http://dx.doi.org/10.1080/10508420701378057

Godlee, F. (2002). The ethics of peer review. In A. Jones & F. McLellan (Eds.), *Ethical issues in biomedical publication* (pp. 59–84). Baltimore, MD: Johns Hopkins University Press.

Goodstein, D. (2010). *On fact and fraud: Cautionary tales from the front lines of science.* Princeton, NJ: Princeton University Press. http://dx.doi.org/10.1515/9781400834570

Greitemeyer, T. (2014). Article retracted, but the message lives on. *Psychonomic Bulletin & Review, 21,* 557–561. http://dx.doi.org/10.3758/s13423-013-0500-6

Grieneisen, M. L., & Zhang, M. (2012). A comprehensive survey of retracted articles from the scholarly literature. [Advance online publication]. *PLoS ONE, 7,* e44118. http://dx.doi.org/10.1371/journal.pone.0044118

Gross, C. (2012). *Disgrace: On Marc Hauser.* Retrieved from http://www.thenation.com/article/165313/disgrace-marc-hauser#

Grubbs, F. E. (1950). Sample criteria for testing outlying observations. *Journal of the American Statistical Association, 21,* 27–58.

Harlow, L. (1997). Significance testing introduction and overview. In L. Harlow, S. Muliak, & J. Steiger (Eds.), *What if there were no significance tests?* (pp. 1–17) Mahwah, NJ: Erlbaum.

Hedges, L. V. (1992). Modeling publication selection effects in meta-analysis. *Statistical Science, 7,* 246–255. http://dx.doi.org/10.1214/ss/1177011364

Hexham, I. (1999). *The plague of plagiarism: Academic plagiarism defined.* Department of Religious Studies. The University of Calgary. Retrieved from http://people.ucalgary.ca/~hexham/content/articles/plague-of-plagiarism.html (Cited in Roig, 2003).

Hoerger, M., & Currell, C. (2012). Ethical issues in Internet research. In S. J. Knapp (Ed.), *APA handbook of ethics in psychology: Vol. 2. Practice, teaching, and research* (pp. 385–400). Washington, DC: American Psychological Association. http://dx.doi.org/10.1037/13272-018

Howard, R. M. (1999). *Standing in the shadows of giants.* Stamford, CT: Ablex.

Hoyle, R. H., & Isherwood, J. C. (2013). Reporting results from structural equation modeling in *Archives of Scientific Psychology. Archives of Scientific Psychology, 1,* 14–22.

Hubert, L., & Wainer, H. (2011). A statistical guide for the ethically perplexed. In A. T. Panter & S. K. Sterba (Eds.), *Handbook of ethics in quantitative methodology* (pp. 61–124). New York, NY: Routledge.

Inter-university Consortium for Political and Social Research. (n.d.-a). *ICPSR: A partnership in social science research.* Retrieved from https://www.icpsr.umich.edu/icpsrweb/landing.jsp

Inter-university Consortium for Political and Social Research. (n.d.-b). *ICPSR data management and curation.* Retrieved from https://www.icpsr.umich.edu/icpsrweb/content/datamanagement/index.html

iThenticate. (2014). *Preventing plagiarism in published work.* Retrieved from http://www.ithenticate.com

Jefferson, T., Wager, E., & Davidoff, F. (2002). Measuring the quality of editorial peer review. *Journal of the American Medical Association, 287,* 2786–2790. http://dx.doi.org/10.1001/jama.287.21.2786

John, L. K., Loewenstein, G., & Prelec, D. (2012). Measuring the prevalence of questionable research practices with incentives for truth telling. *Psychological Science, 23,* 524–532. http://dx.doi.org/10.1177/0956797611430953

Kline, R. B. (2013). *Beyond significance testing: Statistics reform in the behavioral sciences* (2nd ed.). Washington, DC: American Psychological Association. http://dx.doi.org/10.1037/14136-000

LaFollette, M. C. (1992). *Stealing into print: Fraud, plagiarism, and misconduct in scientific publishing.* Berkeley, CA: University of California Press.

Lakens, D. (2014). Performing high-powered studies efficiently with sequential analyses. [Advance online publication]. *European Journal of Social Psychology, 44,* 701–710. http://dx.doi.org/10.1002/ejsp.2023

Levelt Committee, Noort Committee, & Drenth Committee. (2012). *Flawed science: The fraudulent research practices of social psychologist Diederik Stapel.* Retrieved from https://www.tilburguniversity.edu/upload/3ff904d7-547b-40ae-85fe-bea38e05a34a_Final%20report%20Flawed%20Science.pdf

Leviton, L. (2011). Ethics in program evaluation. In A. T. Panter & S. K. Sterba (Eds.), *Handbook of ethics in quantitative methodology* (pp. 214–265). New York, NY: Routledge.

Little, R. A. & Rubin, D. B. (2002). *Statistical analysis with missing data.* Hoboken, NJ: Wiley & Sons.

Macrina, F. L. (2005). *Scientific integrity.* Washington, DC: AMS Press.

Martinson, B. C., Anderson, M. S., & de Vries, R. (2005). Scientists behaving badly. *Nature, 435,* 737–738. http://dx.doi.org/10.1038/435737a

Marušić, A., Bošnjak, L., & Jerončić, A. (2011). A systematic review of research on the meaning, ethics and practices of authorship across scholarly disciplines. *PLoS ONE, 6*(9), e23477. http://dx.doi.org/10.1371/journal.pone.0023477

Maxwell, S. E., & Kelley, K. (2011). Ethics and sample size planning. In A. T. Panter & S. K. Sterba (Eds.), *Handbook of ethics in quantitative methodology* (pp. 159–184). New York, NY: Routledge.

Nagy, T. F. (2012). Competence. In S. J. Knapp (Ed.), *APA handbook of ethics in psychology: Vol. 1. Moral foundations and common themes* (pp. 147–174). Washington, DC: American Psychological Association.

National Academy of Sciences, National Academy of Engineering, & Institute of Medicine. (2009). *On being a scientist: A guide to responsible conduct of research.* Washington, DC: The National Academy of Science Press.

National Institutes of Health. (2007). *NIH data sharing policy.* Retrieved from http://grants.nih.gov/grants/policy/data_sharing/

National Institutes of Health. (2014). *NIH public access policy.* Retrieved from http://publicaccess.nih.gov/policy.htm

National Institutes of Health. (2015). *Rigor and reproducibility.* Retrieved from http://www.nih.gov/science/reproducibility/

National Science Foundation. (2011). *Digital research data sharing and management.* Retrieved from http://www.nsf.gov/nsb/publications/2011/nsb01211.pdf

Novotney, A. (2014). Reproducing results. *Monitor on Psychology, 45,* 32–35.

Oberlander, S., & Spencer, R. (2006). Graduate students and the culture of authorship. *Ethics & Behavior, 16,* 217–232. http://dx.doi.org/10.1207/s15327019eb1603_3

Office of Research Integrity. (n.d.-a). *Data ownership*. Retrieved from http:// ori.hhs.gov/education/products/n_illinois_u/datamanagement/ dotopic.html

Office of Research Integrity. (n.d.-b). *Case summaries*. Retrieved from http://ori.hhs.gov/CASE_SUMMARY

Office of Research Integrity. (2013a). *ORI policy on plagiarism*. Retrieved from http://ori.hhs.gov/ori-policy-plagiarism

Office of Research Integrity. (2013b). *Redundant and duplicate (i.e., dual) publication*. Retrieved from http://ori.hhs.gov/plagiarism-14

Office of Research Integrity. (2014a). *Handling misconduct*. Retrieved from http://ori.hhs.gov/handling-misconduct

Office of Research Integrity. (2014b). *Rapid response for technical review*. Retrieved from http://ori.hhs.gov/rapid-response-technical-assistance

OpCit Project. (2012). *The effect of open access and downloads ('hits') on citation impact: A bibliography of studies*. Retrieved from http://opcit. eprints.org/oacitation-biblio.html

Osborne, J. W., & Holland, A. (2009). What is authorship, and what should it be? A survey of prominent guidelines for determining authorship in scientific publications. *Practical Assessment, Research & Evaluation, 14*, 1–19.

Panter, A. T., & Sterba, S. K. (Eds.). (2011). *Handbook of ethics in quantitative methodology*. New York, NY: Routledge.

Pashler, H., & Wagenmakers, E.-J. (2012). Editors' introduction to the special section on replicability in psychological science: A crisis of confidence? *Perspectives on Psychological Science, 7*, 528–530. http:// dx.doi.org/10.1177/1745691612465253

Perfect, T. J., & Stark, L. J. (2008). Why do I always have the best ideas? The role of idea quality in unconscious plagiarism. *Memory, 16*, 386–394. http://dx.doi.org/10.1080/09658210801946501

Plagiarize. (n.d.). In *Merriam-Webster's online dictinary*. Retrieved from http://www.merriam-webster.com/dictionary/plagiarize

Pocock, S. J. (1993). Statistical and ethical issues in monitoring clinical trials. *Statistics in Medicine, 12*, 1459–1469. http://dx.doi.org/10.1002/ sim.4780121512

Pupovac, V., & Fanelli, D. (2014). Scientists admitting to plagiarism: A meta-analysis of surveys. [Advance online publication]. *Science and Engineering Ethics*. http://dx.doi.org/10.1007/s11948-014-9600-6

REDCap. (2015). *REDCap: Research Electronic Data Capture*. Retrieved from http://project-redcap.org/

Reips, U. (2012). Using the Internet to collect data. In H. Cooper (Ed.), *APA handbook of research methods in psychology* (Vol. 2, pp. 291–310). Washington, DC: American Psychological Association. http://dx.doi. org/10.1037/13620-017

Rennie, D., Flanagin, A., & Yank, V. (2000). The contributions of authors. *Journal of the American Medical Association, 284,* 89–91. http://dx.doi.org/10.1001/jama.284.1.89

Replications and Data Sharing Task Force. (2013, October 6). Memo. American Psychological Association, Washington, DC.

Robinson, W. S. (1950). Ecological correlations and the behavior of individuals. *American Sociological Review, 15,* 351–357. http://dx.doi.org/10.2307/2087176

Roig, M. (2003). *Avoiding plagiarism, self-plagiarism, and other questionable writing practices.* Retrieved from http://ori.hhs.gov/avoiding-plagiarism-self-plagiarism-and-other-questionable-writing-practices-guide-ethical-writing

Rosnow, R., & Rosenthal, R. (2011). Ethical principles in data analysis: An overview. In A. T. Panter & S. K. Sterba (Eds.), *Handbook of ethics in quantitative methodology* (pp. 37–58). New York, NY: Routledge.

Sandler, J. C., & Russell, B. L. (2005). Faculty-student collaborations: Ethics and satisfaction in authorship credit. *Ethics & Behavior, 15,* 65–80. http://dx.doi.org/10.1207/s15327019eb1501_5

Shamoo, A. E., & Resnik, D. B. (2009). *Responsible conduct of research* (2nd ed.). Oxford, England: Oxford University Press. http://dx.doi.org/10.1093/acprof:oso/9780195368246.001.0001

Simonsohn, U., Nelson, L. D., & Simmons, J. P. (2014). *P*-curve: A key to the file-drawer. *Journal of Experimental Psychology: General, 143,* 534–547. http://dx.doi.org/10.1037/a0033242

Simpson, E. H. (1951). The interpretation of interaction in contingency tables. *Journal of the Royal Statistical Society. Series B. Methodological, 13,* 238–241.

Spiegel, D., & Keith-Speigel, P. (1970). Assignment of publication credits: Ethics and practices of psychologists. *American Psychologist, 25,* 738–747. http://dx.doi.org/10.1037/h0029769

Steneck, N. H. (2000). *Assessing the integrity of publicly funded research.* Washington, DC: Office of Research Integrity. Retrieved from http://ori.hhs.gov/sites/default/files/assessing_int_research.pdf

Steneck, N. H. (2007). *ORI introduction to the responsible conduct of research.* Washington, DC: Office of Research Integrity. Retrieved from http://ori.hhs.gov/ori-introduction-responsible-conduct-research

Stern, A. M., Casadevall, A., Steen, R. G., & Fang, F. C. (2014). Financial costs and personal consequences of research misconduct resulting in retracted publications. [Advance online publication]. *eLife, 3,* e02956. http://dx.doi.org/10.7554/eLife.02956

Stern, L. (2009). *What every student should know about avoiding plagiarism.* New York, NY: Pearson.

Sternberg, R. J. (2002). On civility in reviewing. *APS Observer, 15,* 1. Retrieved from http://www.psychologicalscience.org/index.php/uncategorized/on-civility-in-reviewing.html

Stroebe, W., Postmes, T., & Spears, R. (2012). Scientific misconduct and the myth of self-correction in science. *Perspectives on Psychological Science, 7,* 670–688. http://dx.doi.org/10.1177/1745691612460687

Taylor, F. K. (1965). Cryptomnesia and plagiarism. *The British Journal of Psychiatry, 111,* 1111–1118. http://dx.doi.org/10.1192/bjp.111.480.1111

Teaching Copyright. (n.d.). *Fair use frequently asked questions.* Retrieved from http://www.teachingcopyright.org/handout/fair-use-faq

Thomas Reuters. (n.d.). *Web of science.* Retrieved from http://thomsonreuters.com/thomson-reuters-web-of-science/

Times Higher Education. (May 19, 2012). *Muscle from Brussels as open access gets an €80bn boost.* Retrieved from http://www.timeshighereducation.co.uk/story.asp?sectioncode=26&storycode=419949&c=1

Trafimow, D., & Marks, M. (2015). Editorial. *Basic and Applied Social Psychology, 37,* 1–2. http://dx.doi.org/10.1080/01973533.2015.1012991

Tramèr, M. R., Reynolds, D. J. M., Moore, R. A., & McQuay, H. J. (1997). Impact of covert duplicate publication on meta-analysis: A case study. *British Medical Journal, 315,* 635–640. http://dx.doi.org/10.1136/bmj.315.7109.635

Trikalinos, N. A., Evangelou, E., & Ioannidis, J. P. A. (2008). Falsified papers in high-impact journals were slow to retract and indistinguishable from nonfraudulent papers. *Journal of Clinical Epidemiology, 61,* 464–470. http://dx.doi.org/10.1016/j.jclinepi.2007.11.019

Tukey, J. W. (1977). *Exploratory data analysis.* Reading, MA: Addison-Wesley.

Turnitin. (2012). *The plagiarism spectrum: Tagging 10 types of unoriginal work.* Retrieved from http://turnitin.com/assets/en_us/media/plagiarism_spectrum.php

University of Wisconsin–Madison. (2010). *Reporting research misconduct: Policy for graduate students and postdoctoral research associates.* Retrieved from https://kb.wisc.edu/images/group156/shared/ResearchPolicyandCompliance/WhistleblowerPolicy10-22-2007revised1-10-10.pdf

U.S. Department of Health and Human Services. (n.d.-a). *Federal policy for the protection of human subjects ("common rule").* Retrieved from http://www.hhs.gov/ohrp/humansubjects/commonrule/

U.S. Department of Health and Human Services. (n.d.-b). *Health information privacy.* Retrieved from http://www.hhs.gov/ocr/privacy/hipaa/understanding/index.html

U.S. Department of Health and Human Services. (n.d.-c). *Summary of the HIPAA privacy rules.* Retrieved from http://www.hhs.gov/ocr/privacy/hipaa/understanding/summary/index.html

U.S. Department of Health and Human Services. (n.d.-d). *Retention of data.* Retrieved from https://ori.hhs.gov/education/products/rcradmin/topics/data/tutorial_11.shtml

U.S. Department of Health and Human Services. (1979). *The Belmont Report.* Retrieved from http://www.hhs.gov/ohrp/humansubjects/guidance/belmont.html

van Rooyen, S., Godlee, F., Evans, S., Smith, R., & Black, N. (1998). Effect of blinding and unmasking on the quality of peer review: A randomized trial. *Journal of the American Medical Association, 280,* 234–237. http://dx.doi.org/10.1001/jama.280.3.234

Wager, E., Godlee, F., & Jefferson, J. (2002). *How to survive peer review.* London, England: BMJ Books.

Wager, E., Parkin, E. C., & Tamber, P. S. (2006). Are reviewers suggested by authors as good as those chosen by editors? Results of a rated-blinded, retrospective study. *BMC Medicine, 4,* 13. http://dx.doi.org/10.1186/1741-7015-4-13

Wager, E., & Williams, P. (2011). Why and how do journals retract articles? An analysis of Medline retractions 1988–2008. *Journal of Medical Ethics, 37,* 567–570. http://dx.doi.org/10.1136/jme.2010.040964

Washburn, J. J. (2008). Encouraging research collaboration through ethical and fair authorship: A model policy. *Ethics & Behavior, 18,* 44–58. http://dx.doi.org/10.1080/10508420701712917

Welfare, L. E., & Sackett, C. R. (2011). The authorship determination process in student-faculty collaborative research. *Journal of Counseling & Development, 89,* 479–487. http://dx.doi.org/10.1002/j.1556-6676.2011.tb02845.x

Wellcome Trust. (2012, May 19). *Open access policy.* Retrieved from http://www.wellcome.ac.uk/About-us/Policy/Policy-and-position-statements/WTD002766.htm

Werth, J. L., Jr., Welfel, E. R., & Benjamin, G. A. H. (Eds.). (2009). *The duty to protect: Ethical, legal, and professional considerations for mental health professionals.* Washington, DC: American Psychological Association. http://dx.doi.org/10.1037/11866-000

Winston, R. B., Jr. (1985). A suggested procedure for determining order of authorship in research publications. *Journal of Counseling and Development, 63,* 515–518. http://dx.doi.org/10.1002/j.1556-6676.1985.tb02749.x

Index

About the Author

Harris Cooper is the Hugo L. Blomquist Professor of Psychology & Neuroscience at Duke University. His lab mostly conducts research syntheses and meta-analyses but also collects primary data in the area of educational policy and practice. He has taught research methods to undergraduate and graduate students for more than 40 years and has edited two handbooks on research methods and a guide to reporting research in psychology.

Dr. Cooper served as the editor of *Psychological Bulletin* and inaugural coeditor (with Gary VandenBos) of the *Archives of Scientific Psychology,* the American Psychological Association's open-access, collaborative data sharing, open methods journal. After his term as *Psychological Bulletin* editor, he served for 6 years as the chief editorial advisor (CEA) to the APA journals program. The CEA acts as a resource for journal editors, authors, and submitters of manuscripts when (a) disputes arise between editors and authors or between authors and other authors and/or (b) concerns are expressed about the scientific integrity of submitted manuscripts and published articles.

For 3 years, Dr. Cooper served as chair of the Department of Psychological Sciences at the University of Missouri–Columbia, and for 5 years he served as chair of the Department of Psychology & Neuroscience at Duke University.